Moon Journals

Moon Journals

Writing, Art, and Inquiry
Through Focused Nature Study

Joni Chancer
and
Gina Rester-Zodrow

Heinemann
Portsmouth, NH

Heinemann
A division of Reed Elsevier Inc.
361 Hanover Street
Portsmouth, NH 03801-3912

Offices and agents throughout the world

Library of Congress Cataloging-in-Publication Data

CIP is on file with the Library of Congress.
ISBN 0-435-07221-8

Consulting Editor: Maureen Barbieri
Production: Melissa L. Inglis
Cover design: Linda Knowles
Manufacturing: Louise Richardson

Cover illustration: Mixed media collage by Brian Gerrard, age 11
Interior photos and illustrations: The authors and their students

Printed in the United States of America on acid-free paper
00 99 98 97   EB   1 2 3 4 5 6 7 8 9

*To our families
and to past, present, and future Moon Journalists
with whom we celebrate the cycles of life*

Contents

List of Color Illustrations   x

About This Book   xi

Acknowledgments   xv

Introduction   xvii

Part One

The Making of a Studio/Workshop   1

1 A Classroom Story   3

2 Mapping the Journey   27

Part Two

The Process Pages   45

3 The Writing Invitations   49
Writing Invitation #1: I Wonder?: Beginning an Inquiry Study with Poetry   50
Writing Invitation #2: Notes from Nature: Writing About the Environment from a Naturalist's Point of View   53
Writing Invitation #3: Growing Poems from Seeds: Creating Poems from Past Experiences, Ideas, and "Seed Book" Entries   55
Writing Invitation #4: Moontalk: A Dialogue Poem About the Moon   58
Writing Invitation #5: Moon Music: Adding Sounds and Music to Prose and Poetry   62
Writing Invitation #6: Lunar List Poems: Writing a List Poem   64
Writing Invitation #7: Similes by Starlight: Writing Similes About the Moon and the Night Sky   67
Writing Invitation #8: Metaphor Moon: Finding Comparisons in Nature   68
Writing Invitation #9: The Maiden and the Man in the Moon: Using Personification and Active Verbs to Describe the Moon and the Night Sky   71

Writing Invitation #10: Looking Out My Window: Observation and Personal Reflection 75

Writing Invitation #11: Colors of the Night: Using Sensory Description 77

Writing Invitation #12: Lunar Legends: Exploring and Explaining Nature's Mystery Through Storytelling 81

Writing Invitation #13: From Prose to Poetry: Breaking Lines of Prose into a Poem 85

Writing Invitation #14: Draw Me a Story: A Moon Rebus: Recording Observations in Pictures and Words 87

Writing Invitation #15: Moon Facts: A Scientific Observation 89

Writing Invitation #16: Investigating Questions About the Moon: Group Research Projects and Presentations 91

Writing Invitation #17: Moon Mail: Correspondence to and from the Moon 94

Writing Invitation #18: Ode to the Moon: Writing and Scoring an Elementary Ode 97

Writing Invitation #19: The Unexpected Moon: Describing the Moon You Discover by Surprise 99

Writing Invitation #20: Who Am I? Using Personification to Give Voice to the Moon 103

Writing Invitation #21: A Calendar of Moons: Naming the Seasonal Moons 105

Writing Invitation #22: Random Collage Poem: Combining Printed Text with Image 107

Writing Invitation #23: Found Poems: Writing a Poem with Text Found in Moon Journals 108

Writing Invitation #24: Phases of My Life, Phases of the Moon: Writing and Telling Life Stories in Words and Pictures 110

Writing Invitation #25: Nighttime Rituals: Recording a Family Story 112

Writing Invitation #26: Moon Memoirs: Turning Moon Memories into Moon Memoirs 114

Writing Invitation #27: Moon Cycle, Life Cycle: Life Lessons from the Lunar Cycle 117

Writing Invitation #28: Farewell to the Moon: Final Reflections After Completing the Cycle 120

4 The Art Invitations 127

Art Invitation #1: Pencil Sketching: Recording Nature's Details in Simple Pencil Drawings 128

Art Invitation #2: Pen-and-Ink Drawings: Contour Drawings and Field Studies in Pen and Ink 131

Art Invitation #3: Watercolor Wash Backgrounds: Painting a Watercolor Graded Wash 133

Art Invitation #4: Swirling Watercolor Sky: Using Wet-into-Wet Watercolor Techniques 135

Art Invitation #5: Splattered Stars: Using a Toothbrush to Create Splattered Stars in a Night Sky 138

Art Invitation #6: Salt Stars and Clouds: Dropping Salt into Watercolors 140

Art Invitation #7: Bubble Prints: Texture Prints Made with Soap Bubbles 141

Art Invitation #8: Simple Stenciled Shapes: Making Images from Precut Designs 143

Art Invitation #9: The Masked Moon: Using Masking Techniques to Create Shapes with Pastels 145

Art Invitation #10: Moonlit Silhouettes: Landscape Silhouettes Made from Handmade Stencils 147

Art Invitation #11: Handpainted Papers: Painting Designs and Textures 149

Art Invitation #12: Painted Paper Landscapes: Depicting the Environment with Handpainted Papers 151

Art Invitation #13: Tissue Paper Collage: Exploring Color and Texture with Tissue Paper 152

Art Invitation #14: Mixed-Media Collage: Collage Materials and Techniques 153

Art Invitation #15: Crayon Resist: A Mixed-Media Technique Using Wax Crayons and Watercolor Paint 154

Art Invitation #16: The Picture Window: Creating a Composition Within a Lift-up Window Frame 156

Art Invitation #17: Oil Pastel Expressions: Oil Pastel Application Techniques 159

Art Invitation #18: The Moon in Motion: Van Gogh's Starry Night*: Creating Movement in the Sky and Learning About Composition 161*

Art Invitation #19: Mail Art: Designing Envelopes and Postcards 163

Art Invitation #20: Matisse Cutouts: Making Collages from Cutouts and Silhouettes 165

Art Invitation #21: Handmade Stamps: Printmaking with Common Materials 167

Art Invitation #22: Signs of the Season: Creating Nature's Collages with Pressed Leaves, Flowers, and Prints 171

Art Invitation #23: The Moon of the Birch Trees: Creating Birch Trees Using a Variety of Watercolor Techniques 174

Art Invitation #24: Monoprints of the Moon: Printing Painted Designs onto Paper 176

Art Invitation #25: Paper Weaving: Weaving Techniques Using Paper Strips of Text and Image 179

Art Invitation #26: Decorative Borders: Ideas for Framing and Embellishing Moon Journal Entries 181

Art Invitation #27: Ornamental Stitching: Producing Texture and Pattern Using String and Decorative Threads 182

Art Invitation #28: Putting It All Together: Moon Journal Binding Techniques 185

5 A Final Invitation to the Teacher: Keeping a Moon Journal of Your Own   192

Afterword: Beyond Moon Journals   201

Bibliography   203

List of Color Illustrations

Color Plate 1: Watercolor and pastel, Joni Chancer

Color Plate 2: Pastel, Jason Levy

Color Plate 3: Hand-painted paper collage, Haley Boyd

Color Plate 4: Watercolor and pressed leaves, Joni Chancer

Color Plate 5: Watercolor and salt, Candace Camargo

Color Plate 6: Watercolor and felt-tip marker, Gina Rester-Zodrow

Color Plate 7: Hand-painted papers and found text, Gina Rester-Zodrow

Color Plate 8: Tissue paper and watercolor collage, Marisa Duchowny

Color Plate 9: Oil pastel, watercolor and paper collage, Gina Rester-Zodrow

Color Plate 10: Ink monoprint, Joni Chancer

Color Plate 11: Watercolor, Joni Chancer

About This Book

This book celebrates finding uncommon beauty in common things. It has been written by two teachers and two hundred children who shared a purpose and a heartfelt connection: We watched the moon. Our watching was not a passive activity. We took time and made choices, asked questions and searched for answers, noticed and recorded, responded and created. This is the work of Moon Journalists.

As we went about our work, we rediscovered a different type of time clock. We began to think of days, weeks, and months in terms of lunar phases. From the experience of keeping our Moon Journals, we developed new understanding of and appreciation for the people who came before us. We knew our ancestors did not rely on calendars, clocks, wristwatches, or computer screens to tell them the hour or the season. They marked time by the colors of the leaves, the feel of the wind, the growth of their crops, and the changing face of the moon. In our journals we found that it is possible to slow life down, to take notice of the natural world, and to mark the passage of months simply by learning to observe small changes.

Like the phases of the moon, this book gradually developed over time. As a self-contained classroom teacher at Red Oak Elementary School, Joni teaches academics and the arts to thirty fifth grade students. Gina, a Writer-in-Residence, works with children in kindergarten through sixth grade at St. Patrick's Day School. This multigraded teaching situation provided a unique opportunity for cross-age research and a context for experimenting with various approaches to keeping Moon Journals. We hope that our combined classroom stories offer a variety of entry points and options to colleagues who choose to join us in watching the moon.

Like a lunar legend, our story grew out of observations of nature. Several years ago we both began keeping Nature Notebooks with our students. These combined sketch pad–notebooks contained observations, poems, stories and drawings that sprang from watching trees and clouds, rain and insects, animals and other elements in nature. David Sobel (1993) writes about "touchstone memories" of childhood that you can "tuck away in a comfortable pocket in your mind, accessible so you can pull them out at a moment's notice. Smooth to the touch, they glint with the original brilliance of the moment of their inception. Dip them in water and their sheen awakens." Nature Notebooks, we discovered, can become a place for children to store memories of wonder and can provide a structure for immersion in the natural world. They inspired us to introduce different types of journals to our students. We began to select focused topics for investigation rather than generalized themes.

During the peak of the wildflower season, for example, we coordinated a day hike to La Jolla Canyon, which borders Southern California's coastline. The children followed the trails up the gentle slopes of the mountain, discovering waterfalls, springs, blooming yuccas, Prussian-blue lupine, orange poppies, and golden sunflowers. In addition to sketching and writing in their journals, our students took photographs of the landscape with its flowers, lizards, moths, frogs, and grasses. The snapshots added an important new element to our discoveries.

When the photographs were developed, the children passed them around the classroom, comparing those images to their sketches and field notes. Several children talked of creating collages and writing poems to accompany their images. We realized they needed time to re-enter their experience. We gave it to them. For days, the process continued in writing workshop and art studio. Ultimately, each child created a unique picture book of our day at La Jolla Canyon.

When we took this hike, we had no idea that we would soon be recording the story of the lunar cycle in Moon Journals. But this is where our story begins. We learned the power of individual and collaborative response to focused observation, and we discovered the importance of devoting consistent periods of time to playful improvisation. Revision and creation happen simultaneously in a studio/workshop environment. We recognized the importance of staying open to all of the options that are available to teachers and students, both within and beyond the walls of our classrooms. Thus were seeds planted for our study of the moon.

Moon Journals: Writing, Art, and Inquiry Through Focused Nature Study is divided into two parts that describe the beginnings, the development, and the extended applications of this project. Also included is a sample Moon Journal. It is filled with a selection of student art and writing entries. We have included first drafts and final products that represent the contents of an actual Moon Journal. We also included artwork from our own personal Moon Journals for two purposes. First, we wanted to show that teachers such as ourselves, without formal art training, can feel comfortable using the simple methods described in the Art Invitations. More importantly, we included our pieces as a way of inviting teachers to become part of a collaborative learning environment and to explore these techniques with students.

Part One presents an overview of the inquiry process that is an inherent part of keeping Moon Journals. In this section we describe how the study arose from the questions posed by children and how their continued queries sustained the investigation. In Chapter One, "A Classroom Story," Joni gives a personal account of her students' experiences during the development of their first Moon Journals. This presents an opportunity for teachers to step into a colleague's classroom and see the evolution of a studio/workshop environment.

Chapter Two, "Mapping the Journey," explains how the study of the moon becomes a focused-inquiry project, operating within the structures of writing, reading, and art workshops. We describe how Moon Journals develop into "working portfolios," demonstrating the students' growing confidence, versatility, and skills in writing and art. Just as the moon casts back the light of the sun, our students' Moon Journals reflect the words and insights of colleagues and researchers whose stories have instructed and inspired us.

Part Two, "The Process Pages," contains fifty-six art and writing minilessons that a teacher may use during writing and art workshops, or as classroom demonstrations, throughout the course of keeping Moon Journals. They need not be introduced in any particular sequence, but may be used flexibly. Each classroom account demonstrates how the invitations were developed in response to our students' writing, artwork, interests, questions, and discoveries.

Chapter Three, "The Writing Invitations," has twenty-eight writing minilessons. As we followed the moon, our students experimented with a wide range of genre, including field notes, poetry, scientific investigation, memoir, legend, and personal reflection. They also learned to apply various writing techniques to their entries, such as the use of similes, metaphors, and personification. The classroom stories, samples of student writing, and descriptions of instructional process suggest ways that teachers can adapt our experiences to fit their individual situations.

Chapter Four, "The Art Invitations," has twenty-eight art minilessons using various media such as pencil, pen and ink, watercolor, pastel, stencil, printmaking, and collage. Each invitation provides easy-to-follow step-by-step process instructions that serve as a starting point for extended individual exploration.

Chapter Five, "A Final Invitation to the Teacher: Keeping a Moon Journal of Your Own," includes journal entries contributed by teachers from across the United States. Whether their form is poetry or prose, within each piece is a common thread: the beauty and mystery that is an inherent part of watching the moon. We hope our readers will come to discover, as we did, that beauty is a natural part of science and wonder is at the heart of nature study. In this spirit, we invite you join us in following the moon.

Acknowledgments

Sheridan Blau and Maureen Barbieri lighted the fuse that began this book. We are grateful for their faith in this project, guidance, suggestions, and frequent e-mailed notes of support.

Toby Gordon believed that a Moon Journal could make a difference to teachers and children. Scott Mahler, our editor, traveled with us on this writing and art journey. His expertise, advice, and sense of humor have been invaluable. Melissa Inglis led us through the production process with gentle and meticulous care.

Our students, young writers, artists, and collaborators asked the questions, discovered the answers, and taught us new ways to see the world. A special thank you to Hailey Boyd, Pete Burns, Sara Charleston, Jacki Chou, Cleavant Derricks, Marisa Duchowney, Brian Gerrard, Jason Levy, Nicholas Rester-Zodrow, Ashley Tindall, and Luke Wilken, whose artwork appears in this book.

The staff at Red Oak Elementary School, especially Enid Miller, Rebecca Coger, Rich Stewart, and Kim Coufal, offered interest, insights, and heartfelt support.

Jeff Hamlin, administrator, artist, and friend, provided encouragement and enthusiasm and created an environment where art can flourish.

The teachers at St. Patrick's Day School, particularly Carol Clarke, Joan Jones, Diana Knapp, Jani Knotts, Timma Koepke, Brigid Marshall, Miriam Ritchey, and Penny Robison shared their experience in planning for surprises.

Aline Hontos and Patricia Morris understood the importance of exploring possibilities and setting and reaching goals.

Bronte Reynolds offered the gifts of understanding, patience, and renewed opportunity.

Fellows of the South Coast Writing Project demonstrated how to create and reflect, revise and respond, and pass along the pleasures of the process.

Lois Brandt, Gwen Dawson, Pat O'Brien, Linda Rief, Marolyn Stewart, and Sue Whisenand, our colleagues and fellow moon journalists, shared their poetry and classroom experiences and reminded us why we should invite children to look up at the sky. Michelle Safer taught us to make stars with a toothbrush, clouds with a sponge, and moonscapes with painted papers.

Darlene Appleford, Heidi Craine, Sue Nan Douglass, Tricie Krim, Karen Taylor, Michele Weston-Relkin, and Jo Woolery turned life into painted stories.

Joseph Wells gave insight and counsel.

Carol Boysen made each moment a work of art and taught us how to see in both directions at the same time.

Harriet Bender, Rosemary Cabe, Gaby Edwards, Sue Perona, and Jack Phraener celebrated, instructed, nourished, and believed. Their stories, poems, and friendship sustain and renew.

The teachers who attended our writing and art academies inspired and amazed us with their creativity, heartfelt response, and enthusiastic participation. Each hour spent in their company was a gift.

Mary Littell, owner of our favorite independent bookstore, unknowingly acted as our research assistant. A person who knows good books is a treasure.

Kathy Asher, Melodee Cane, Denise Carroll, Beverly Charleston, Margie Chespak, Candace DePuy, Judy Forman, Jackie and Dennis Fox, David Frazee, James Griffin, Nancy Hawfield, Lisa Hawthorne, Donna Nakashima, Marea Otter, and Andrea Porterfield are friends who provided the hands that sustained us during the months of writing this book and who encouraged our creative process day to day.

Robert and Helen Killeen and Virginia Brehm demonstrated how to pluck poetry seeds from a garden of wildflowers and alfalfa.

Len and Edith Chancer believed that dreams can happen.

John and Leona Zodrow reminded us that each detail in the landscape is a small gift of life.

George, Virginia, Taira, and Licia Rester proved that a kitchen table is not just for eating, but a place to learn drawing, painting, and storytelling.

Our families and fellow moongazers, Jeff, Kylie, and Josh, and John, Joshua, and Nicholas, gave their love, patience, and support throughout this project. We are blessed and are thankful to be on this journey with them.

Introduction

Warm colors of a crimson sunset fade into the cool, dusty purple sky. From window, sidewalk, and hillside observatories, young writers and artists watch as the delicate crescent of the new moon appears on the horizon. Its faint curved light is barely noticeable, but the children have anxiously awaited its appearance. With journals in hand, the moon watchers record the beginning of this lunar cycle.

Every night for the next four weeks, these students will watch the moon's transit and transformation across the sky. In so doing, they join a long line of scientists, astronauts, sailors, farmers, hunters, storytellers, musicians, poets, timekeepers, and painters. The children join these others in discovering how the moon tugs on imaginations, promotes artistic growth, inspires expression, and celebrates the cycles of their lives. This will occur, we have learned, as these student writers and artists fill the blank pages of a book we call a Moon Journal: a twenty-eight-day written and illustrated record of the moon's travels.

A Moon Journal begins on the first night of the new moon and continues through the next seven phases of the moon's elliptical journey: waxing crescent, first quarter, waxing gibbous, full moon, waning gibbous, last quarter, and waning crescent. As the shrinking crescent finally disappears into darkness, the lunar cycle is complete and so are the Moon Journals.

These journals take on as many shapes as the face of the moon. No two are alike. Each nightly entry begins in a similar way: The time, date, and weather are noted; a brief written observation is recorded; and a simple sketch is drawn to illustrate the scene. What happens next is up to the journalist. There are a multitude of choices. Often the written entry is expanded into a story or a poem and the sketch becomes the catalyst for artwork in another medium.

We think you'll discover, as we have, that when students spend a month of daily lunar observation they become *experts* in their field. Presented with the challenge of seeing something new, unique, and compelling in the moon every night, they become active learners, questioning scientists, patient researchers, expressive artists, and detailed writers.

By discovering finite differences in the nightly skies, moongazers stretch their creative boundaries. As they dig into previously unexplored realms, most achieve a new sensitivity for life's cycles and an appreciation for their own ability to depict the world through writing and art.

The Moon Journal is a place for learning, reflection, and response. It is a book of poems, a collection of stories, a set of facts, a gallery of art—an anthology of surprise.

In many ways a Moon Journal is not about the moon. It is perhaps better described as a book about questions and discovery, about seeing and wonder. The moon is simply the illuminated vehicle that allows us to journal this journey of life.

Part One

The Making of a Studio/Workshop

To Make a Difference

I asked the sun . . .
why do you come each day
wheeling across the sky
hot fire
warmth
light
a daily toil
a daily gift?

He answered:
I know what I can do to make a
    difference . . .
to the farmer,
to the artist,
to the cactus wren,
to the morning glory.
It is my work,
it is my reason,
it is my dignity.

I asked the moon . . .
why do you come each night
gliding across the sky
white fire
coolness
reflected light
a nightwatch
a constancy
a gift?

She answered:
I know what I can do to make a
    difference . . .
to tides,
to owls,
to lovers,
to clouds that cover me with veils in
    the indigo sky.
It is my work,
it is my reason,
it is my dignity.

I asked myself . . .
why do you begin again, each year
with new faces, new children?
Books and stories,
read and told,
pictures and puzzles . . .
daily lessons and daily decisions.

I answered:
I know what I can do to make a
    difference . . .
to minds that wonder,
to eyes that see
and not just look.
For the children,
for myself,
it is a shared gift.
It is my work,
it is my reason,
it is my dignity.

Joni Chancer

Chapter One

A Classroom Story

What started as a question ended in a journey into writing, art, science, nature—into life. It began quite simply when Joni and her students made a place for the moon in their lives. This is Joni's classroom story about their first twenty-eight-day Moon Journal cycle.

BEGINNINGS

At Red Oak Elementary School we begin each day with announcements, celebrations, and the flag salute. We line up, class by class, on the playground. My habit is to look up at the Southern California sky during this time, especially in the month of October, and watch the clouds move over the canyons behind our school. Lindsay, our classroom naturalist, followed my eyes one morning. As we began our short walk to the classroom, she pointed out that the moon was visible if you looked closely. Other children were surprised to see that paper-thin disk in the bright blue eastern sky. Conversation about the moon continued as the students took their books and papers out of their backpacks. While I took roll and wrote the day's agenda on the board, questions surfaced across the room:

> Why do we see the moon in the day? Does the moon rise like the sun? Is the moon visible every night and every day? Does it give its own light? Why does it change size and shape? What makes it orange and yellow? Does the moon look the same all over the world?

I started jotting the children's comments on the chalkboard. In September I had worried about finding an engaging topic for an inquiry study. As Short, Harste, and Burke (1996) describe, "instructionally, inquiry means that instead of a single theme as an excuse to teach science, social studies, mathematics, reading, and writing, these knowledge systems and sign systems become tools for exploring, finding, and researching student questions." Now my antennae were up. I felt an almost tangible interest taking shape.

With strong possibilities brewing, I left our initial questions on the board. I knew that the children would read them over throughout the morning. After lunch we revisited the questions. Andrew, Adam, Lindsay, Kirsten, and Brian seemed to know a lot about the moon and made sketches showing the moon in relationship to the sun and the earth. Tracy and Nadine used the questions as a springboard for metaphorical writing and suggested ideas for legends and stories with the moon as a central character. But most of the children (and their teacher) still had many unanswered questions.

Half in jest, I invited the students to personify the moon by asking, "Do you think it is male or female?" Some children called out, "What about the man in the moon?" This was direct evidence, they felt, of its masculinity. Courtney remembered a Chinese folktale about the Lady of the Moon, and other legends were recalled about moon maidens. I jotted on the board: Look for legends at the library! This would become a new genre study in our reading workshop.

By the time the children left for the day, our project was loosely defined and offered several options for investigation. The connections to science, social studies, and literature were obvious. Moon legends and folk tales, cultural tie-ins, and poems about the moon were easy to find. The moon was readily available for observation and focused study over time. The lunar phases provided a dynamic factor that would fuel interest and inspire continued questions. The weather and seasonal considerations added spice to the mix and a welcome degree of unpredictability. At this early planning stage, my main objective was to find a common vehicle for exploration that would connect all aspects of the study.

Several possibilities ran through my mind, and I recalled a recent meeting of my teacher-researcher group. Lois Brandts, a second grade teacher, shared the pocket-sized sketch pads she gave her young scientist-writers. With them they drew pencil sketches of the moon each night, along with brief written entries. Something she told her students struck me: Write like a scientist and then like a poet. I thought of that morning's conversation in my fifth grade classroom. Our talk about the moon had crossed the language line between prose and poetry.

Lois's sketch pads reminded me of the Nature Notebooks my students and I keep throughout the year. These journals contain field notes, drawings, and observations of flowers, birds, insects, rain puddles, clouds, animals, and constellations. A past nature study focused on the Monarch butterflies that spend the winter in a nearby eucalyptus grove. Last year my students investigated a single oak tree on the hill behind our school, recording seasonal changes and the animals and insects that make it their home. When the children focused on a particular subject in their Nature Notebooks, their entries were often richer and more reflective.

I gathered resources at the school library. While turning the pages of moon-related picture books, my hands twitched with excitement. The illustrations were inspiring. Eric Carle's *Papa, Please Get the Moon for Me* (1991), Ed Young's *Moon Mother* (1993), and Myra Cohn Livingston and Leonard Everett Fisher's *A Circle of Seasons* (1982) captured the beauty of the moon in their own distinctive styles. Just like these published authors and artists, my students could make meaning through words and images in their Moon Journals. From watercolor to collage, prose to poetry, observing the moon offered a context for integrated writing, reading, art, and science.

FOCUSING AND ORGANIZING: DECISIONS

At this point I had important decisions to make. Would knowing facts about the moon enhance the children's observations? Or should we observe first and then engage in research? I opted for the second choice. Short, Harste, and Burke (1996) describe how "the focus of an inquiry is not always in the form of a specific question, but can be a 'wondering' about something we want to pursue. As we work through inquiry, we do not usually end with one answer or even a set of answers. Our problem solving does not narrow our perspective, but gives us more understandings, questions and possibilities than when we started!"

Even though excitement was high, I decided to delay the actual daily journal process until the next new moon. It was important for children to observe and record cyclical lunar changes, and we needed to begin with the discovery that a "new moon" meant no visible moon. I wanted my students to feel the excitement of observing the growing, waxing moon and to anticipate with a sense of drama and wonder the eventual full moon.

A new lunar cycle would begin in one week. In the interim, to keep our interest peaked, we continued reading moon legends and poems. During this week I was busy. Because I planned to follow the moon with my students, I purchased a blank journal with a crescent moon smiling from its cover. Having a special journal would be like publishing my own book and I could hardly wait to begin my entries. I wanted the children to feel the same way about their journals, but I could not afford to purchase thirty blank books.

I set out to design an easily constructed but inviting alternative. Using rubber stamps and my computer's fonts, I created a cover and reproduced cardstock copies (see Art Invitation #28: *Putting It All Together*; Figure 4-24 shows a photograph of the journal covers). Later, I cut these copies down to a comfortable size for writing and sketching, laminated them, and set them aside. I composed a preface page with open-ended instructions for keeping the journal. (See Figure 1-1, the preface page of the Moon Journal.) Two parents helped by binding together thirty-five blank sheets of paper per student book, more than enough for the nightly entries. When we finished, we knew we had made the children books they would fill with pictures, poems, and discoveries.

BEGINNING THE JOURNEY: DAY ONE

Our greatly anticipated day arrived on November third, the night of the new moon. I passed out the journals. The children decorated the preface page with illustrations of stars and moons, and each book took on an individual character. I reminded the students of the Moon Journal procedures they would follow that

Moon Journal Preface

In your Moon Journal you will observe the night sky every night for one month, from new moon to new moon. Be sure to record the date and time of your observations. Even though the moon is the star of your journal, pay attention to other nighttime wonders. Let your eyes adjust to the darkness and then—look up! What do you see? Are there clouds? Is it a foggy or misty night? Is the wind blowing? Is the sky dark or filled with moonlight? Do you see constellations or planets? Shooting stars? What do you hear? Crickets? Birds? Animals? Raindrops or wind? Cars or airplanes? Do you smell flowers, trees, or the smoky scent of a fire?

What does the moon look like? What shape is it? What time does it appear in the sky? What position is it in? What stars are near it? Does it change from night to night? How? What does it remind you of? A banana? A silver dollar? Jot down an observation. What were you doing when you discovered the moon? What were you thinking? How did it make you feel? There are many ways to record your impressions: scientific observations, poems, questions, diary entries, legends—the choice is yours.

Words will help you describe many of the things you see, but pictures will allow you to add color and mood to your journal entries. Looking carefully at the sky will guide you in choosing the right art materials to use: watercolors, chalk or oil pastels, crayons, colored pencils, collage papers, cotton balls, foil, tissue papers, or tempera paints. Look around your house and the classroom until you discover interesting ways to represent your impressions. Be creative! You might want to start with a simple sketch and then experiment with different media until you find satisfying ways to illustrate your observation. Daily class time will be reserved to share your entries, learn new techniques from your friends and your teacher, and revise your art and writing pieces. You will be able to check out some of our art materials to take home, including colored construction paper cut to the size of your Moon Journal pages. Many students like to glue in their art entries so they can use different types of paper.

Just as important as your words and pictures are the questions that come to mind when you make your observations. Be sure to record the things you want to know. Your questions will help all of us learn about the moon, the night sky, and—who knows what else? Your journal is a place for discoveries, a place to watch and wait for surprises. Look up at the stars, focus your eyes on the moon, and let your journey begin!

FIGURE 1-1   *Moon Journal preface*

evening. Because we kept Nature Notebooks earlier in the year, they were already familiar with recording the day, date, and time of each entry. They could begin with either a sketch or a written observation. I encouraged them to use all five senses and to notice more than the moon in the sky.

My closing words were, "Look carefully for clouds, stars, silhouettes of trees, houses and bushes, flowers, and other signs of the season. Remember, your journal is portable and you can take it with you wherever you go." Several children made plans to meet for moongazing that evening. At the end of the day, not a single journal was left on a desk. I took my journal home, anticipating personal time for observation, sketching, and writing.

The next morning, while standing in line on the playground, the children were already buzzing about their first entries. When we entered our classroom, hands shot up. Everyone wanted to share observations. In my plan book I had penciled in about fifteen minutes for sharing, so after taking roll we took out our journals. The first entries described clouds, stars, sounds of the night, and the absence of the moon. Ashley wrote:

> I'm sitting here listening to sounds and staring up at the sky. Planes and stars are floating by. I wish the moon were out, so he could give some light to show the silhouette of the hills and brush. But there is no moonlight to reflect in the puddles of water. So now the stars will do all the work and shine so bright throughout the night. And as this night passes I say good night to all the stars, but not the moon.

Cleavant recorded:

> Tonight there is no moon. I feel the cold breeze brushing against my face. I also see a blanket of fog rising over the hills. I can hear the cries of the coyotes. I like seeing the moths and going outside to look for the moon.

Jacki observed:

> I was about to go to sleep when I remembered to look for the moon! I went to the front room and looked out the window. I looked for one certain star that is always next to the moon. The moon was invisible to my naked eye. The sky looked so beautiful, bright and clear, it seemed like I could reach out the window and touch the stars.

Tracy raised her hand and asked to share her perceptions—a poem. The children and I knew Tracy as a writer who delighted in imagery, so we were very interested to hear how she translated her prose to poetry. She walked up to the author's stool, sat down, and waited for the audience to listen attentively. With her natural dramatic flair she began.

Where Is the Moon?

Giant fireflies that dance in the night sky.
These are the stars.
Candles that go out with the first stream of light.
These are the stars.

Tiny light bulbs that flicker and flash in the night.
These are the stars.
Silk worms that slither slowly across pastures of gray and black.
These are the stars.
But . . .
where is the moon, I say?
I've been looking for it all day.
I've looked for it high and low,
but I don't know where a moon can go.
I've looked for it all day and all night,
but I've had to use a large flashlight,
because without the moon tonight
there is nothing to make the world seem bright.
I loved that moon,
its shine and its glow—
why did that moon
have to go?
Look up there in the sky,
is that my moon floating by?
Please, moon, please don't go.
I want to tell you how I love you so.
Because without you
there is no light.
Without you I can't read
in the darkness of night.
Well, in the end
it all worked out—
in the next few days
the moon was floating about!

We applauded when she finished and I asked her to read it aloud one more time. The students responded to this second reading and repeated lines they especially enjoyed. We noticed Tracy's use of repetition and how she seemed to be talking to the moon, engaging it in dialogue.

Tracy commented that her poem would sound even better if some of the children created a chorus and read certain lines along with her. Her poem struck me as one that would be enhanced by sound and musical instruments and I asked Tracy if she might want to "score" her poem. She wasn't quite sure what that meant, but was eager to learn; so we made plans to discuss choral techniques during writing workshop.

The children shared a few more entries. Although most of then were brief, we heard several examples of "show not tell" (Caplan, 1984) and sensory descriptions:

The sky is as clear as a piece of glass.
Maybe the new moon is somewhere in the night's bright sky.

There are widely scattered stars. They are very faint.
The sky is full of grayish white clouds that look like sheets!
Night birds sang songs to the new moon, asking it to come out and visit.
I decided to share my entry.

> First night of my moon journal—new moon, so *no* moon. It's cold, and I turned on the heater for the first time this season. I woke up thirsty and went into the kitchen for a glass of water. Now I look out one of my windows and see bright stars. They actually twinkle, just like the words of the nursery rhyme. It's quiet. Semibare branches of our alder tree peek out from the edge of the window. I think how in August they still have brownish-green leaves that rustle in the wind, and I can hear the owl call out the story of a summer night. Not now—it is still. No insects, no birds.

The children commented that I didn't write just about the moon but that I had also included my thoughts. I explained that when I keep a journal I often write down what I am saying to myself. This type of writing is called "internal dialogue" or "reflection." I noted that, although I began by simply describing what I saw out the window, my observations gradually evolved into personal reflection.

My house was very quiet when I started this piece. It made me think of the beginning lines of one of my favorite poems by Wallace Stevens: "The house was quiet and the world was calm." I borrowed that first line and used it as a springboard for my own poem.

> The house is quiet and
> the world is calm
> and the sky is washed in purple
> and indigo.
> Fall stars
> in the clear sky
> twinkle and light the heavens
> with their cold fire.
> I listen for the wind in the trees,
> but it is quiet.
> I listen for insects
> or my friend the owl . . .
> only quiet.
> Can you hear a star twinkle?
> Do the constellations sigh or sing
> as they wind their way across the sky?
> My window is a frame
> for the brilliance,
> and I imagine I hear
> chimes . . .

star chimes
that lull me to sleep.

I read the poem twice, following our established writing workshop procedures for giving response (Graves, 1983). The first reading was an opportunity for my students to "receive" general impressions. The second offered them a chance to notice specific parts that impressed them. They verbally "pointed," or said back the lines that struck them, noting the repetition of some words and commenting on my questioning technique near the end of the poem. I told the students that tomorrow I would put the poem on an overhead and they could help me read it as a poem for two voices. Perhaps we would accompany our reading with a few musical instruments. Some of the children suggested using wind chimes to enhance the lines about the twinkling stars.

The recess bell rang. We were all surprised that an hour and forty-five minutes had passed. The fifteen-minute time allowance I originally penciled into my plan book caused me to smile. I looked at the words and pictures that covered the chalkboard and copied them into my notebook (see Figure 1-2).

There were enough minilessons spiraling out of the first day's experience to keep us busy for a week, and tomorrow we would have even more entries to share! Fifteen minutes would not be enough time for our Moon Journals. I reconfigured the initial ninety minutes of the day, reserving more time for surprises, in addition to the lessons and demonstrations.

The afternoon's writing workshop provided us with an opportunity to revisit our initial entries. I looked forward to conferencing with Tracy and several other students about their poetry. In this small group we prepared a "poetry present" for the rest of the class. We recorded Tracy's poem on chart paper and I showed the children how simple it is to create musical notations. We matched common symbols to specific sounds and instruments. (See Writing Invitation #5: *Moon Music*, Figure 3-2.) For example, an illustration of three little stars represented wind chimes, and a picture of rain falling from a cloud represented a rain stick.

After experimenting with several instruments, Tracy added notations with the help of her friends. The group went outside to practice tomorrow morning's performance. Later that day, I looked for other published poems that lend themselves to sound enhancement and I bookmarked their pages. I knew that after hearing Tracy's group perform her poem, many of the children would be eager to "score" poetry.

AN OLD TOOTHBRUSH: A CATALYST FOR INTEGRATED RESPONSE

That night I found myself listening for sounds as I recorded observations in my Moon Journal. The Pleiades, a star cluster in the constellation Taurus, impressed me with its distinct configuration. A poem took shape, this time with written notations for musical instruments:

FIGURE 1-2

Planning book

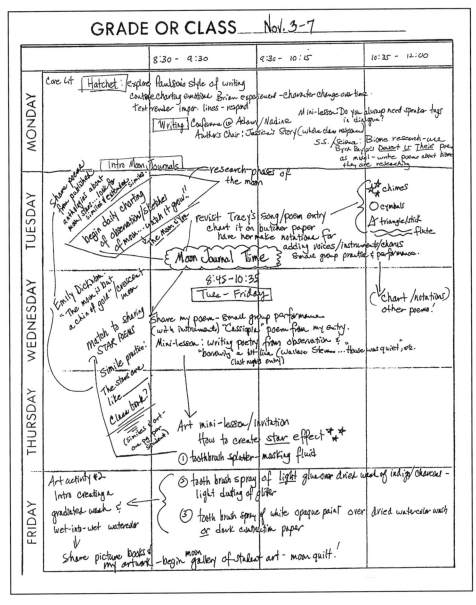

(soft shake of a tambourine)
The Pleiades (shake.............)
Seven sisters of the night, (shake.............)
Tightly clustered, (wind chimes)
Punctuating the velvet of the indigo sky. (wind chimes)

The Pleiades (flute.....)
Seven sisters of the night, (flute.....)
Dancing, trailing their veils through constellations. (chimes and flute)
The Pleiades (soft tambourine.....)
Seven sisters of the night, (soft tambourine.....)
A sisterhood, (high octave twinkling keys of piano)
A small tight company, (high octave twinkling keys of piano)
Embracing in the November sky.
The Pleiades (chimes)
The Pleiades, (chimes and flute)
The Pleiades. (chimes and flute softly fade, final shake of tambourine)

My sketching changed as I became more attuned to sensory images. A pencil alone couldn't possibly capture the dimensions and colors that surprised me. The night sky wasn't actually black; it was a mixture of colors, shades, and tones. The stars were shining and the sky was indigo, ultramarine, and gray, with wispy, white, barely visible clouds. I felt particularly limited in trying to render the shining stars contrasted against the sky. When I returned to my study to complete the entry, I played with silver pens. The stars did shine, but the look was too metallic and not realistic enough.

To achieve a softer, more natural effect I experimented with colored pencils. The color names imprinted on the side of the pencils looked promising; indigo, midnight blue, and cloud gray matched my visual impressions. I applied strokes of color over the original pencil sketch.

Although satisfied with the general effect of the colored pencils, I was still unhappy with the stars. How could I create a galaxy of brilliance and pinpoints of light? I remembered a watercolor technique that produces a splattered-paint effect. After taping a piece of watercolor paper to my Masonite board, I dug through a drawer and found an old toothbrush. I took the brush back to the table and dipped it into a masking fluid mixture. I splattered the fluid onto the paper by brushing my thumb across the bristles.

When the splatters were dry I spread clear water over the paper with a wide, flat brush. Mixing black and blue pigment together in my palette, I produced a deep indigo blue. I applied the pigment to the watercolor paper with a paintbrush. The drops of color bloomed on the wet paper, diffusing and swirling as they created an abstract colorful background. I tilted the Masonite board from side to side, continuing to blur and blend the colors until they resembled the sky I had observed. (See Art Invitation #4: *Swirling Watercolor Sky*.) When the paper was completely dry, I gently rubbed off the masking-fluid splatters with my fingers. The white paper underneath the small spots was revealed.

I smiled with satisfaction. The white splatter marks looked like the real stars I had described in my poem. With very diluted bluish-gray watercolors I added a final touch: an almost transparent wash over a few of the white splattered areas. I remembered that some of the stars had been blurred by the veil of clouds, and this final pale blue wash helped me achieve that effect. (See Art Invitation #5: *Splattered Stars* for instructions, and Color Plate 1 for a sample of this entry.)

But my picture was not complete. In my written observation I had described the silhouette of my neighbors' houses against the sky. I sketched a simple pattern of a roofline on a piece of construction paper and cut it out. Using the top portion of the pattern, I applied black-chalk pastels along the cutout edge. I positioned my stencil in the location of the roofline and gently wiped the pastel dust onto the watercolor painting using a tissue. (See Art Invitation #10: *Moonlit Silhouettes*.) When I lifted the construction paper mask, I saw a clean-edged silhouette of my neighbors' houses against the starry sky. (See Color Plate 1 for a sample of this technique.)

I was pleased with this simple piece, but I needed to find a way to add the watercolor paper to my journal. I suspected the children would also want to try these techniques, so the method of including them in the journal needed to be quick and easy. I decided not to open the binding. Instead, I simply cut the watercolor paper down to size and glued it on top of the thinner bound paper.

As I packed my Moon Journal into my canvas school bag, I realized that my old toothbrush had become a catalyst that added an entirely new dimension to the journal. Something important had occurred when I connected the indigo sky and splattered toothbrush stars with the words of my entry. Now I was seeing the night sky through the dual lenses of art and writing. Thinking about which techniques, tools, and art media could help me depict an observation caused me to look at the landscape more carefully. For example, I saw thin, transparent clouds as torn tissue papers, softly diffused moonlight as a watercolor wash, and a bed of flowers as a mixed-media collage. I began thinking metaphorically. Now my verbal descriptions were enhanced by visual comparisons. Words from an artist's vocabulary spilled over into my prose and poetry.

> Tissue paper clouds
> Float through watercolor moonlight,
> Casting sepia shadows
> Over a garden collage.

These words pointed to the art materials that I could use to represent the scene. I knew, for example, how to use pastels to create an iridescent moonglow, how to use a toothbrush to splatter stars, and how to mix indigo blue paint for the night sky. Sometimes words led to pictures and sometimes pictures wrote the words.

Our Moon Journals, I realized, could contain a diverse selection of entries that demonstrated a process approach to writing and art. The initial pencil sketches acted as a first draft for more developed art pieces. Likewise, recording a visual response in writing often turned factual observation into prose and poetry, flavored with imagery and imagination. The children could use a variety of materials and writing and art techniques to match the mood, colors, and emotions of a particular night's observation. I wondered whether my students had likewise been inspired to add dimension to their sketches and entries. I could hardly wait for the next morning.

EXPLORING OPTIONS FOR MEANING MAKING: DAY TWO

Once again excitement whipped through the room as the children took out their journals and asked to share their work. Tracy was already in position with her group of accompanists. We waited until everyone was silent, and then the group began their performance of her poem. The students delighted in hearing the sound instruments and begged to take turns in providing the accompaniment. Tracy's instrumental notations were easy to follow. Marnie played her flute, Jessica tinkled the wind chimes, and Kerstin hit the tambourine. Brian added the sounds of the rainstick, and Adam crashed cymbals together to create the effect of lightning.

The sounds, I realized, did more than enhance the oral presentations. As we selected just the right instruments and effects to add to the words, our understandings and interpretations of the poem changed. The musical accompaniment added feeling and atmosphere and pulled on our emotions in the same way a sound score enhances a film, adding suspense, excitement, mystery, and mood. (See Writing Invitation #5: *Moon Music*.)

As we listened to written entries and admired the artwork, I was struck by the power of the children's response. Today's entries were blossoms from seeds of yesterday's sharing. Although I did not assign the writing of poems with musical notations and accompaniment, many of the students chose to experiment with this new approach.

In the same spirit, I shared my watercolor splatter painting. I did not initially tell the children how I produced the effect. I wanted them to see if they could guess the process. Several students recognized the watercolor wash technique from previous art demonstrations. They guessed that I splattered white paint onto the paper, but were puzzled by the flat quality of the white spots or stars. Paint splotches, they decided, would have a slightly raised surface. I took out the materials and quickly demonstrated the process.

Because there were so many of us in the classroom, I hesitated about using masking fluid, which can produce an odor and possible health concerns in a closed area. Therefore, I demonstrated a second approach to achieving the same effect. This time I put down the watercolor wash first, waited for it to dry, and then splattered opaque white tempera paint across the paper. Some children decided they could just as easily splatter the paint onto dark construction paper, achieving the same effect of stars in a cloudless black sky.

Since the children were eager to try the technique themselves, we set up stations and soon had galaxies of stars appearing in our classroom. Christina even created specific constellations by applying minute dots of white paint with the end of a toothpick before splattering the rest of the stars.

Before the day was over, many students asked to check out sets of watercolor paints and pastels overnight. They also requested some heavier colored papers to glue into their journals. I commissioned a small group of organizers to devise a checkout system and prepare Ziplock baggies of materials. The children left for home with their Moon Journals, construction paper, watercolors, and pastels packed safely into their backpacks. Tonight we hoped to see the moon—the star of our celestial production!

"I WANT TO SHOW YOU WHAT I SAW AND TELL YOU HOW I FELT": DAY THREE

As the sun set in the western sky, the thinnest possible crescent appeared. I first spotted the moon while traveling north with a group of friends for a poetry reading. As we followed the coastline, I followed the moon. It hovered over the ocean, creating a silver path over the water. I was struck by a contrast in colors. Earlier in the evening the sky was filled with vibrant colors that made the landscape glow with golden warmth. Orange had blended into yellow and then into a pure color that was a combination of blue and white.

But now the moon, sky, and sea created a palette of cool colors: deeper blues and shiny silver light. As the reflection of the moon made a path on the inky waters, I recalled Greek myths of another world, where crossing the waters became part of a spiritual journey. The lines of a poem played in my mind.

When I returned home, the contrasting colors of the sunset and moonscape nudged me to work. I began by painting a watercolor sky of the sunset colors, using a graded-wash technique. (See Art Invitation #3: *Watercolor Wash Backgrounds.*) When I finished the sunset painting, I began a second piece. After mixing a palette of cool ocean colors, I painted the moon's reflection on the water. I mentally composed the poem that began in the car. Once again I observed how art and writing were working together as complementary processes.

> A sickle moon
> hovers above the sea.
> A silver path shimmers over the moving waters.
> Spirits could walk across that pale trail . . .
> Into the stars,
> up to the moon,
> and look down on me.

As I put away my paints, I anticipated reading about the appearance of the moon in my students' journals. The hills of Agoura offered another background for the setting crescent moon. I imagined thirty children looking up into the night sky from different locations, yet finding common delight in making their varied discoveries.

It was fortunate that Moon Journal time was now an established first-thing-in-the-morning event. The children couldn't wait to share their entries. "Did you see the moon last night?" was asked over and over again as they walked through the door. We heard descriptions of the night sky, the sunset, and the crescent moon.

I can see all the colors like yellow, orange, black, light blue, a little purple, and even pink.

The sky looks like a picture made out of watercolors or pastels.

The stars are like paint splattered on my mother's new carpet.

The sky is a dark navy blue, and it is a satiny look.

Tonight I can see the waxing crescent of the moon. It's the first part of the new moon.

The moon is what you can look at, unlike the sun.

Both scientific descriptions and poetic improvisations were filled with the excitement of the first sighting. Although we had all viewed the moon many times before, watching, anticipating, and drawing the moon gave us a sense of ownership. This moon belonged to us.

The sliver-shaped moon offered the perfect invitation for writing similes. (See Writing Invitation #7: *Similes by Starlight*.) An impromptu writing minilesson elicited several responses to the sentence frame I wrote on the board: A crescent moon is like a _____.

This was a new way of thinking about the moon, but the children caught on and offered a variety of comparisons to complete the open-ended sentence. Jessica contributed "It's like a slice of pineapple!" Our chalkboard was quickly filled with similes.

A crescent moon is like _____.

a cat's claw

an angel's smile

the tail of my cat

magic in the night sky

Each simile could be featured as a page in an illustrated class book, a possibility I jotted down in my planning notebook.

As we continued discussing the moon's appearance, several children reported that the crescent seemed to grow larger and more golden as it dropped lower in the sky. They wanted to describe the moon with greater scientific accuracy and explain what caused the change in size and color. This was the perfect time for research. A trip to the library provided us with several sources of information, and I brought out three new additional books I had found at the bookstore. We went to work as scientists, researching these questions:

What do you call this moon?

Why does it move in the sky?

How much bigger will it appear each night?

What makes it look so small at first, and why does it seem to grow?

When will we have a full moon?

Will it appear at the same time every night?

Does the moon give light like the sun?

As answers to the questions emerged, the children made notes in their journals. We added new vocabulary words to help us describe the moon as it moved through its phases. *Waxing*, or growing, and *waning*, or shrinking, were just the words we needed. Stephen suggested we also add "quarter moon," which, he explained, was really half a moon. The moon at this point would be one quarter of the way through its cycle.

We attempted to demonstrate the cause of the changing shape of the moon. Different children took the positions of the sun, moon, and earth in the sky. With a bright flashlight as our light source and two basketballs representing the moon and the earth, we were able to duplicate a waxing and waning moon. We decided to keep a classroom wall chart of the changing moon, with a small square representing each night of the cycle. This would help us watch the moon grow and provide us our own resource for comparison.

Right before recess the children asked me to share my journal. As soon as they saw the brightly colored watercolor wash, they wanted to try this technique themselves. "We need to know how to do this—for the sunsets!" they urged.

FROM OBSERVATION TO IMAGINATION: DAY FOUR

The following day, we had watercolor workshop. First, we looked at many examples of watercolor illustrations in picture books. We reviewed Moon Journal entries that described the sunsets and listed the colors on the board. I introduced the children to some of the color names found in an artist's palette: indigo, ultramarine blue, vermilion, burnt umber, cerulean blue, and cadmium orange. (See Writing Invitation #11: *Colors of the Night*.) Next, I demonstrated how to create a multicolored wash on wet watercolor paper. Watercolor skies of different combinations appeared: oranges, reds, and yellows over warm brown hills and the deeper blue shades of a night sky over an ocean. At the end of the day, watercolors were checked out of the classroom once again.

In the children's written entries, what Brown and Cambourne (1987) term "linguistic spillover" was becoming a regular phenomenon. We had begun reading legends about the moon as part of a focused genre study during reading workshop. The language and imagery of these stories spilled over into students' responses to their observations. When they described the moon, an interesting cloud, or even a particular star in the sky, many children extended their literal observations into imaginative speculation. They began seeing drama in the sky, with the moon, stars, and clouds as the cast of characters. (See Writing Invitation #12: *Lunar Legends*.)

Jacki, for example, was struck by the very bright star she noticed near the moon on several consecutive nights. She wrote in her journal:

> There always is a lone star by the moon. This star has a special story. Stars get older and older over centuries. When they get too old they fall to earth,

to the end of the world where there are islands called the Star Islands. Retired stars go there and bathe every day in a golden waterfall of youth. When they are young again, they can go up into the sky and be young stars once more. But one star was impatient. So after begging the moon for a long time, the moon lifted it up to the sky and it became a star again. But, on account of the bargain, it may not go out of the moon's gaze. So in the day it cannot play with the other stars. It is lonely. Now the star wishes it had been patient, so it could play with its friends.

PICTURE WRITERS AND STORY PAINTERS: DAY FIVE

We became very impressed with the art and writing of one author-illustrator in particular: Eric Carle. We read and examined his picture books daily. My friend Lois Brandts had e-mailed news of "Picture Writer," an Eric Carle videotape in which he describes his journey as an artist and writer that began when he was in kindergarten. Lois and her students loved the video, and her second graders reveled in a day of creating handpainted "community papers" like Carle's to use in making collages. I bought a copy of the tape and screened it for my class. We watched Eric Carle at work in his studio, listened to him delight over his creations, and observed him working with uninhibited creativity. As he described it, he "is just like a little kid, having fun!" He told the story of how his mother and father encouraged him and how his kindergarten teacher had brought his artistic gifts to their attention. As we listened to him talk, we watched his painted tissue papers come alive with vibrant color, pattern, and design. We understood his message because we, too, knew about "picture writing." Our journals were filled with it.

I knew the children would want to create their own treasure box of handpainted papers to cut up later for collage. As Carle demonstrated, it is useful to have piles of predominately green, yellow, red, blue, brown, purple, and orange papers available. So we turned our classroom into our own version of Eric Carle's studio. (See Art Invitation #11: *Handpainted Papers*.)

Lois had suggested setting out paper plate palettes of warm and cool analogous colors, so we organized painting stations throughout the room. On each table I placed wide and thin bristle brushes, plastic palette knives, and small pieces of sponges attached to clothespin holders. The children could produce swirls, squares, and blots with the materials, depending on the pressure and movement of their wrists and fingers. In the video Eric Carle used different objects to create textures, so we brought in our own assortment of small carpet squares, wide-toothed combs, netting, needlepoint canvas, and bottles. Most of the children used tempera paints, but some wanted to create handpainted papers with watercolors. We played music and moved from table to table creating small masterpieces. "Look at this!" I kept hearing. "How did you do that?" quickly followed. Minilessons erupted all over the room and I couldn't begin to keep up with my students' activities and discoveries.

The freedom of creating abstract designs was invaluable to the children's artistic development. They felt free to experiment with color, shape, pattern, and design. As the papers dried, we ooohed and aaahed over the variety, the bold colors, and the dynamic designs. Our classroom was a glorious mess, but the experience more than justified every minute of cleanup! Linguistic spillover, I discovered, had a correlation in art. Visual spillover was occurring every day in our classroom.

SKYSCAPES AND CLOUD PRODUCTIONS: DAY SIX

The next morning the bright blue November sky was gobbled up by heavy cumulous clouds. Nadine began to point out creatures she found in the clouds: dragons, feathers, birds, and faces. Soon many children were finding castles, ships, vegetables, and animals in the clustering formations.

When we entered the classroom, the students wrote and illustrated the action in the sky. Some children created dropped-in watercolor clouds, but many chose to use our handpainted papers to create collages. Davey decided the white and gray clouds in his painting were feuding. "The sky was in a war between good and evil," he described. As the children talked about their paintings, I heard poetry in the making.

Imagery such as "the clouds are like ships" and "the clouds look like bunnies hopping across a blue pasture" offered another opportunity for experiments with simile and metaphor. I wrote "The clouds are_____" on the chalkboard, and the children called out comparisons:

a soft warm blanket for the heavens
spirits of people who have gone away
a grand canyon of clouds

The list became a found poem of thirty different metaphors. (See Writing Invitation #8: *Metaphor Moon*.) Later that day I typed each metaphor in very large letters on the computer and printed out the pages on construction paper. Each child painted or collaged his or her individual page and we created an illustrated class book of poetry.

That night the moon wasn't visible. Instead, the sky was covered with the same shifting clouds we had observed during the day. The next morning, I wasn't surprised to find that the children developed individual poems from the lines of the class book. Sheila's and Timothy's poems describe the cloud-filled skies:

Illuminated

The clouds are a pure white.
They're fluffy with

no distinct edges.
They're layered
like sedimentary rock in white.
They blend in with the sky,
like a baby kangaroo in his mother's pouch.
The clouds cover the sky
like a blanket over a person.
It's beautiful.
All of the sky is illuminated
through the clouds.

Sheila

Bulls

Today I saw clouds moving fast
like a herd of bulls at a rodeo
chasing clowns.
I closed my eyes for a few minutes and wondered
what it felt like
to be a cloud.

Matt

THE JOURNEY CONTINUES: HIGHLIGHTS FROM DAY SEVEN THROUGH DAY TWENTY-EIGHT

Cloudy skies gave way to crisp, clear mid-November nights. In the beginning of its cycle, the moon was briefly visible in the western sky just before sunset. Each night, we discovered, it appeared later and later. Now we could watch the moon rise in the eastern sky and follow it as it traveled slowly across the heavens. Drawing and painting the growing crescent and gibbous moon offered a challenge to some of the students. How could they create the misty quality of the sky or the soft glow of the moon? What technique would allow them to represent a pale moon contrasted against the darkness of the night?

Previously, the children had learned to use pastels and paper-masking techniques to create the silhouettes of houses. (See Art Invitation #10: *Moonlit Silhouettes*.) Pastels are easy to blend and overlap. When used with a crisp-edged paper mask, distinct forms easily appear, or, when gently rubbed with a tissue, soft, blurred images evolve. These methods gave many students the confidence to attempt illustrations that depicted the mood of the sky.

To help the students represent the crescent moon, I introduced a minilesson on using paper masks or stencils. (See Art Invitation #9: *The Masked Moon*.) The children watched a crescent moon shape appear on the chart paper as I played with the positive and negative forms. They experimented with changing the position of the masks, adding overlays of color to the sky and creating a halo around the moon. Some students made a silhouetted roofline in the foreground. (See Color Plate 2 for an entry that incorporates this technique.)

As I walked around the room that day, I was struck by the power of choice. Some children created abstract images that conveyed a feeling or mood. Others selected media that helped them render realistic representations. The students were looking at the world through a new lens, focusing on color, contrast, outlines, and forms. They were coming to know how to translate their observations into composition.

Our anticipation grew daily as we recorded the changing appearance of the moon. In just a few nights the full moon would appear. We researched and told full moon stories and enjoyed identifying popular superstitions as fact or fiction. Are more babies really born on the night of a full moon? Are more crimes committed when the moon is full? Hospitals and police departments helped us with a new kind of research.

On the day of the full moon it seemed as though we were preparing for the arrival of a special visitor. The children carefully considered how they might illustrate their entries. Would the moon be white or gold? Would we see shadows on the moon of the lunar mountains, valleys, and seas we had discovered in our research? What would be the best time for viewing the moon? We would have the answers to our questions within a few hours.

That night I walked to the top of the hill where I live. As I watched the moon rise I was struck by the powerful connection between the moon, my students, and me. I knew that, at that moment, thirty children were likewise witnessing the moonrise. Their fingers were sketching and recording the very same spectacle that I was seeing.

The poems and observations that were shared the following morning celebrated the grand arrival of the full moon. The illustrations were varied and creatively composed. They ranged from pastel, watercolor, marking pen, and colored pencil drawings to collages made of cellophane, foil papers, and even coins attached to a page. (See Color Plates 7, 8, and 9 for samples.)

The written entries reflected the same diversity. Kerstin reported how the moon's light illuminated her room and actually "lit up her prism." She wrote about "moonbows of color" that danced around her room and described how she recorded her entry by moonlight! Many children were impressed by the brightness of the night and discovered that moonlight created distinct shadows.

About this time parents and other family members became involved in the project. I started finding slips of paper tucked into the journals with late-night sketches of the moon. Under the drawings were little notes describing the sky, the moon, and the time, signed by Mom or Dad. Marnie's mother told me about taking a group of girls in bathrobes and slippers out for a walk to observe the moon; it was the hit of that slumber party. Other parents reported pulling off the freeway to watch the moon rise over the mountains or shine over the sea. At parent conferences many parents inquired about art supplies that would make well-appreciated holiday gifts.

Later that week Brian presented a collage that showed the moon resting above the houses in his neighborhood (see cover illustration). We were very impressed with his use of negative space, the repetition of pattern, and the tonal quality of the sky. Brian taught the demonstration that day, and I learned new techniques along with the children. We decided to make a large-scale version of Brian's entry as a bulletin board display. Under the leadership of Karen Taylor, our student teacher, a small group went to work with sponges, scissors, paint, and glue. With great pride, Brian saw his entry turn into a mural that graced the walls of our classroom.

Karen commented that our room had changed dramatically within just a few weeks. The walls were covered with illustrations, poems, and questions about the moon. New pieces were posted every day. It was a combination workshop-gallery in the making, and our principal, other staff members, students, and parents began dropping by regularly to see the latest additions.

As the weeks progressed and the lunar phases changed, I watched the children's confidence, imagination, and skill take root and blossom. I realized that my role was diminishing along with the moon. The students were demonstrating new ideas and approaches to composition every day. Their attention to both process and technique empowered them to become the facilitators of small- and whole-group minilessons.

I recall having heard Nancie Atwell speak at the National Council of Teachers of English Convention in San Diego in 1995. She described a "hand-over phase," during which the teacher provides demonstrations to students who learn from the instructor's experiments, drafts, and published pieces. Eventually the children internalize the process, creating their own unique pieces. As she spoke, I thought of the phenomenon I observed in my classroom while we kept our Moon Journals. I recalled student-led minilessons that succeeded in "handing over" new approaches in writing and art to other children. The demonstrations also served as examples of revision. The Moon Journals, I realized, were becoming filled with more than first-draft sketches. They were evolving into working portfolios and provided evidence of developing skills and strategies, versatility, voice, response, and reflection.

I became aware of a chain of events that began with the daily sharing of art and writing entries. When one student demonstrated an art technique, work-in-progress, or completed piece, other children became motivated to attempt a similar experiment with a new medium or design idea. If at first it seemed challenging, the classmate's advice, demonstration, and encouragement motivated the other students to take a risk and play with something new.

Ashley, for example, particularly enjoyed an art minilesson on paper weaving. The previous day we studied a watercolor weaving by the artist Sara Steele. Steele's design elements and techniques seemed approachable. We experimented with dropping sunset colors onto wet paper. (See Art Invitation #4: *Swirling Wa-*

tercolor Sky.) When these vivid abstract designs dried, the children cut them into half-inch strips and wove them together to create intricate designs. (See Color Plate 6 for an example and Art Invitation #25: *Paper Weaving*.)

At home that night, Ashley recorded the colors of the evening sky in her Moon Journal. Then, using small bottles of fabric puff paint, she "scribbled" an abstract design across construction paper. She achieved an exciting effect of both movement and color. Using the techniques she learned in the paper weaving minilesson, she created her own abstract weaving to represent the colors and movement of the clouds she observed in the sky. The following day, Ashley taught a minilesson to the rest of the class on how to use puff paints in a variety of ways, ranging from paper weaving to creating beaded-looking designs. (See Figure 1-3.)

On a cloudy night, Jason glued cotton balls onto construction paper and made a lift-up flap of thick clouds. Underneath the flap was a drawing of the moon, accompanied by a poem. (See Figure 1-4.)

His demonstration to the class the following day gave many students new options for adding dimensional elements to their illustrations. A new cycle of integration thus emerged in our classroom from the children's observation, improvisation, revision, exhibition, and publication of these elements.

FIGURE 1-3   Ashley's paper weaving and puff paints

FIGURE 1-4

Jason's cotton
clouds

As the month progressed and the moon continued to diminish, we wrote with regret about the passing of our lunar friend. We could no longer watch the moon in the evening because the children were asleep before it made an appearance. Toward the end of the cycle we wrote our observations in the daytime, when the pale morning moon was visible. We came to understand that the phases of the moon are transitory, each with its own pleasures and promises, each giving way to a new version of itself.

Likewise, from day to day, month to month, and year to year the children change. Friendships and interests wax and wane just like the lunar cycle. Recognizing and understanding their "phases" helps children gain a sense of their own personal journey toward maturity. They can look back on their younger years and mark how they have grown and developed both outside and inside. (See Writing Invitations #27: *Moon Cycle, Life Cycle* and #24: *Phases of My Life, Phases of the Moon.*)

As we try out our wings, we experience highs and lows. On some days children feel like they are on top of the world and on others they feel left behind. Understanding that there will be times to shine and times to enjoy someone else's brilliance is an important part in building a community in the classroom. Children need a sense of wonder for their spirits and imagination, but they also need the resiliency to know that if today is a bad day, tomorrow can be better. Watching the phases of the moon provided an entry point for a discussion about sharing the spotlight and celebrating each child's turn to shine. "It's a full moon day for you!" became a phrase we all understood.

Keeping a Moon Journal is a metaphor for teaching. When you start the journal you cannot predict whether the sky will be filled with clouds or stars. You don't always know where you will be as you watch the moon move across the sky. You can't anticipate the exact events in your life that will be reflected in your poems and paintings. And yet you know the moon will predictably change; it will grow from a crescent to a golden orb and gradually diminish until its cycle is completed.

Similarly, I know that as a teacher I cannot predict the moments when the best connections are made for students. Though it seems to be an oxymoron, I do believe that teachers can plan surprises. As Short, Harste and Burke (1996) write, we can "plan without predicting." By extending invitations and encouraging creative response, we can offer children opportunities to discover and develop their strengths and skills. By turning a poem into a scored, orchestrated performance; by developing questions into a research project; and by introducing children to scientists, artists, and writers not just as models to follow but as collaborators in investigation, an important change takes place. The children take ownership of their learning.

Years from now, I hope my students will look back through the pages of their Moon Journals and will discover, somewhere amid their poems and paintings, ten-year-old children who found beauty and wonder in the sky and the writer and artist in themselves. While the moon will wax, wane, and disappear, their words will not. This, I learned, is the true magic of our shared experience.

How to Be a Writer and Artist

Look at the world
and wonder why.
Pay attention to details.
Find the adventures
that scream
to be explored.

Think about living—
all that you have learned,
all that you've been told.
Consider
the what-ifs.
Invent problems.

Squat
and take another look.
Touch the earth regularly.
Rub texture
from the grass,
the wind and the clouds.

Pull colors
from rain puddles,
then use the moon
as a canvas.
Leave your wordprints
on the wet landscape.

Watch people closely.
Follow the lines
on their faces.
Listen to conversations,
you have permission
to eavesdrop.

Live fairy tales.
Uncover mysteries.
Remember
your childhood,
it is rich.
Dream often.

Be brave.
Take risks.
Jumping without parachutes
is part of the process.
Most importantly
be honest.

Even strangers
will know
your truths.
Your heart
was meant
to be shared.

Gina Rester-Zodrow

Chapter Two

Mapping the Journey

Like the children we teach, we grow by pausing and reflecting on what we have learned. In this chapter we present a collaborative overview of what we have discovered after years of keeping Moon Journals with many students. We discuss the theoretical underpinnings of this focused study and the broader scope of our combined experience.

KEEPING A MOON JOURNAL: A PORTFOLIO PROCESS

"Did you see the moon last night?"

This question, asked again and again by the students in our classes as they keep their Moon Journals, becomes the starting point for inquiry, writing, and art. Although it can be answered with a simple *yes* or *no*, a one-word response is not what the students want or need to hear. They ask the question to begin a conversation.

Ashley: "Did you see the moon? Venus was so bright! It was right on top of the tiny crescent moon!"

Pete: "The crescent moon looked like a smile last night, kind of a mischievous smile—like my cat's!"

Taylor: "I never saw the crescent moon on its back before. I wonder why it was like that—maybe it was tired and needed a rest!"

Rachel: "In October the crescent was sideways and the bright star was to the left of the moon. I'll draw a picture of it on the board."

Cleavant: "The moon turned bright yellow when it was low in the sky, and it even looked bigger. Why?"

Rob: "I want to use the Eric Carle papers to make a collage of it."

Tyler: "How do you know that the bright star was a planet? Maybe it was Jupiter! Let's find out . . ."

Luke: "I have my stargazer's book. We can look at what the night sky looks like in February. There's an astronomy club on the internet that gives a weekly star and planet report. We can check that in the computer lab."

Pete: "I drew it in my journal. Let me show you."

Cleavant: "I used watercolors to make it."

Ashley: "I used salt in the watercolors to make stars."

"Did you see the moon last night?" What the children are really seeking is a response from someone else who witnessed the same beauty, excitement, and wonder in the sky. Although the children creatively break off into different directions, the Moon Journal provides the common ground, or context, for inquiry. While the Moon Journal often contains quickly written entries and simple pencil sketches, it also provides a vehicle for improvisations in art, writing, and music. In one sense, it evolves from a simple sketchbook into a working portfolio, showcasing students' self-selected art and writing compositions and chronicling their growth over time.

After keeping Moon Journals with several classes of students, we became aware of a consistent process.

- The children begin by looking into the night sky. They notice stars, planets, clouds, fog, wind, colors, and the shape and position of the moon. They also pay attention to sounds, smells, birds, insects, animals, objects, and voices.
- Next, the students record their observations. The initial entries are rough and sketchy, written or drawn in the journal itself or on another piece of paper. Later that evening, or in school the following day, a child may choose to develop the initial entries using various art materials and writing techniques.
- During the four weeks of the lunar cycle, the teacher and students share entries and demonstrate techniques during a daily Moon Journal studio time—a combination of art and writing workshop. Students are invited to experiment with the variety of art media available in the room (watercolors, chalk and oil pastels, tempera paints, crayons, markers, colored pencils, construction paper cut to the size of the pages of the journal) or to work on composing and revising written entries. Children also use different reference materials and resources to develop and verify their hypotheses about the moon, constellations, and planets.
- When a child is satisfied with an entry in writing and/or art, the piece is glued into the Moon Journal. The process approach is not assigned or required; a few students prefer to record only the initial sketch and written description in their journals. However, as the demonstrations and minilessons are introduced, most students enjoy experimenting with the new approaches they learn and decide to develop at least some of their rough drafts and sketches.

It is not surprising to find students revisiting their Moon Journals in the same way that they update their portfolios. Turning the pages of their journals, they see evidence of their growing versatility and the development of their personal voice and style. They can tell you the story of each piece, beginning with the initial observation and ending with their final decisions regarding the composition's form and technique. The poems, observations, legends, memoirs, sketches, paintings, and collages create a self-evident body of work that gives the journalist a clear message: I am a writer, and I am an artist.

Teachers who are familiar with portfolio assessment know that there are no recipes for this process. Portfolios are part of a larger picture. Their design, function, and value are determined by the opportunities made available to students and the philosophical approach to learning that is in place in the classroom. The same considerations regarding the importance of underlying context can be applied to Moon Journals when they are viewed as working portfolios. This focused nature study operates under the umbrella of curriculum as inquiry and within the existing structures, philosophies, and classroom cultures of writing, reading, and art workshops.

FIGURE 2-1

A Portfolio Culture

Students participate in reading, writing, and conversation on a daily basis; revise and reflect regularly; and take ownership of their learning. They create portfolios to demonstrate their process, growth over time, skills, pride, and achievement.

Inquiry

Children learn about themselves and their place in the world. They make connections to their lives and past experiences and pose and pursue new questions through investigation. (Personal and Social Knowing*)

Children make use of knowledge systems,* that is, ways that human beings have structured knowledge to make sense of the world. These knowledge systems reflect a certain stance or perspective in researching and looking at the world (i.e., through the lens of a scientist, historian, astronomer, and so forth).

Students use the sign systems* of language, art, music, dance, drama, and math to make meaning, communicate response, and develop unique interpretations.

As students read about and research their topics and communicate through writing and art, they work within the philosophies, structures, and classroom cultures of
Writing, Reading, and Art Workshops

Contributing to the art and writing process are "seed book" journals including
Writers' Notebooks   Artists' Sketchbooks

An integrated journal and sketchbook focused on observation of the natural world
Nature Notebooks

A focused Nature Notebook and inquiry study that integrates art, writing, and music and incorporates elements of all of the above-listed approaches
Moon Journals

*Short, Harste, and Burke use these terms in describing curriculum as inquiry (*Creating Classrooms for Authors and Inquirers*, 1996)

In subsequent sections of this chapter, we will explore the relationship of Moon Journals to these process-based approaches to learning and will share the research that has guided us in developing the breadth and scope of this project.

INQUIRY

Like the fine skin of an onion, the layers of inquiry provide form, shape, and dimension to the entire Moon Journal experience. Each observation spawns questions, and each answer inspires new queries. The study is powered by ongoing curiosity.

Inquiry is a constructivist approach to learning characterized by dynamic, collaborative investigation. Along with their teacher, children pose questions about an engaging topic. They employ the multiple "sign systems" of art, dance, music, language, drama, and mathematics as they investigate and research their queries, and they represent or communicate their personal response to new learning (Short, Harste, Burke, 1996).

Throughout the Moon Journal study, children learn about the world primarily through personal experience. But they extend their understanding by tapping into various "knowledge systems" (Short, Harste, with Burke, 1996). They learn to use the questions, tools, and research methodologies of scientists, naturalists, historians, or astronomers to conduct their investigations. The teacher's role is that of facilitator rather than technician, helping students pose questions, consider options for problem solving, learn techniques, use tools, and, ultimately, make meaning.

Each time the students ask "Did you see the moon last night?" they are actually asking a new question and expecting a new answer. The moon changes nightly, and so do the opportunities for investigation. For example, one cold night the moon was surrounded by rainbow rings of colors. The children came to school the next day, excited and mystified by this phenomenon. Of course, they wanted to know what caused it! This question led to other questions. What causes the rainbows we sometimes see in the sky when it rains? Why do rainbow colors spill over our desks when the sun lights the prism in our window? How are these rainbows connected to the bands of color that circled the moon last night?

The children listed the other conditions they noticed on the night of the rainbow moon. It was unusually cold. Even though there weren't clouds, it felt as though it might rain because the air was damp and heavy. The moon was nearly full and very bright. At this point the students wondered what role, if any, these various factors played in determining the cause of the rainbow rings.

The children continued to investigate their questions and support their speculations in collaboration with published authors and researchers. They learned an important lesson about how discoveries in science are made. Discoveries often start with wonder, followed by questions, observations, hypotheses, and more questions. Whether the subject of the study is the moon or any other natural object, the procedures and processes are constant and transferable. Children do more than learn about science; they learn the behavior of scientists.

Immersion: Dipping into the World

The students' questions move the investigation beyond the four walls of the classroom. The concept of immersion expands to include more than daily experiences with visual and written language. As the children research their questions, they discover a need for diverse resources. Our students quickly became limited by the available books and periodicals in our classroom and school libraries. They extended their investigations to the computer lab and the outside world. Our ongoing list of information sources steadily grew to include

- almanacs
- weather reports and the weather channel
- the internet (especially the on-line astronomy club, weekly planet and star reports, NASA and Jet Propulsion Laboratory [JPL] reports)
- e-mailed messages and observations from people throughout the country and the world
- newspapers (moon phase and moonrise information, tide tables)
- observations using binoculars or telescopes
- observations from parents and friends (especially when the moon appears late at night)
- interviews with local astronomy enthusiasts
- interviews/phone calls to scientists and college instructors
- radio programs
- magazines
- videos
- television programs (especially on the Discovery Channel)
- visits to planetariums and museums
- prints of the art work of various artists
- books and videos introducing art techniques
- visits from local artists and writers
- picture books about the moon and space
- reference books about the moon and space
- books of legends about the moon from around the world

In recent years, educators and the public have recognized the importance of bringing technology into the schools. A focused-inquiry project can use the internet for obtaining information and comparing observations from across the country. Students have specific queries in mind when they explore CD-ROM programs or use word processing and art-related software. More importantly, multimodal inquiry provides students with an experience in real life—the kind of learning they will encounter outside of school. They are discovering how to pose questions, find answers creatively, and employ a variety of resources that are not always stacked together on a single shelf in the library. They experience the excitement and satisfaction of probing deeper into a topic. Through inquiry, literacy extends beyond reading and writing, and students learn to understand their world.

INQUIRY INVITES A WORKSHOP APPROACH

Reading and Writing Workshop

As students engage in inquiry, they are empowered by their abilities to discover and communicate meaning. They function as readers and writers with a purpose. We discovered early on that the time set aside for sharing entries, demonstrating techniques, reading stories and legends, and creating compositions of individual choice began to look and feel like "writing and reading workshop" as described by Graves (1983) and Atwell (1987).

This approach to literacy addresses the importance of time, choice, response, and predictable structures in developing a community of writers and readers. Regularly scheduled blocks of uninterrupted time allow children to participate in a process, to stay with a piece of writing, to read and sometimes reread a particular book, to explore a particular genre or the works of a favorite new author, and to seek response and collaboration.

Children are offered opportunities to make choices. They self-select writing topics and determine which books to read. Choice also implies decision making and problem solving. Jane Hansen (1987) writes "Decisions about how to put together a piece of writing and what information to include present writers with a constant barrage of problems to solve." Options include "what to write about, what form the writing will take, what information to include, whom to share it with, and whether it will be buried in a folder or labeled as a final draft."

Response from teacher and peers in the form of conferences, conversations, and Author's Chair sharing (Graves, 1983) provides more than an audience. It plants the seeds of revision, demonstrates effective writing, and helps a student learn what "works" in his or her piece. Likewise, when students personally respond to the books they read, it moves them from reading passively to engaging actively with the characters and their problems, decisions, and dilemmas. When opinions and ideas are shared, reading becomes a social act, inviting children to become "members of the club of literacy" (Smith, F., 1992) as they learn from each other.

Predictable structures allow for open-ended instruction. Children know the procedures for getting started, requesting assistance, organizing drafts, participating in response circles, publishing pieces, and maintaining portfolios. Eventually, the children themselves take on the roles of advisors, demonstrators, editors, and respondents as they work with their peers. Ultimately, the students make decisions and take responsibility for formulating and representing meaning.

In both its function and structure the Moon Journal experience is an extension of writing workshop, but with a specific focus. For example, the ongoing procedures of keeping the journal establish predictable structures and address the issue of time. The guidelines are simple. Regular time is set aside each evening for observation, sketching, and writing. Scheduled classroom time is devoted to sharing, responding to entries, demonstrating new techniques, revision, and research.

Although the moon provides a common focus, students are offered a variety of choices in composition, technique, and performance. Words, pictures, music, and dance are available as options for personal response as the children make their nightly observations of the moon. As writers, students are invited to experiment in different genres. One entry may take shape as a poem, while another may include a detailed scientific observation.

The techniques that are introduced are not one-time-only exercises to be used exclusively in the Moon Journal, but constitute many of the basic minilessons that are part of an ongoing writing workshop approach. Trish Doerr, for example, suggested to one of her fourth grade students that she might consider adding a very descriptive entry from her Moon Journal to an adventure story she was writing. The detailed and poetic prose from the journal greatly enhanced her fictional piece. Using similes and metaphors, planting seeds for poetry, writing detailed observations, using sensory descriptions, including dialogue, and adding personal reflection to a piece are all minilessons that carry over into personal writing, whether it be fiction or writing in content areas.

Art Workshop

In *Seeking Diversity* (1992), Linda Rief writes, "I think too often I forget the name of the course I teach—language *arts*, not language *art*. Too often I forget that there's more to the arts than the written word." In her book she describes ways "to allow students to respond to their world in ways other than just 'the word.'" Through murals, paintings, and drawings, her students create more than writing—they create meaning.

Like Rief, Karen Ernst takes the philosophy and structures of writing workshop and applies them to what she terms "artists workshop." In *Picturing Learning* (1994), she describes how choice, sharing, response, demonstration, collaboration, exhibition, portfolio, and reflection were essential to her students' learning process. Choice, in particular, was at the heart of her artists workshop. Ernst writes, "When students make their own choices for pictures, projects, stories, or problems to solve, they engage in their work with enthusiasm and ownership that cannot be matched when work is assigned. They have a stake in the outcome, in their learning, and can move toward becoming creative individuals."

In order for young artists to know and understand the scope of their choices, they need time to explore and experiment with various media and art techniques. In our classrooms we have tools and media available for both school and home use. Art materials, including colored pencils, pastels, watercolors, fabrics, rubber stamps, collage supplies, hole punches, scissors, and glue, can be "checked out" in shoe boxes or Ziplock bags. Drawing, painting, printmaking, and collage techniques demonstrated in class show our students some of the options open to them as artists.

Students have repeated exposure to this decision-making process while making their nightly observations. For example, as journalists see foggy skies, the sharp silhouettes of trees, or a multicolored halo around the full moon, there are choices to make. From experience the young artists know that each scene can be illustrated using many familiar materials and techniques. A foggy sky can be made with cotton balls and a sponge loaded with gray paint. Tree silhouettes might be created with pen and ink, stencils, or paper cutouts. A rainbow-colored stamp pad, a tissue paper collage, or stitched embroidery floss could depict a moon's halo. Artist, writer, and teacher Mona Brookes (1986) tells her students, "Be brave and try it all." She notes that the children often opt "for challenges instead of the things they know they can be successful at."

We are continually surprised by the variety of visual images children come up with in their Moon Journals. Once students are comfortable with the characteristics and applications of specific media, they will challenge themselves to go beyond work produced in classroom demonstrations. As they do with their written journal entries, students engage in several drafts of art work before selecting a final piece for their Moon Journals. We have often seen students take the subject of a single pencil sketch and reproduce it two or three times using different media. This appears to be more than an experimentation with materials. These students seem to be searching for a way to "say" accurately what they mean.

We encourage teachers to do their own artwork with the students. It is not necessary to be an art expert in order to teach the invitations in this book. For example, we ourselves do a few drafts of an art technique ahead of time and share them with the children whether or not we are satisfied with the outcome. We then discuss the process: the trials and errors, the frustrations and how we work through them, and, finally, the finished art piece. Brookes (1986) writes, "Students can be very supportive to the teacher and each other when they are aware that you are all equal and learning together. How well you draw isn't the point anyway. You are only providing the general structure that is needed to get everyone involved and give them permission to make their own interpretation."

Choice in the Integrated Writing and Art Workshop

In an integrated writing and art workshop, choice and response flourish in an atmosphere that honors improvisation. In addition to the minilessons that we offer students, we feel it is important to provide unstructured time for experimentation. Drawing from past experiences in art, dance, and music studios, we labeled this daily opportunity for demonstration and practice "studio time."

The choices offered to the students during Moon Journal studio time are not choices between two or three teacher-determined activities. Rather, during a minilesson, such as those described in Part Two of this book, students participate in a demonstration of some new technique that will become a common tool for writing and/or art. Yet even at this instructional phase, each child produces unique words and pictures in response to the invitation.

For example, the teacher may demonstrate simplified techniques for creating monoprints. (See Art Invitation #24: *Monoprints of the Moon.*) The children do not just watch the teacher, they experiment along with the teacher as she or he guides them through the process. Even though the procedures of the process are presented in step-by-step instruction, each child chooses colors and shapes that are individually appealing. As Short, Harste, and Burke (1996) explain, "An invitation means that the children have the right to turn down an option and to justify how their own idea is an equally valid experience. Choice is the propeller that gets the whole process started. . . . The thinking about available options is crucial; it allows one to focus on a topic and, because alternatives have been weighed and rejected, to know what can be done with a topic before really beginning."

Studio Sharing: Reaping a Harvest

As the students respond to each other, they discover new ways to respond to the moon. Through shared demonstrations they learn options for expanding their initial observations. Studio conversation invites experimentation, application, and revision. "How did you create that effect? I'd like to try it, too" and "I like the way you painted a night sky. Maybe I'll try my own version of that!"—these replace "Is this right, teacher?" As children gain confidence, they rely less on their teacher and more on their own imaginative and decision-making initiative.

In a sense, response to Moon Journal entries works in the same way that news of a "hot" new book spreads around the room during reading workshop (Atwell, 1987). When children discuss favorite books in small-group conversations or read about an interesting book in a "lit letter" written by another student, they are motivated to try new titles.

The same qualities of respect and trust are evident when children learn from each other during Moon Journal studio time. Luke, for example, drew a quick sketch of the moon while driving home from school with his mother. He jotted a few words underneath his pencil drawing to remind him of what he was thinking when he first spotted the moon. Later that evening he considered which art medium he could use to depict the scene with greater clarity. After he decided on oil pastels, Luke experimented with his design until he found just the right way to represent his visual impression (See Figure 2-2.)

The following day Luke brought his Moon Journal to school and shared his revised writing and art entries with the rest of the class. He discussed his choice of using oil pastels, and the other students commented on his effective use of perspective. "I like the way he made the hills look far away and the way the road gets smaller and smaller" was the comment that began a discussion and demonstration about vanishing points, foreground, and background. All of the children

FIGURE 2-2

learned from Luke's independent work in art, just as student writers learn from their peers while giving and receiving response to a written piece.

Discovering teachable moments is an ongoing opportunity for teachers during Moon Journal studio time. Looking at the child's work, the teacher might say, "Tell me about this. Where did your idea come from? Will you show this to the rest of the class?" Pointing out an element in a piece of art that truly impresses the viewer is specific, sincere response. The comment is recognition of the student's ability and imagination and gives him confidence to continue developing ideas, skills, and techniques.

When looking through their children's Moon Journals, parents sometimes ask, "Did my child *really* do this? I didn't know she was such an artist!" or "I can't believe he wrote this poem just from looking at the moon!" We have learned that the beauty that shines through journal entries is not simply the result of newly acquired skills and techniques. Rather, it is a reflection of the child's honest response, unique voice, and heartfelt appreciation of the natural world.

NOTEBOOKS, SKETCHPADS, AND SEEDS

When students become immersed in a workshop approach, they quickly learn that creating compositions in writing and art does not start and stop when they enter or leave the classroom. Artists and writers come to see the world as their studio and learn ways to collect the seeds of stories, poems, and pictures for future development.

In *Bird by Bird* (1994), Anne Lamott writes, "One of the things that happens when you give yourself permission to start writing is that you start thinking like a writer. You start seeing everything as material." The caution here, as she explains, is that she might "stand there trying to see it, the way you try to remember a dream, where you squint and it's right there on the tip of your psychic tongue but you can't get it back. The image is gone. That is one of the worst feelings I can think of, to have had a wonderful moment or insight or vision or phrase, to know you had it, and then to lose it. So now I use index cards."

Joni keeps a small notepad in her purse, and it is filled with sketches, ideas, lines from movies, quotes from favorite late-night reads, and sometimes scraps of paper taped onto a page. Gina's notebook is a collection of "writers' material." It contains snippets of conversation written on napkins and stapled onto a page, torn-out and glued-in newspaper articles, the titles of books, random momentary reflections, pressed leaves, and drawings of the moon.

In *Living Between the Lines* (1991), Lucy Calkins shows teachers how to share the practice of keeping "writer's notebooks" with children. She encourages us to "begin living our lives with the consciousness that 'my life belongs to me, it matters. I need to put scraps of time and thought away in order to take them out later, to live with and linger with them.'"

The pages of a Moon Journal invite children to live life with their eyes wide open. The journal itself establishes a daily habit of noticing the world, with entries that extend beyond the observations of the moon. In our students' journals we often find jotted comments from parents, friends, or siblings; newspaper clippings showing weather conditions or the time schedules for the moonrise; and records of unexpected discoveries made when glancing up from playing tennis, skateboarding, or driving home.

Marisa used a scrap of paper to record a quick note and sketch featuring an airplane and the growing crescent moon she spotted from her car window. Later that evening she drew a detailed color pencil drawing and a more developed entry that was a combination of prose and poetry.

Out the Car Window

Out the car window, a plane do I see, and more of a moon looking down upon me. Over the mountains the growing moon sits—I see several more planes, and . . . the picture fits! The streetlights hit us with light just like the moon, and I can see all of this in my little car room.

The adjoining page in her journal featured a pastel composition, celebrating the bright yellow crescent in a lavender sky. Marisa saw so much looking out the window of her "little car room"! Her classmate, Pete, summed up experiences like these when he said he "presses the pictures in his mind until he can get home and draw them in his sketchbook."

NATURE NOTEBOOKS

Nature Notebooks are a combination of writers' notebooks and artists' sketch pads. They are journals filled with drawings and written observations about the world of nature. Their pages contain accounts of discoveries or observations about trees, wildflowers, insects, birds, reptiles, the backyard, the beach, a pond, clouds, or even a particular season. In words and pictures students give focused attention and notice small details, in order to know a creature or a natural object from the "inside out."

We delight in the diverse collection of Nature Notebooks that are available for teachers to use as demonstrations. From the classics we celebrate Thoreau's *Walden* (1991) and entries from John Muir's personal journal. From our bookshelves of picture books by contemporary writers and artists we pull Byrd Baylor's *I'm in Charge of Celebrations* (1986), Thomas Locker's *Sky Tree* (1995), and Jean Craighead George's *Dear Rebecca, Winter Is Here* (1993). For suggestions and instruction we frequently dip into Lorraine Ferra's *A Crow Doesn't Need a Shadow* (1994) and Cathy Johnson's *Creating Textures in Watercolor* (1992). *Orion Magazine* is always filled with inspirational essays and articles by naturalists, writers, poets, and artists. To explain to parents the philosophy and importance of keeping Nature Notebooks with children, we often share *The Sense of Wonder* (1984) by Rachel Carson.

Introducing children to majesty often happens through intimate encounters with nature. We continually remind ourselves to honor the notion of small beginnings and recognize the importance of simplicity. Written inside the cover of Joni's personal Nature Notebook is a quote from Frederick Franck (1993).

> All that is needed is a little sketch pad in your pocket and a pencil or pen, and to let the hand follow—whether brilliantly, or awkwardly at first— what the eye perceives, and to keep on doing this with eyes and mind and heart wide awake. Epiphany of the commonplace.

And so, with pencils in their pockets and journals in their hands, our students venture out into the world.

MOON JOURNALS: START SLOWLY AND SEEK CONNECTIONS

A solitary star can easily be lost in the pinpoints of light that make up the galaxy. Yet a star that is part of a constellation contributes to creating a recognizable image; it becomes a marker in the night sky for stargazers and navigators. Like a single star, Moon Journals have a place in the larger picture created by inquiry, writing workshop, artist studio, and Nature Notebooks. We value the breadth and scope of these approaches to learning and the choices they offer to teachers and students. The message is clear: Take ownership, be active participants, and find a way to make it your own. There is no one way to create a classroom program, and there is no recipe for learning. As Linda Rief (1992) advises, seek out and celebrate diversity as you build the structures and patterns of learning in your classroom.

We have found different ways to approach this study within our individual teaching situations. Joni teaches a self-contained class of thirty fifth grade students. They stay with her for the entire day. She has the flexibility to schedule uninterrupted blocks of time for focused study. The first year Joni's students kept Moon Journals, she scheduled studio time in addition to the established writing and reading workshops. In the second year, the study developed into broader opportunities for extended inquiry. Half the day revolved around demonstrations, research, independent studio time, and presentations connected to the students' questions about the moon. Writing minilessons were generated from the observations. Genre studies including moon legends, myths, poetry, and nature observations were explored in the integrated reading workshop. Science and social studies became part of the research conducted by students. Art, music, and dance were common threads woven throughout the experience.

As a writer-in-residence, Gina works with children from kindergarten through sixth grade. Interacting with students at many levels of development and experience gives her repeated opportunities to adapt the process of keeping Moon Journals. Not surprisingly, the product, or journal itself, frequently takes on different forms. For instance, her kindergarten and first grade students are very expressive verbally, but they are just beginning to communicate through writing. A language-experience approach, with students talking about their illustrations and dictating observations and responses, is often a way to begin Moon Journals with young children. They create a classroom Moon Journal, filled with contributions from all of the students.

One year, the students in Gina's first grade class volunteered to record journal entries on certain nights of the week. Their job was to draw pictures and compose entries using invented spellings or observations dictated to parents and to bring them to school the following day for whole-class sharing. For example, Camille, Anthony, Chris, and Jessica wrote and illustrated entries on Monday and Thursday, and Sebastian, Casey, Vanessa, and Nicholas became responsible for Tuesday and Saturday. The rest of the class members and days were assigned in the same way. By the end of the week, seven nights of lunar observation were covered by different children. Moon Journal studio time gave all of the students an opportunity to share updates on the moon's progress.

Our experiences have taught us that the development of a classroom inquiry study is influenced by each teacher's individual situation. The number of students in a class, the age of the children, scheduling options, time considerations, departmentalization of the curriculum, location, and available resources are factors that influence the design and implementation of the study.

In both of our situations we learned an important lesson: *Start small* and let the program develop slowly. We learned along with the students. We needed time to develop organization and management strategies as well as confidence and techniques in writing and art. We are still adding new ideas to our studies and changing the notes in our plan books as we grow along with our students. Although change is a challenge, it is also the joy of the experience.

The invitations in the process pages of this book invite a teacher to "start small" and engage with students in a focused nature study like Moon Journals from a variety of entry points. These options apply to any focused study and can support or enhance student participation in reading, writing, or art workshop. In the following paragraphs, we summarize the components we have gradually added to the initial procedures of keeping the Moon Journal.

Students can begin with simple sketchbooks filled with pencil drawings and short written entries. Even at this baseline level of involvement, they will learn about the lunar cycle and begin to discover the world of nature. Their sketching and drawing will most likely develop as they find better ways to represent their observations. Research and rich discussions will stem from the drawings and notations. A part of the day, or a period of time every other day, can be set aside for sharing observations and discussion.

From this point, possibilities expand. During the weeks of the Moon Journal study, a teacher can experiment with the following options, remembering to let the students' questions and interests provide the road map for investigation:

- Introduce literature genre studies, incorporating books related to the study, i.e., legends, myths, the writings of naturalists, poetry, memoir, and so forth.
- Offer writing minilessons that connect with the observations, i.e., writing similes, metaphors, writing legends, memoirs, focusing an entry, adding sensory description, and so on.
- Demonstrate techniques in art that allow students to represent their observations more creatively.
- Introduce students to various art media.
- Help students locate a wide range of resources to assist them in their research.
- Collect and demonstrate music and sound instruments that can enhance the students' compositions in writing and art.
- Demonstrate simple methods of adding musical notation to compositions.
- Encourage students to use dance as a way of representing their messages (poems, songs, entries).
- Introduce drama (readers' theater, choral readings, short plays, or puppet shows dramatizing moon legends and other moon observations) as a way of presenting composition or research.
- Conduct scientific demonstrations and experiments to test the students' hypotheses.

- Present information, poetry, and art in exhibitions, programs for parents, or classroom visits.
- Encourage students to reflect on their work in the journals as part of a portfolio process.

A teacher does not have to work alone when introducing children to any of these components. Working with partners and sharing the introduction of minilessons based on individual experience and interest can provide support for the teacher and introduce the children to different perspectives. Specialist or support teachers (music, art, drama, or science) can present minilessons, demonstrate techniques, or provide resources and instruction to the teacher. Parents who have a background in the arts or sciences can share their expertise. They don't need to be experienced instructors; just watching an artist or musician in progress can be a lesson in itself.

Start slowly. Select carefully. Ask questions, and observe. Take time to reflect and to connect with others. The procedures for keeping a Moon Journal can guide teachers as we develop a classroom community that supports inquiry and learning.

FINAL REFLECTIONS: RETURNING TO PURPOSE, RESPONDING TO LIFE

Students fill the pages of their journals with evidence of creative and critical thinking—demonstrations of active minds at work. But there exists another important reason for keeping the Moon Journal, a purpose we have come to believe is just as significant as the many instructional opportunities. If children listen to each other's poems and stories simply to develop skill, or study their teacher's and peers' experiments in art for technical reasons only, they will miss the essence of the experience.

Author Katherine Paterson, in an address to teachers at the 1995 National Council of Teachers of English Convention, asked the question, "When did we begin, as a society, to turn our backs on beauty?" She described three essential elements of literature, science, and art: simplicity, harmony, and brilliance. Simplicity is in observation, in giving children opportunities really to "see" by watching something over time and noticing details. Harmony is found when we connect with nature and realize that we are part of the experience. Brilliance is in the discovery and appreciation of beauty and in the essence of the object that is viewed.

Artist and writer Frederick Franck, in *Zen Seeing, Zen Drawing* (1993), writes, "Art is the most profound, most irrepressible response to life itself, whether that art is drawing, dancing, playing a flute, or acting on a stage. Seeing/drawing is, for me, that response. It is the response of the artist-within." He describes how seeing-drawing becomes a breakthrough, an "awakening, a new openness for and insight into the livingness of living things, a reborn capacity for empathy, wonder and reverence, for awe for the simplest things of nature, for a leaf, a scallion. It may be momentary, but it could also be a lasting awakening. . . ."

Pete, a fifth grade student, experienced such a moment when he illustrated his discovery of the moon one winter night:

FIGURE 2-3

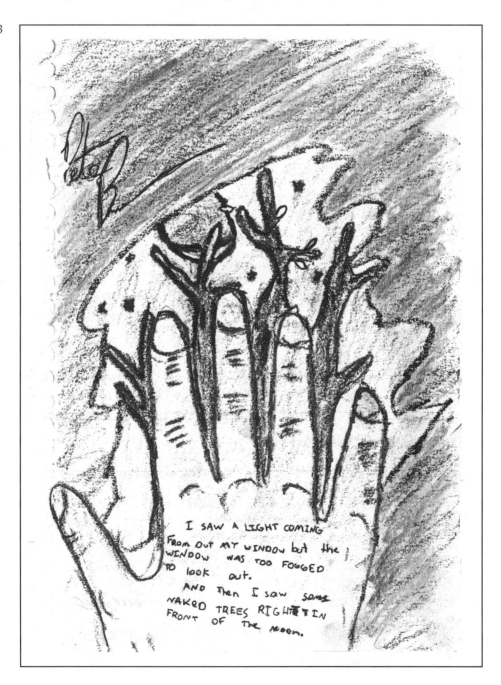

His drawing shows his hand clearing away the fogged-up window of his car, revealing the gleaming moon. Peter succeeded in capturing four important elements that tell a story: his hand, the foggy window, the cleared space, and the distant moon in the sky. The excitement of the instant the moon was revealed is captured, a record of his response to beauty. The illustration serves as a metaphor for the awakening described by Franck.

Jack Borden is the founder of *For Spacious Skies*, a nonprofit venture that fosters awareness and appreciation of the heavens. Borden believes that for most people the sky has become "visual Muzak" instead of "a symphony of contrasting movement, a composition of light and color." In an article about this project, Cornelia Schwartz (1984) writes

> To experience in full the beauty, variety, and majesty of the sky requires seeing it as object, not as background, in shades of white on blue, in tones of gray against gray, until raising one's eyes, even if only for a few minutes daily, becomes a habit. Establishing the habit requires a conscious effort of attention, because the sky is always there, and is easily taken for granted.

There is a computer command in desktop publishing for moving the "background to the foreground." In a sense, this is what Moon Journals are all about: taking something that we see daily, moving it to the foreground, and finding it incredible. It is a natural impulse to want to share discovered beauty with someone else. But it is not always easy to express it. "Did you see the moon last night?" is a hand and a heart reaching out, seeking to share a developing sense of wonder.

As our students experiment with written entries and drawings, the focus is not on creating a piece to be praised by someone *else*. Instead, we ask the students to inquire of themselves: Does this represent what *I* experienced? Does it capture *my* response? Does it tell the story of what *I* discovered? Does it help *me* find or make meaning?

Orion Magazine (Spring 1993) reprinted an article written over twenty years ago by physician and psychologist Franz Winkler titled "The Wisdom of Childhood." In this piece Winkler asserts

> As a rule, no one is very much interested in the names and habits of strangers, and will not remember them for long. Names and habits of friends, however, are important. The child who knows a flower, who learns to love it and watch it climb toward the sun, will have no difficulty in recalling its name and the details of its life. . . . Every piece of information transmitted by the teacher should be met by an imaginative-artistic activity on the part of the pupil. . . . In this manner, the creative in the human responds to the created in nature, and knowledge becomes alive through comprehension.

Winkler's message touches upon an important aspect of learning about science and nature—words that are even more applicable to the child of the late twentieth century. When children respond to the world and use their senses to notice their surroundings, they intimately know the object or creature that has invited their focused attention. Through intimacy comes caring and, ultimately, responsibility.

Our students know that the natural world is becoming increasingly endangered. They read books and watch videos about animal species that are threatened, rainforests that are disappearing, and oceans that are becoming more and more polluted. We talk about saving the whales and healing our bays. And yet, as David Sobel (1993) points out, "If we want children to flourish, to become truly empowered, let us allow them to love the earth before we ask them to save it."

The pages of a Moon Journal can become a place for children to forge a friendship with the moon and stars, crickets that chirp in their yards, leaves that fall from trees, and the rain that wets their windows. They enter a world that grounds them in creativity, imagination, and wonder.

Kimmy's poem "Night Dream" speaks collectively for our students.

Night Dream

I watch the world at night
through sleepy eyes
and I look up
at the star-filled skies.
I dream about
the wondrous things
that tomorrow promises
to bring.
I keep my secret hopes
and dreams
tucked far away
on bright moonbeams.
Out beyond the horizon far
my dreams take me where rainbows are—
when I follow my own star.

Part Two

The Process Pages

When we were children, the world seemed new and promising. Discovery and adventure waited for us behind every rock. It was tucked away in knot holes, lurking through hedges, and hidden in snail shells. What happened to us as we grew? As we became taller, why did our creative capacity grow smaller? As our knowledge of the world increased, why did our emotional response to it diminish? Is there a way that childhood's wonder can be sustained for a lifetime?

Writer Charles Augustin Sainte-Beuve may have answered these questions when he wrote, "With everyone born human, a poet—an artist—is born, who dies young and who is survived by an adult." Perhaps it is possible for adults to revive the artist that has been buried since childhood. But how can we teach our children ways to nourish and protect the artist that already flourishes within them?

Art, whether it be the art of drawing, painting, or writing, is a way to preserve a child's wonder of life. Writers and artists make a habit of looking closely at things while gathering seeds for their work. Simple observations become catalysts for creative expression. As they paint with words and pictures, their imaging becomes their reply to the world and to life.

While the visual artist uses pencil or paint and the writer uses language, both create in the same ways to achieve their end result. Here is an example. Both an artist and a writer sit in a studio looking at the same teapot. The artist does a contour drawing. He looks at the edge of the teapot and draws lines to represent that edge. As his eyes slowly follow the contour of the pot, his pencil re-creates the peak formed by the handle and the valley formed by the spout. Every curve, every bump, every straight edge is depicted on the paper. In this way, the artist discovers the unique and subtle aspects of the object's shape. Later, he may "color it in," adding volume through texture and shading. Interestingly, several artists may draw the same pot but every drawing will be different because each artist responds to the subject using his own imaginative abilities to create an individual interpretation.

The writer does the same. She will use words to follow contour, to explore, define, and depict the features of the teapot, selecting words such as round, shiny, iridescent, chipped, delicate, mauve, and Limoges. Later, she too may "color it in," adding a written form of volume, shading, and texture. She might describe the owner of the pot, the hands that have held it, the dusty shelf it sits on, the memories pouring from its spout. Many writers can write about a teapot, but each writer will use her own imagination and creative response to present a unique view.

What inspires someone to write, draw, or paint? It's an uncontrollable emotional reaction. It's so strong, so consuming, he wants to document it, record it, create an impression of it. It is this response, driven by emotion and wonder, that becomes the poem, the story, the painting, or the sketch. In this process, the response becomes the creation of something unique, not just a mere copy or rendering of that which was observed. The creation holds in it not just what was seen but what was felt.

In this way, the connection between art and writing is a powerful creating and re-creating force. In fact, there are so many similarities between the two disciplines, the line of distinction in terms of the creative process becomes blurred.

The process pages that follow contain twenty-eight Writing Invitations and twenty-eight Art Invitations that give students an opportunity to explore a wide range of options for integrating words and pictures in their Moon Journals. Although the moon provides a common focus, the children have a variety of choices in composition, form, and technique as they make their nightly observations. We use the word *invitations* very deliberately. Students are introduced to many art and writing genres during workshops or Moon Journal studio time, but it is up to them to decide if they will incorporate these techniques into their journal entries.

Often the children in our classes use the invitations as springboards or entry points for their own writing and art ideas. Individual students frequently elect to use the same invitation more than once. The scientists in the class may have several journal entries devoted to *Moon Facts*, just as the young musicians might choose to use the instrument notations in *Moon Music* to score all of their poems. While we do not assign invitations, we do encourage our students to try different genres in both writing and art throughout the course of the study.

How you decide to use the invitations in the process pages is a matter of personal preference. You can choose to introduce them in the sequence suggested or you can vary their order. It is important to note that each Writing Invitation does not necessarily correspond to a specific Art Invitation. However, you may discover that some work especially well together. For example, we like to introduce the Writing Invitation *Similes by Starlight* and the Art Invitation *The Masked Moon* as soon as the waxing crescent appears in the sky. We do this for two reasons. First, both invitations are simple and our students are usually very pleased with the art and writing pieces they produce. Secondly, we know that similes and masking techniques are two basic tools that the children can use repeatedly throughout their journals. Numerous choices for written and visual expression are immediately available to students just by introducing these two versatile invitations. You will undoubtedly come up with your own favorite combinations.

Do not feel that you need to introduce fifty-six Art and Writing Invitations in one four-week study. We do many of the invitations in our writing or art workshops before the children begin Moon Journals. Consider selecting a handful of invitations based on your students' needs, interests, and previous experiences in writing and art. You'll know when and if to add more. Remember that while some of these invitations are completed in class during Moon Journal studio time, others are carried out at home as students respond to what they see during nightly observations.

We suggest that you read through all the invitations and become familiar with the choices. See which ones appeal to you. Which are best suited for your students? Which are appropriate to the season and the weather conditions you are experiencing? Depending on the night, one Art Invitation might be better than another. For example, a rainy night would be wonderful for watercolor. A hazy sky might best be depicted with pastels. No moon but lots of clouds? Try a tissue paper collage.

The same holds true for the writing invitations. Perhaps the full moon reminds you of an evening you spent under another moonlit sky long ago. Consider sharing that memory with your students and introducing *Moon Memoirs.* Maybe the moon won't rise until most of your students are asleep, but the clear sky is perfect for constellation viewing. This might be a good night for writing odes to the stars. Have your students been asking questions about planets, night birds, or the harvest moon? *Notes from Nature* and *Moon Facts* invite students to write from a naturalist's or scientist's point of view.

Regardless of how you choose to work with the invitations, encourage your students to keep an accurate record of the moon's performance by completing one art and one writing entry on a daily basis. It doesn't matter which entry is done first. Some children prefer beginning with a picture, others like to start with words. Either way, consistent observation of the lunar cycle is important. This can come in the form of a quick pencil sketch and field notes or expanded writing and art pieces such as those described in the invitations.

You may want to experiment with these invitations in your own Moon Journal before sharing them with your students. This will give you an opportunity to adapt our techniques to your particular needs. The invitations tell our classroom stories. But just as a storyteller varies his tale every time he tells it, so too must the teacher change her story for each class of students. We invite you to make *our* stories *your* stories. Use these invitations as guidelines, suggestions, or seeds for your own ideas. Before long the Moon Journals will take on the unique characteristics of your young authors and illustrators. The invitations are extended. Come and play in the light of the moon!

Story Painter

The writer slips back into life
like water dropped into a painting,
disturbing the pigment,
seeking depth,
adding dimension.
Refashioning events
with words chosen
as carefully as colors.
Shadow and light
juxtaposed,
images reformed,
a focal point emerges.
It is yours, it is its own,
it is given to someone else
and the story connects
with another life
like sunlight
filtering through leaves,
casting patterns on the ground.
Is it revision
or creation?
It's a way to paint a story.
It's a way to live a life.

Joni Chancer

Chapter Three

The Writing Invitations

As the moon grows, so does the plant.

The calendar pages in farmers' almanacs suggest specific times for moon-phase planting and harvesting. For centuries, lunar gardeners have followed this advice, believing that a growing moon causes seeds to sprout, then flourish. As a teacher, you may find yourself closely tied to this notion of lunar farming throughout the phases of the Moon Journal process: looking for just the right time to plant the seeds and knowing that, with nourishment, patience, and a commitment of time, they will blossom into a garden of unique delights.

The Writing Invitations in this chapter are the seeds that we have used with our classes. Within the pages of our students' Moon Journals, we have watched these ideas develop into poems, legends, lyrics, stories, memoirs, letters, and reflections. In moon-phase farming terms, it was our evidence of an abundant harvest.

Included in the Writing Invitations are classroom stories that will give you a flavor of our experiences and show how we approach writing with our students. The invitations are not meant to be used as directive, step-by-step models, but as open-ended opportunities for exploration. We present them during our Moon Journal studio time demonstrations or during our ongoing writing workshops. The details of this process are discussed in "Inquiry Invites a Workshop Approach: Reading and Writing Workshop" on page 32 in Chapter Two.

The samples of student writing in each invitation are taken from the children's Moon Journals. You may wish to share these with your students as part of your classroom demonstration. We have found that when children hear the writing of other children they respond to it very differently from when they hear the writing of adult authors. The work is better received when it has been written by a fellow member of the children's writing community, even if the student-author is not a part of the child's immediate class. Their thinking seems to be, "If another kid can do it so can I" or "I'd like to try that." Students make a personal connection with other children.

Typically, when we present student writing samples to our classes, we read them and ask, "What did you notice about this? What was the student doing in this piece? What can we learn from it? Is there something that this writer did that you might want to try?" This gives children the chance to make their own discoveries and choices. Over time they accumulate many writing tools and techniques that can be adapted in their own work. Some of our students have an envelope glued to the back cover of their Moon Journals that contain ideas they have gotten after listening to another child's written piece or after experimenting with an Art Invitation during studio time.

Moon Journal entries result from observing life, feeling a personal response, and determining the precise way to communicate the experience with others. Response from teachers and peers lets students know that what they've expressed in written language is understood and valued by others. As young writers learn to capture the moon night after night in words, they also come to understand that they can share their minds, their hearts, and their personal visions of the world through their work. They learn that writers plant seeds and harvest them for a lifetime.

WRITING INVITATION #1

I Wonder? Beginning an Inquiry Study with Poetry

Questions provide a road map for inquiry. They keep the momentum going, inspire us to keep observing, recording, and investigating, and lead us to where we want to go next. As students patiently observe the moon and elements of nature, subtle changes take place. The children make discoveries that inform and puzzle them, often at the same time.

For example, students discover that the *new* moon is not visible. This information leads them to wonder why we don't see the moon. Is it hidden? Is it visible in other places? Does it appear while we sleep?

Knowing the importance of questions and the part they would eventually play in this nature study, Joni and her students began their Moon Journals by making an initial entry of everything they wanted to know about the moon. At first the questions were scientifically based.

- How far away is the moon?
- How did it get there?
- What is it made of?
- Does it come out at the same time every night?
- Is it in different places in the sky?
- Why does it change color, shape, and size?
- How do scientists name places on the moon?
- What is on the other side of the moon?

Her students were surprised when Joni added a question of her own: Is the moon made out of cheese? They laughed, thinking her silly, until she began composing a poem of whimsical questions about the moon. Because Joni writes frequently with her students, they were not surprised to see her experiment with a poem on the chalkboard. The children read the poem aloud as she composed, anticipating words and lines. When Joni became uncertain about a new line, she played with verbal strings of rhyming words. The students called out suggestions, and before long the poem became a cooperative piece.

Mr. Moon, I have a question
on this clear October night:
do mice and owls read bedtime stories
by your soft, glowing light?
Is the nighttime news printed
on the brilliant falling leaves,
recording your conversations
with the sycamore trees?
If I make a date to watch you
up in the night sky,
will you tell me your secrets?
You know I can't fly!
I want to know everything
you see from up above,
I want to know all about
the things that you love.
Are your friends the stars?
Is your rival the sun?
Or do you all work together
so your job is more fun?

If the only demonstration offered was of a rhyming poem, the students might feel that they needed to make their poems rhyme too. The next step, therefore, was to record questions that didn't rhyme but still felt like a poem.

Mr. Moon, are the clouds white rivers you cross every night?
Do your sighs make the stars twinkle and shine?
If I stand very still, will you talk to me?
Do flowers grow in your light?
Will I grow, too?

This second poem suggested a slightly different tone, colored by reflection. The students had questions of their own, and their first entries took shape in their journals.

I Wonder

When the moon gets dull,
who shines it?
If the moon is made out of cheese,

when does it turn old?
When the stars get dim,
does the moon turn them to gold?
Does the moon drink from the Big and Little Dipper?
Does the moon fish with moonbeams, looking for kipper?
If it's yes, then tickle me pink,
and wash all my questions right down the sink!

Jacki, age 10

I Wonder

Is there a man on the moon?
Did the car really jump over it?
Is there water on the moon?
Is the moon made out of cheese?
Is there life on the moon?
Where do you go when there is a new moon?

Stacey, age 8

Eye in the Sky

I'm looking at the sky
in the cold night air,
The moon so high up,
and me down here.
I wonder if I
will ever travel to space,
See people from another planet
face to face?
For now
I just dream of
what I might see,
And just imagine
what those people
would think of me.

Alyson, age 10

Asking these questions helped to make the moon seem more personal to the children and nudged them to begin thinking metaphorically about nature. They left for home ready to make detailed factual observations but also willing to play with their ideas and thoughts.

As you and your students begin Moon Journals or other focused nature studies, try recording your initial questions, both factual and fanciful. See what happens when you set aside time to wonder.

WRITING INVITATION #2

Notes from Nature: Writing About the Environment from a Naturalist's Point of View

As you step outside under the night sky you see the shadows of a tall pine touching the darkened sky, you hear the sounds of a raccoon digging through a trash can, and you feel a chilly breeze rubbing the side of your face. You look up and see the creamy crescent moon glowing in a sea of glittering stars. The moon, the air, and every plant and animal that you observe can be described in your Moon Journal from a naturalist's point of view.

Naturalists look at the ecosystem as a balanced web of life. Each strand on the web is critical to the health of the entire environment. The web loses its strength even if one link is weakened. *Notes from Nature* invites students to pay close attention to nature's details. Everything they observe is an important silky thread in the web of life that exists in their own backyard.

To begin this invitation, our classes looked at *Sketching Outdoors in Summer* (1988b) and *Sketching Outdoors in Autumn* (1988a) by Jim Arnosky and *The Sierra Club Guide to Sketching in Nature* (1990) by Cathy Johnson to see examples of field journal pages written and illustrated from the perspective of naturalists. Both authors include next to their sketches detailed remarks concerning weather, season, animal and plant life, and art techniques.

Next, we shared our own journal entries to demonstrate how this type of writing might be approached in the environment where we live. Obviously, every region will assume unique characteristics. This example, taken from Gina's journal, is written from a naturalist's point of view.

> It is a damp November evening, probably 45 degrees outside. The wind is blowing from the northwest. The sky is a deep, midnight blue. The nearly full moon is lighting the sage-covered hillside, causing the Douglas Firs, Ponderosa, and Sugar Pines to cast tall, eerie shadows on the earth. The valley below is filled with deciduous trees that are dropping their leaves; only the inky red ones remain on their branches. The fog is starting to roll in—an earth-bound cloud hugging the ground. I can hear the coyotes howling in a pack not far away, perhaps yipping about a recent kill.

The students saw that there were many other elements that a naturalist might note in an observation, including
   exact time and date
   identification of lunar phase
   climate
   season
   animal/insect activity
   flower/tree/shrub identification and growth

cloud cover
wind direction
weather prediction
night bird/insect sounds

We asked the children to list a few of these ideas in their journals to use as future reference points.

The following *Notes from Nature* were taken from student Moon Journals:

> It's a full moon. It's a little bit foggy and I see a lot of stars. There are bright yellow lights, green trees and big, big mountains. I hear coyotes howling.
>
> *Brian, age 8*

> The sky is so blue. The moon looks so bright. I hear a soft meow and a dog howl. Not too many stars. It's a little cloudy tonight. I feel the wind. It blows against my face. I see the wind blow in the sky.
>
> *Danielle, age 8*

> I am writing this entry by candlelight out in my backyard. There are many stars but no moon. I see long white clouds in the sky. It was very dark except for the candle. I found the constellation Orion among the many stars and each time I look up I see more and more stars. It is pretty cold tonight but it is nice. Even though there is no moon it is still nice. It is silent except for something scurrying in the bushes.
>
> *Rob, age 9*

Sometimes *Notes from Nature* are enhanced with imagery. The beauty of the observation can be very moving and often leads to free verse or prose poetry.

Fall Moon

> I see the fall moon.
> I see dry hillsides,
> pale colors fading in the distance,
> bare rose bushes,
> and crows circling,
> like a black ring in the air.
> I see lizards gazing hungrily
> at the flies
> and squirrels storing their nuts
> for the winter.
> I see the wind blowing
> leaves off the trees
> for little kids to play in.
>
> *J.D., age 11*

This selection from Joni's journal is another variation on the form.

> The hills were brown, like baked loaves of bread. The trail was newly cleared, no flowers bordered its sides. It felt stark and bare. The smell of sage and salt brought back memories of my spring hikes in La Jolla Canyon. As the sun set over the ocean, the hills took on a golden cast. The shadows lengthened. The only sounds I heard were bird cries, small skittering animals, and the waves pounding on the rocks. The setting sun made a golden trail over the sea and when I squinted, the water sparkled like brilliant coins. As I crested the hill I saw a gleaming white disc peek over the canyon. "The moon!" I thought with excitement. I wondered if my students were watching this moon too.

We demonstrate *Notes from Nature* in conjunction with Art Invitation #1: *Pencil Sketching* and Art Invitation #2: *Pen-and-Ink Drawings*. A brief observation accompanied by a sketch or drawing is the simplest form of a Moon Journal entry.

WRITING INVITATION #3

Growing Poems from Seeds: Creating Poems from Past Experiences, Ideas, and "Seed Book" Entries

Poems are often the blossoms of past experiences, conversations, observations, sketches, or journal entries. These experiences—pictures or words—may often take root consciously or unconsciously. Later, the writer may find the idea or image emerging in prose or poetry.

Many writers and artists keep "seed books" for their ideas, filled with improvisational sketches and written entries. The pages of a combined writer's notebook and artist's sketch pad may contain images of anything that catches the journalist's eye: leaves, buildings, an interesting window or doorway, a sunset, a flower bordering a path, a bird on a fence post, a blade of grass, or perhaps a contour drawing of a friend. In addition to the sketches, you might find quotes from favorite poems or lines from books, snippets of conversations, interesting signs, brief observations, or character descriptions. At the time the entries are made, the writer-artist is engaged in giving focused attention to an object or idea. Often the observation or sketch is recorded for no other purpose than "saving" an impression. Later, however, a description of the sketch or only one word of the writing may surface in a composition.

One example of a "poem grown from a seed" involves the full moon, a telephone conversation, and a journal entry. During one summer, Joni visited the city of Idyllwild in the San Jacinto Mountains of California. The second night of her visit she walked down a quiet street in the moonlight. When she came to a clearing she looked up into the sky and was treated to a view of the full moon.

Later that night she recorded her impressions, accompanied by a simple sketch (Figure 3-1A).

When Joni returned from the mountains she received a phone call from Gina, who began their conversation by exclaiming, "You missed the moon! We had a harvest moon, in July!"

Joni smiled and told Gina she saw the *same* moon up in Idyllwild. Although the conversation turned to laughter, the delight in knowing that the moon was enjoyed and appreciated by two friends standing in very different locations underscored more than the words of the conversation could express: their shared sense of celebration and friendship.

Joni drew lines in her sketch pad, connecting the full moon to Gina (in the city) and herself (in the mountains). That sketch (Figure 3-1B), combined with her journal entry of July 12th, became the seeds of the poem found in the next writing invitation, *Moontalk*.

As students keep their own Moon Journals, invite them to keep a sketch pad or notebook for ideas, observations, snippets of conversations, quotes from books, lines from poems or songs, headlines from newspapers, or perhaps even the daily weather report. Look for connections.

For example, Jacki, one of Joni's fifth grade students, discovered a connection between two lines from a favorite book and the stars in the dark sky. She jotted down two lines from Eleanor Coerr's *Sadako* (1993): "When the candles were burning brightly, the lanterns were launched on the Ohta River. They floated out to sea like a swarm of fireflies against the dark water." Later, on the night of the full moon, Jacki wrote a poem that included the "seed" words from the book.

Stars

Little fireflies
flying in the sky—
these are the stars.
Lantern fish
swimming in the dark vast sea,
these are the stars.
Glowing, glowing lanterns,
these are the stars.

When students borrow lines, record observations, and jot down questions, their ears soon become attuned to the "seeds" that may blossom into later poems. Gina's poem "Pack Rat" tells the story of one writer's habit of saving scraps of life.

There's a pack rat in me,
Gathering, collecting.
Roaming and scrounging
For stories to tell.

FIGURE 3-1

I wander through hallways
Down alleys and rain gutters
Looking for something
Shiny and rare.

I listen for voices
And word of your travels
For memories, for gossip,
For the news of your day.

I steal all your treasures
And write them on napkins,
On matchbooks and wrappers
And cash register receipts.

I take them to nest,
I guard them and watch them,
I percolate and boil them
'Till the stewing is done.

I cherish you in tales
And poems of my writing,
I am a pack rat
With stories to tell.

The more writers and artists pay attention to common things, the easier it becomes to find poetry in the heavens *and* on the earth.

WRITING INVITATION #4

Moontalk: A Dialogue Poem About the Moon

In a recent interview, poet Naomi Shihab Nye commented that poems often contain the "juxtaposition of ideas." The notion of putting different ideas next to each other, side by side, and then discovering an unexpected connection is the power and fun of a dialogue poem. In natural dialogue, one speaker often picks up the conversational threads of the other speaker, agreeing or disagreeing or adding a personal experience or opinion about a topic. Sometimes, after each have had their say, the speakers come to consensus or find a common conclusion to their discussion. Other times the speakers may agree to disagree, appreciating each other's opinions and points of view.

Keeping a Moon Journal offers writers an opportunity to engage in a dialogue about the moon—a conversation that may later develop into a poem. The seeds of the poem are in the daily observations. The journalists are recording their different impressions of the same moon in their own unique styles. What one person notices in one location may be slightly different from the observations of another.

In this example, Joni and Gina are having a conversation about the moon. Joni was in the mountains and Gina was in the city, but they both observed the same full moon on the night of July 12th. (See Writing Invitation #3: *Growing Poems from Seeds.*)

Moontalk

"You missed the moon,"
my friend informed me,

"there was a harvest moon . . .
while you were gone.
So round and orange
it felt like October—
trick-or-treat,
but in July.
I watched it rise.
Here, in the city.
You would have loved it . . .
I thought of you."

"I saw that moon.
Yes, in the mountains.
I watched it, too . . .
I saw it rise.
It climbed the heavens
on a ladder of branches
and turned the charcoal sky
to indigo blue.
It paled as it rose,
orange faded to white
until it gleamed
like a newly minted dime.
It dimmed the stars,
an altar boy in white linen
snuffing out candles,
and I stood there in peace.
The cathedral was silent,
the canyon cast shadows,
raccoons huddled in pinetrees
watching me . . .
watch the moon."

So what is it,
I wonder,
why do we both pause?
It's a piece of rock, after all,
just floating in space.
What is the connection?
We stand in different places . . .
let our eyes both focus
with the same delight.
Our friendship is stitched
in shared appreciation

of simple, small gifts
that mark our days.
Moments, ideas,
a painting, a flower,
poems, a sentence,
memories and thoughts.
Embroidered together
a tapestry in the making
threaded with moonbeams
worked with four hands.

Joni Chancer

The structure of the poem was easy, because it followed what actually occurred in their conversation. The first verse contains Gina's comments to Joni about the harvest moon she saw in the city. In the second verse, Joni answers her by commenting that she saw the same moon. At this point Joni adds observations from her summer journal to the poem. The gleaming moon, the peace she felt, even the raccoon she noticed in the tree behind her—they all made their appearance in the poem. The final verse is the "so what" of the poem: the big idea or lasting reflection. In this case, Joni and Gina agree about the connections the moon offers in their friendship.

Helping Students Write Their Own Dialogue Poems About the Moon

To begin, invite students to meet with a friend and compare Moon Journal entries from particular nights. Encourage them to find observations from the same night that are *slightly different*. For example, one evening Marnie and Kerstin both observed the same cloud-covered sky. Marnie's entry described a fading blue sky that was quickly disappearing as darker clouds moved in. She turned her observation into a poem as she wrote

A pastel picture, that's what it is.
A dolphin-blue sky waving good-bye right before my eyes.
A soft, warm heavenly blanket
casting a shadow on the deep mysterious mountains.
Dark clouds are illuminated
by the bright golden sun
peaking out behind them.

Kerstin recorded an observation that same night, and she also noticed the dark clouds moving in. But the sky she observed was threatening, filled with ap-

proaching thunderclouds. Her observation and poem sound slightly different
from Marnie's.

> Thunderclouds, big and dark,
> Thunderclouds, growing darker and darker,
> Thunderclouds, moving like smoke across the sky,
> Thunderclouds, carrying rain and more rain,
> Thunderclouds, windy and dark and cold.

The contrast between these two poems creates an interesting juxtaposition of the
same night, the same sky, but different observations and responses.

The fun part of this process is the next step: combining the two short pieces
into a longer poem. First, one must decide who will be the first speaker in the
poem. Will this speaker write several lines together or just an initial line of conversation? The second speaker might "answer" the lines of the first speaker in
true conversational style or choose to write an entire, uninterrupted second verse.
Here is an example of how Marnie's and Kerstin's separate entries become combined to create a new poem:

> "Did you see the sky?
> Last night, at sunset . . .
> A pastel picture, that's what it was.
> A dolphin-blue sky, waving good-bye
> right before my eyes.
> A soft, warm heavenly blanket
> casting a shadow
> on the deep mysterious mountains.
> Dark clouds were illuminated
> by the bright golden sun
> that peaked out behind them."

> "I saw the sky.
> I sketched it in my journal,
> but the palette was different,
> no blues or gold.
> Instead I saw thunderclouds, growing darker and darker.
> Thunderclouds, moving like smoke across the sky,
> Thunderclouds, carrying rain and more rain,
> Thunderclouds, windy and dark and cold."
> Lightning cut through the sky
> followed by a loud clap of thunder
> that stirred the eerie silence.

> Then rain,
> rain, rain.

And blue, blue sky
reappeared.
A rainbow of colors filled the sky.

In their combined poem, Marnie and Kerstin engaged in a conversation about the cloud-covered sky. They decided to place Marnie's poem first because it seemed to precede the action in Kerstin's poem. Kerstin's poem continues the dialogue and the story. The final verse, with lines from both entries, brings the reader to the resolution of the events described in the combined poem.

After their two entries are pieced together, your young writers will have a choice. Will they end the poem after the written conversation in the two verses, or will they compose a third verse together? Will the new verse tie the preceding verses together? Will it contain a reflection? The choice belongs to the authors.

These pieces can easily be performed as poems for two voices. For example, Marnie could read the first verse and Kerstin the second. The final verse could be read in unison. The completed piece might be enhanced by "scoring" the poem. See Writing Invitation #5: *Moon Music* for a description of this process.

WRITING INVITATION #5

Moon Music: Adding Sounds and Music to Prose and Poetry

Poems often come alive when they appeal to the senses. Whistling wind, rustling leaves, soft rain pattering across a window pane, or lightning and thunder crashing through a stormy night—can you hear these sounds in your mind? By producing the sounds described in a poem, the music and rhythms of language and the interpretation of the message are enhanced and celebrated. All it takes are simple instruments.

Many of these instruments are disguised as common household items: paper bags, an empty tin can filled with marbles, rice in an empty jar, pie tins smashed together, blocks of wood rubbed against each other—the possibilities are endless. The instruments enhance the performance of poetry and offer a sensory vehicle for interpretation. Triangles, chimes, xylophones, keyboards, lummi sticks, cymbals, drums, tambourines, flutes, and recorders cast magic on the lines of verse and/or prose. For example, a lonely flute melody or minor chords played on a keyboard can convey the feeling of sadness. The words of an exciting poem can be punctuated by cymbals, snapping fingers, or the rhythmic beating of drums.

Once students have assembled and gathered musical instruments and made their own homemade sound devices, they are ready to look for Moon Journal entries that invite enhancement. Children enjoy working with classmates who later become the orchestra or chorus for their poetry readings. They don't need the ability to read music in order to score a poem. Students can develop a simple code to represent particular sounds (Figure 3-2). A cluster of stars, for example, can

FIGURE 3-2

bell	cymbals	wind chimes
triangle and a stick	drums	keyboard
lummi sticks	sand paper blocks	pencils tapping table tops
fingertips tapping on a metal cookie sheet	rain stick	flute
rice in an empty can	recorder or flute	wood blocks
tambourine	xylophone	crunched plastic grocery bag

"Did you see the sky?
Last night, at sunset...
A pastel picture, that's what it was.
A dolphin blue sky, waving good-bye
right before my eyes.
A soft, warm heavenly blanket   (softly)
casting a shadow
on the deep mysterious mountains.
Dark clouds were illuminated   (trill across)
by the bright golden sun
that peaked out behind them."

"I saw the sky.   (minor chords)
I sketched it in my journal,
but the palette was different.
No blues, no gold.
Instead I saw thunderclouds, growing darker and darker.
Thunderclouds, moving like smoke across the sky,
Thunderclouds, carrying rain and more rain,
Thunderclouds, windy and dark and cold."

Lightning cut through the sky   (loud crash!)
followed by a loud clap of thunder
that stirred the eerie silence.
Then rain,
rain,
rain.
And blue, blue sky
reappeared.
A rainbow of beautiful colors filled the sky.

denote tinkling wind chimes. Demonstrate to students how they can create their own musical code, and then record their suggested symbols on chart paper. Figure 3-2 is an example of a musical code from one classroom. In this demonstration, Marnie and Kerstin's dialogue poem has been scored by a group of students. (See Writing Invitation #4: *Moontalk*.) Encourage students to follow the code and practice performing Marnie and Kerstin's poem with sound and musical instruments. Once they feel comfortable reading the notations, they are ready to try scoring and performing some of their own Moon Journal poetry.

WRITING INVITATION #6

Lunar List Poems: Writing a List Poem

Staring at a white sheet of paper or blank computer screen can be a stressful experience for any writer. It's no wonder that teachers and parents often hear young authors, faced with the challenge of an empty page, say, "I can't think of anything to write." Often what they really mean is, I don't know where to begin. One simple writer's tool that can be used as an initial step in writing poetry or prose is to create a list.

Here is an example. You have just returned from an evening walk. You want to write a poem about your experience but you're not sure where to begin. Try writing a list of words about everything you recall from the walk. Let your ideas tumble—no editing at this point. Just jot down any word that comes to your mind. Sometimes it's fun to see how many words you can write without stopping. Perhaps your list will include words like these:

path	stars
shadows	silent
crickets	fog
full moon	clouds

Now it's time to *fill in* the list. Look at each word. What other words or phrases can be added to each list word to describe your experience more fully? Let's consider the word *path*. What kind of path was it? Steep, spooky, narrow, rocky, dark, quiet, moonlit? Where was it? In the mountains, desert, field, park, your neighborhood? Think about your five senses. Are there any smells or sounds that struck you?

Describe the path. Let your readers step onto it with you. Take them on your journey. Write these new words or phrases under the word *path*. Continue this process for each word on your list.

Once the list has been expanded in this manner, you can begin playing with what you've listed, adding or deleting words as needed. There are many choices at this point. You might choose to tell the *story* of your evening walk from beginning to end by placing your list entries in chronological order. Or you might choose a selection of the words or phrases from the list and rearrange them until you find a sequence that suits you. Perhaps one phrase will jump out at you and become the seed for something totally unexpected. (See Writing Invitation #3: *Growing Poems from Seeds*.) There's no right or wrong way to do this. Ultimately, you will find a poem waiting to be discovered within your list.

In one first grade class, students kept a community Moon Journal. They all contributed to a list poem as one of their journal entries. This was their initial list of lunar words:

moon	stars
face	earth
cookie	solar system
eyes	outer space
finger nail	planets
banana	holes
volcanoes	bedtime
full moon	sun

You can see how the children developed the poem "Space" by adding words, phrases, and sentences to the list above.

Space

The moon shines on the Earth
And has a face.
It is big,
Like a half cookie,
A finger nail,
A banana,
Or round like your eyes,
With interesting shapes inside
And lumps and holes from volcanoes.
We see it at night,
It reminds us it's bedtime.
The sun shines
And you see different moon parts.
There are full moons,
Half moons,
Or no moons.
Not really,
It's still there,
Covered by clouds.
Stars in space,
Little dots of light,
Really high in the air.

Tiny, twinkly, blinking.
Stars sparkle but planets don't.
They make pictures
Outside my window
Over my tree.
Shooting stars,
Zooming past the moon,
Moving all around in outer space,
Sometimes shooting to the ground,
Going up and down like an elevator.
Make a wish
On a falling star.

Roseanne, a kindergartner, developed her list poem in a different way. First, she *drew* her list of words, depicting stars, the sky, and the moon. Then Roseanne described her pictures as she dictated ther list poem "Stars."

Stars

Stars,
Up in the air.
They sparkle
And look like diamonds.
They make the moon
Turn around
To look at them.

Michael, a second grader, wrote a list of silly words: macaroni, flying squirrel, frogs, and monster; then he "filled in" his list to create "Under the Moon."

Under the Moon

Under the moon
Someone might be cooking
Macaroni and frog legs.
A flying squirrel
Might be crashing into a tree.
Or maybe
There's a monster
Lurking under your bed!

Whether you are planning a trip to the market or watching the moon, writing a list will help you remember little things that are too important to forget!

WRITING INVITATION #7

Similes by Starlight: Writing Similes About the Moon and the Night Sky

The moon has been celebrated in similes for hundreds of years. Each lunar phase is characterized by a distinctive shape that invites comparison. Popular music, for example, has likened the full moon to "a big pizza pie"!

Although the new moon is not visible, this lunar phase provides an excellent view of a starry sky. Constellations shine like jewels. One of the first rhymes children learn is a simile about a star.

> Twinkle, twinkle, little star
> How I wonder what you are
> Up above the world so high
> Like a diamond in the sky.

The challenge of creating similes is to discover uncommon comparisons, to rub unlikely ideas against each other. For example, what else do stars look like? Perhaps stars shine in the sky like sunlight dancing on the water, or sing in the sky like tinkling wind chimes.

To get the students started, we write the following sentence frame on the board: The stars are like_____.

As the students suggest comparisons, we record their ideas also on the board. Next, we read a few published poems that contain interesting similes about stars. Sometimes creating artwork showing stars in the sky helps students visualize what they will later express in writing. (See Art Invitation # 5: *Splattered Stars* and Art Invitation #6: *Salt Stars and Clouds*.)

After listening to the poetry and after drawing or painting stars, students are often inspired to experiment with new similes. We then add a second round of comparisons to the original list. At this point, a class book of star similes can be created, featuring an illustrated page from each child.

The appearance of the crescent moon provides another opportunity to explore similes. As a warm-up lesson, pass out small crescent-shaped cutouts. Encourage the students to position the moon in different ways. What does it look like? Again, using a simple sentence frame is an easy way to begin. The crescent moon is like a_____. Some of our students have responded with:

comma on a page of sky
a sly smile in the sky
a piece of pineapple
a slice of cantaloupe

At this point, invite students to break away from the sentence frame and play with extending their comparisons, perhaps stringing a number of similes together to describe the night sky they observed while writing in their journals. Jessica wrote the following entry in her Moon Journal:

> The sky is as clear as a piece of glass
> and the stars are as bright as a child on Christmas.
> Tonight the moon looks like a piece of pineapple,
> right above the twilight that looks like fire.
> It looks like magic in the night sky—
> it's a miracle.

Student entries often contain a mixture of scientific description enhanced by poetic comparison. Sheila, who took her Moon Journal with her to Denver, Colorado, wrote:

> A quarter moon again tonight. It is 32 degrees and freeeezing! In the north there are long stratus clouds that are stretched across the sky like smoke drifting away from a chimney. The sky is a deep navy blue color, but there are still some specks of brighter blue left over from the day, like morning glories that are about to close up.

Consider introducing your students to similes early in its cycle. As the moon continues to grow, new comparisons will add interest and mood to journal entries.

WRITING INVITATION #8

Metaphor Moon: Finding Comparisons in Nature

In Writing Invitation #7: *Similes by Starlight*, we explored the comparison of two things not commonly connected with each other. Once children are familiar with writing similes, they find it easy to compose metaphors (figures of speech that compare two different things without using a word of comparison such as *like* or *as*). Again, juxtaposition adds interest and imagery to prose and poetry.

The process is simple. The simile "the clouds are like mashed potatoes" is easily changed into a metaphor by writing "clouds are mashed potatoes." Sometimes a metaphor feels stronger than a simile when the word of comparison is dropped.

One gloriously cloudy day in October, Joni's students went outside to watch the action overhead. They sketched the clouds and discovered creatures in the shifting formations. Some of the children drew pictures of the dragons, ships, and teddy bears they saw appearing in the sky.

When they returned to the classroom, Joni wrote the following sentence frame on the board: Clouds are _____.

Earlier, when students were naming the creatures and objects they spied in the clouds, Joni took notes. Now she was able to begin the metaphor minilesson by writing some of their earlier comments on the board:

Clouds are

fluffy cotton balls
spirits of people who have gone away
ice cream and snow cones
marshmallows, soft and melting

The students called out additional comparisons, and before long the chalkboard was filled with metaphors. Without knowing it, the children had composed a class poem. Later, they gave the poem a title by selecting one of the lines of the poem: "Waves on an Ocean of Sky." The entire poem, which could have resulted only from observation, sketching, and discovery, became a metaphoric tribute to clouds.

Waves on an Ocean of Sky

Fluffy cotton balls,

Soft warm blanket for the heavens,
Waves on an ocean of sky,
God's pillow,
A flock of puff-ball sheep
moving across pastures of blue,
Mary's little lamb,
Smooth feathers floating by,
Teddy bears,
Spirits of people who have gone away,
White sheep and black lambs,
The artwork of God's palette,
Cauliflower and whipped cream,
Mashed potatoes,
Castles of old in the sky,
Teddy bears,
Heavenly gray boulders,
Heavy and still,
Pastels smeared across an illuminated
     sky,

Pillow stuffing,
Oranges, tangerines, the fruit of the
     heavens,
Or monsters changing shapes,
Creating a grand canyon of white,
     grey and blue
Marshmallows, soft and melting,
A mound of mashed potatoes with
     sunny butter melting down,
Cups of thick clam chowder,
Crumpled up pieces of paper,
Ghost ships, crossing the ocean sky,
Ice cream and snow cones,
Snowballs and waterfalls,
Winter's wonder,
Or summer's surprise,
Ever-changing skies,
God's poetry . . .
Clouds.

Using a large point size on the computer, Joni typed each line as an individual page and then printed them on construction paper. The children illustrated their comparisons with watercolors. The pages were bound, a cover was created, and the book became part of the classroom library.

When the students recorded Moon Journal observations later that evening, many chose to extend their cloud metaphors into developed poems.

Jousting Match

A tidal wave
A wave moving across the sea
An army of falling rain
All coming down on me.
A jousting match between the clouds
All charging at each other,
What will happen when they get closer,
Closer to one another?
Someone is crying in heaven up above;
The rain will stop,
The sun will shine . . .
When that person gets love.
And then the match will stop
And the clouds will move away . . .
The moon appears,
The stars dance along,
It's the end of the day.

    Tracy

Clouds

Cotton balls
a blanket over an azure sky
a scorpion's tail
continents and islands
an ocean with huge waves
a slingshot, an anchor, a head of a cobra
manholes and flying squirrels
a box of crayons in a row.
No fog . . .
just beautiful clouds.

    Davey

Changing Seasons

Nights are getting foggy,
days are getting colder,
a warm cotton blanket of clouds blocks the sky from view.

Leaves are falling,
and brilliant colors of red, orange and gold
are carpeting the ground in a lush texture.
The mountains
wear hoods and jackets of light fog.
Animals are running away,
looking for shelter.
Earlier this month,
summer was blowing its last breath . . .
But now,
it is colder.
Rain will soon be dancing around the ground
like little butterflies,
chasing each other around.

Megan

Megan's poem, "Changing Seasons," began when she compared clouds to a "warm cotton blanket" but grew to include other metaphors. It was later, after the poems were written, that Joni labeled the technique as "writing metaphors." Observations, sketching, class sharing, Moon Journal entries, watercolor compositions, and informal conversations were the components that came together to create these poems. Students write what they know and understand. As always, experience is the best teacher.

WRITING INVITATION #9

The Maiden and the Man in the Moon: Using Personification and Active Verbs to Describe the Moon and the Night Sky

Is there a Man in the Moon looking down on Earth? Or a moon maiden dancing across the sky? Once students begin thinking metaphorically, it is a natural progression for them to begin giving the moon, the clouds, and the stars human characteristics.

Personification invites the use of active verbs and breathes life into a piece, allowing the reader to visualize the action more specifically. What is the moon doing? Chomping, dancing, whispering, singing, frowning, smiling, marching, tip-toeing—the descriptions evoke exciting mental pictures and emotional connections. A frowning moon is sad or disparaging, whereas a singing moon is joyful or playful.

When the moon is personified, it becomes a player in the drama of the night sky. Who are the other actors? Stars and clouds also take on human characteristics, entering the action. The moon may be whispering to the stars or singing sunset clouds a lullaby. The settings are as limitless as a child's imagination. For example, Amanda described the moon as a dancer.

The moon dances in the glow of her light.
She sparkles and glitters as she shines in the night.
Her grace and beauty are admired by all.
Her dress glows with stardust,
and the mist is her shawl.

Amanda, age 9

Another student takes us to the circus in her Moon Journal entry.

The sky
has just been to the circus.
He went on all the rides,
he played all the games,
but the best thing he did
is eat his cotton candy!

In this poem, the writer celebrated how the sky was "eating" the cotton candy clouds so she could see the full moon. Her poem stemmed from an earlier Moon Journal observation.

November 14th, 8:00 p.m.
You can barely see the moon, but there, underneath all those clouds, is a navy blue sky and the full moon. It's really neat! I'm sooooo happy it's a full moon! You can hardly tell that the moon is there when the clouds creep over it, but I KNOW it is there. Tonight is a peekaboo night. The clouds keep covering the moon up!

In *Light and Shadow* (poetry by Myra Cohn Livingston with photographs by Barbara Rogasky, 1992), each poem begins with the noun *light* and is followed by an action verb such as *swims*, *hikes*, or *drifts*. The rest of the poem is an elaboration of the original thought and creates a written image as striking as the accompanying photograph. It is a delightful book that helps train one's eye to look for small pleasures in usual and unexpected places.

When Joni visited the Hawaiian island of Kauai, she established a daily ritual of watching the sun disappear into the ocean as the first stars appeared. In her sketch pad she experimented with the structure of Livingston's poems and created her own ode to light.

Dusk

Light slips between the sheets
and pulls the covers slowly up around its cheeks

burrowing into a velvet blanket of evening
until it yawns . . .
looking out on the world
through half-closed,
heavy-lidded eyes
caught between dreaming and reflection
savoring the rest
the peace
the silence
not wanting to lose awareness
but
slipping
    slipping
        slipping
into the night
where it sighs . . .
its gentle breath
rustling the stars
that chime in the stillness.

Joni used *Light and Shadow* as a literary model when she introduced a minilesson on the use of vivid verbs. The students began by clustering verbs plucked from Moon Journal entries. They also made a selection of verbs that are not commonly associated with the moon but are used to describe people or animals.

the moon	*moonlight*
grazes	searches
drinks	paints
snoozes	beckons
tiptoes	washes

After creating the cluster, the children thumbed through their journal pages looking for observations to transform into poems about personified moonlight. A few students needed assistance and met with Joni in a corner of the classroom with their Moon Journals. They decided to begin with the verb "watches." What would the moon be watching? The children suggested people, nocturnal animals, owls, falling leaves, lights going off in houses, and children falling asleep. They were ready to draft a poem using verbs from their list.

The moon watches
the creatures of earth.
Some are getting ready to sleep,
and others are waking up.
The owl stretches its wings
and calls to its friends:

"The moon is here! Come out and play!"
Leaves drift down from the branches of trees,
and children fall asleep in their beds.
One by one,
lights are dimmed in houses.
Moonlight illuminates
a nighttime world.

Two of the children in the group copied this poem into their journals, underlining their specific contributions. Others were ready to take off on their own.

The moon is tiptoeing around the earth
while the stars are left behind,
glowing in the dark indigo sky.

As the moon passes the stars
they whisper
Ssssh! Sssssh!

The moon swims
in a sea of stars
lighting up the water
with its bright light.

The moon paints a picture
on the canvas of night.

The moon is a cake of soap,
washing the sky clean.

The moon is roller-blading around the earth,
night-dreaming that it could be
zooming around Saturn's rings!

One student used the following moon-verb combination as the beginning of a moon legend:

The moon is patiently sewing a great sparkling cloth. One day it will be big enough to cover the sun. Sometimes it almost does, but the sun gets out! Yet, each time it is harder for the sun because the moon uses her moonbeams to hold down the cloth.

Because the children experienced the power of this technique while crafting their poems in class, they subsequently included active verbs in their Moon Journal observations. Let the moon guide you in deciding when to introduce this writing invitation. You will know it is time when you experience a moon breaking through the mist, fighting with rain clouds, or illuminating the neighborhood. Sketch the action and then paint a picture with words!

WRITING INVITATION #10

Looking Out My Window: Observation and Personal Reflection

Observation and personal reflection are at the heart the Moon Journal process. As students observe the moon and the environment, they learn to *feel* their response and then document it. In *Wild Mind: Living the Writer's Life* (1990), Natalie Goldberg says to writers, ". . . notice your mind and begin to trust it and understand it." Taking notice is how this writing invitation begins.

Look out your window. What do you see? The moon, the night sky, darkened trees, bushes, rooftops? The silhouette of a swing set, a car, a street sign? Beyond the obvious objects, beyond the things observed at first glance, what else do you notice? Look closely at the scene. Pretend you are a detective looking for clues in the night. Are grasses moving in the wind? Is there a cat taking an evening stroll? The distant lights of a jet zooming through the night sky? Clouds beginning to cover the moon?

Do you hear anything? Maybe there are loud sounds that you hear immediately, like traffic on the street or your neighbor's crazy dog. What about the quiet sounds? Is there a cricket symphony in progress? A radio playing in the apartment downstairs? A conversation coming from the alley? Jot down some of these things in your journal. Consider beginning your sentences with "I see . . . ," "I hear . . . ," "I notice. . . ."

This *Looking Out My Window* entry was taken from a third grader's journal.

> Tonight it was a banana moon. I felt very cool air. I smelled nothing. But I heard crickets across my street. I could taste the air. I heard a story about the stars. It's like a bird poking through this big black blanket that God puts over us every night. The bird poked and poked and he pulled out a lot of the blanket which we call the moon.
> *Christie*

Hollie, a sixth grade student, wrote about events happening outside her window and inside her house.

> When I look out my window I see the moon smiling down on me, the stars dancing, the trees swaying in the breeze and the hills lying down to sleep. Oh, and what is that? I see a coyote over there on the grass and beside him sits his shadow. When I look out my window I hear a cat meowing and my

dog pawing at the back door. My mom's computer printer, my sister's blaring stereo, and, of course, the washing machine are all going at once. I feel at home. There is not one night at my house when things are quiet.

Two first graders dictated the following observations to their parents:

It's raining. I hate it because you can't play baseball and your game gets canceled because there's too much mud in the field. And you can't see the moon either because of the clouds.

Nicholas

I saw the banana moon lying on its side. It looked like it fell over. I saw a star above it. My dad said it wasn't a star. He said it was Jupiter. We drew a picture of it together.

Jonpaul

Alternate Ideas

After your students write their observation or reflection, invite them to use it as material for a poem. Ryan observed the moon over his garden one evening in spring, then wrote "The Night Garden."

The Night Garden

The trees are hiding their blossoms
Under their leaves,
With the grass waving.
The flowers are swimming
In a slither river of weeds,
Sunflowers asleep under the moon,
Waiting to crawl up to the sun.
Then the rain pounds down and
I have to move from the garden.

Breana, a first grader who loves to dance, saw the full moon out her window and said that it reminded her of a white stage. Later, she dictated the following poem:

The moon is a place
for angels to dance,
dressed in gowns and capes,
with sparkly, glittery wings
softly swaying.
They are like ballerinas
on a round, white stage.

Stories also develop from these observations. This *Looking Out My Window* entry was taken from Gina's journal.

> A spider joined our family for dinner tonight. She watched us eat our meal from her web outside the dining room window. My children, Joshua and Nicholas, decided that the spider was hungry too. From where we sat, the spider's web looked like a fine silvery picture frame that broke up the sky beyond into a multitude of miniature portraits. A silhouette of a Sugar Pine was featured in the center of the delicate frame. The moon's image was hung in the upper left-hand corner. The pearlescent moonlight illuminated the spider's silky stitches.
>
> A moth flew into the web. Its frantic fluttering wings allowed it to escape capture, but not before it tore a huge hole in the weaving. Any hopes for moth dinner had disappeared into the night.
>
> After the commotion was over, the spider inched her way toward the tear. She crawled all around its perimeter like a building inspector assessing property damage. Then slowly she began to spin again.
>
> We watched as her endless spool of thread unwound from within her abdomen. The moon spotlighted the tiny quilter as she meticulously duplicated the exact pattern of the previous web. When she finished her work, the spider went back to her waiting area.
>
> Several times throughout the evening I returned to the dining room window to see if this patient creature was having any luck. For hours she was motionless. But finally, right before I was about to give up, a small fly got caught in the sticky strands. The spider rapidly approached her prey. I assumed she'd gobble it right up, but instead she bundled the fly into a ball of silk string and left him there; a treasure she'd enjoy later.

The poem "Creative Patterns," which precedes Chapter Five, and the stitched spider web described in Art Invitation #27: *Ornamental Stitching* resulted from this entry. Together, these three pieces can be used as an example of how a single observation, in this case a spider's web outside a window, can lead to a story, a poem, and a picture.

WRITING INVITATION #11

Colors of the Night: Using Sensory Description

Paying attention to detail is critical to the writing process. Writers train their eyes, ears, nose, fingers, and even their tastebuds to explore the world around them. Their discoveries turn into words rich with imagery and expression. *Colors of the Night* is an activity that helps sharpen student-writers' senses as they notice the multitude of colors in the environment around them.

Consider taking a nature walk with your students on the school grounds or perhaps on a field trip. First, find an interesting tree or bush. See how many colors the children can find in the leaves, branches, and bark. A leaf might appear green, but if you look at it closely you may see many shades of green from dark to light. What about the tip of the leaf, the edges, the stem, the veins? Often there are hints of red, brown, black, or yellow on a leaf that at first glance looks green. Continue the same color observations for several other natural objects: the grass, a flower, rocks, a spider web. You are teaching your students to *see*, not just *look*.

After your field study exercise, invite your students to discover the colors in the sky. Which ones do they see as night approaches? Most likely there are many shades of blue and gray. Perhaps they can find purples, oranges, and pinks too. Is the moon out yet? Occasionally the moon and sun can be seen sharing the sky together.

Artists have precise names for all of the colors. Some names like indigo blue, mauve, or burnt sienna may be familiar to your class. If not, it might be helpful to look at color charts found in many art technique books. Sometimes students may choose to use the artists' names for colors, but sometimes they enjoy making up names. Does the night sky look like elephant-ear gray, octopus-ink black, or fruit-punch fuchsia?

While observing the sky and landscape, have your students write a list of all the colors that they see. Next, ask them to go through the list and write a descriptive phrase using each of the colors. Finally, have them write a poem using some or all of the colors listed. The children can experiment with word selection and the order of their phrases until they are satisfied with a final version.

One fifth grader's list of colors included gold, red, orange, brown, yellow, violet, and rainbow. From that list, the student wrote these phrases:

gold crescent
giant rainbow sky
brown hills
clouds like red strawberries
macaroni-and-cheese orange
yellow dandelions
cerulean and violet

These phrases were used in "Rainbow Sky," a poem that describes the sunset. Notice that some of the words in the writer's list were cut from the poem's final draft.

Rainbow Sky

The sky
is like a giant rainbow.
First, the
brown hills,
Then the
red

like fresh strawberries,
Then the
orange
like macaroni and cheese,
Then some
yellow
like dandelions,
Then there's
cerulean violet,
a beautiful ending.
The sky is like a rainbow!

Sheila

After observing the full moon one evening, Gina decided to write a list of all the colors she could see in the moon. This is what her list included:

moon silver
dusty white
eggshell white
ivory
yellow ocher
pale yellow
umber
multigray speckles
soft black

As Gina read over her list, she realized that the moon is often described as white, but in truth it isn't white at all. That idea developed into the following poem taken from her journal:

The Moon Isn't White

The moon isn't white,
The night is not black,
And clouds aren't gray,
These are the facts.
A star isn't yellow,
The sunset's not pink,
The dirt's never brown,
But that's what some think.

The moon might be ivory,
Yellow ocher, or umber,
Indigo blue describes
Night in the summer.
Leaves on the branch

Should not be called green,
When chartreuse or viridian
Is often what's seen.

Colors aren't simply
Red, yellow and blue,
Colors have names
Just like you and I do.
Names that are cool,
Warm, hot and snazzy,
Monochromatic,
Complementary and jazzy.

There are wonderful ways
To describe every scene,
Mauve, burnt sienna,
Or ultramarine
Create the palette's
Vivid hues, subtle shades,
Put pen to the tablet
In words that don't fade.

Look very closely,
Keep the earth near,
Watch as the words
And the colors appear
For writers in phrases
And artists through sight
Show that night is not black
And the moon isn't white.

Another approach is for students to focus on one color. Joni chose to explore the color gray in this entry from her journal:

Nov. 6
This morning the sun was shining, but a bite in the wind foretold a cool day. I never appreciated gray until I watched the sky production today and thought about painting the sky.
Blackish-gray
    Blue-gray
        Watercolor-edged gray
Dolphin-gray
    Steel-gray
        Heavy gray

Pale gray
> Dove-gray
>> White with gray smoke
A veil of wispy gray
> A heavy, threatening gray
>> All there above the canyons of Oak Park.

Ethan, a kindergartner, also focused on the color gray when he wrote the poem "Clouds."

Clouds

Clouds over the trees,
They're gray,
Like gray birds
Whose feathers are so bunched together
You can't see their bodies.

Ethan

A fifth grade student found the first line of the couplet "Blue" in one of his written observations. He developed it into the following poem:

Blue

Blue is the long stretching night.
Blue is a bird that flew out of sight.

Blue is the purr of a baby kitten.
Blue is your hand fresh out of a mitten.

Blue is the sound of a soft jazz melody.
Blue is walking down a silent alley.

Brett

WRITING INVITATION #12

Lunar Legends: Exploring and Explaining Nature's Mystery Through Storytelling

Dragons and dogs eat the moon, gradually changing its shape in the night sky. Children, maidens, eagles, and toads are lunar residents, giving the moon's full face human and animal characteristics. Stars and fireflies receive or even steal lunar magic and interact with the moon like characters in a folk tale. Ancient Greeks and Romans, Aztecs and Mayans, Australian Aborigines and Africans, Native Americans and Eskimos, Chinese and Japanese, and many other cultural groups have written and told moon legends. These stories are often an attempt to describe how the moon was created, why the moon changes shape, how people have been affected by the moon, and how creatures relate to the moon and each other. There are many beautifully illustrated moon legends and myths to use as literary models. Some of our favorite books are *Moontellers: Myths of the Moon from Around the World* (Moroney, 1995), *Moon Mother* (Young, 1993), *The Moon Lady* (Tan, 1992), *Dancing Moons* (Wood, 1995), *Keepers of the Earth* (Caduto and Bruchac, 1988), *Keepers of the Animals* (Caduto and Bruchac, 1991), and *Thirteen Moons on Turtle's Back* (Bruchac and London, 1992).

A natural part of keeping a Moon Journal is to compose lunar legends based on observations of the night sky. Discovering the characteristics of the genre while reading and discussing other moon legends can be an effective way to begin. In their book *Read and Retell* (1987), Brown and Cambourne suggest a model for genre investigation, or "planning for retelling," that supports what they describe as "linguistic spillover."

These authors describe an immersion process in which students hear and read a variety of stories in a particular genre. Each oral reading is followed by a discussion. As they compare the stories, the children discover the characteristics of the genre. These practices help students develop strategies for reading and writing. The teacher sets the stage by focusing on the cover and title of the book and asks questions such as, What might this story be about? What words might we find in this story? What do the illustrations on the cover suggest?

During the first telling, the teacher "chunks" story passages, asking prediction questions as the plot unfolds. A teacher might ask, Why would the chief of the tribe want to shoot an arrow at the moon? How will the moon maiden help the flowers grow? How will the dragon get up to the moon? What will keep the dogs from eating all of the moon? This type of interactive discussion prepares the children for developing their own characters, settings, plot, and problems to be solved in the legends they will write.

During this immersion period we use sheets of butcher paper to create wall-sized retrieval charts like the one pictured in Figure 3-3.

As the legends are read and basic story elements recorded, the students discover for themselves the similarities among the legends. They compare and contrast various stories and distill the characteristics of the genre. Other considerations we investigate during and after the read-aloud sessions include

Leads: How do the different legends begin?

Character Descriptions: What are the characters like? How are they described physically? Do their physical descriptions match their personalities?

Settings: How are the settings described and illustrated?

Problems: What are the problems in each of the legends?

Writer's Craft: Are there particular lines or descriptions that strike you? Images, similes, or metaphors? Personification? Action or suspense? Dialogue?

After reading several legends as a class and engaging in the activities described above, a student may choose to read moon legends independently, with another child, or in a small guided-reading group with the teacher.

After reading a legend several times, the child writes or tells the story in his or her own words. This is when "linguistic spillover" occurs. Frequently, a student who has internalized a story will incorporate some of the author's language in the retelling, but often the spillover will not be an exact quote. For example, the retelling may contain a student's version of a simile or metaphor embedded in the original story, or a child may borrow a few lines of dialogue from the text of the legend and then invent new dialogue for the rest of the story.

Brown and Cambourne describe many options for presenting the retellings. For example, two children read the same story and then write independent retellings. When they compare each version, they comment on original story elements that were included or left out. They also note ways each student-author added new details and descriptions. Based on their discussion, they often choose to revise their retellings. Finally, students meet in small groups to read and tell different stories.

Name of Legend	Culture or Country of Origin	Characters	Setting	Problem	Solution	What It Explains About the Moon
Why There are Fireflies	Japan	Woodsman Wife Fujiyama Lady in the Moon Moonchild Emporer's Son	Edge of forest behind Mount Fujiyama	Woodman/ wife want a child. Lady in the Moon sends a child, but child needs to return in 20 years to the moon.	Lady in the Moon sends a moonchild to them (she may stay for 20 years). She goes back to moon and cries silver tears.	Fireflies are the tears of the moon princess, who had to return to the moon.
Weaver and the Cat	Iroquois, North America	Old Woman Pet Wildcat	The Moon	Old Woman weaves a headband, and moon gets larger as the weaving grows. Cat unravels the weaving.	Old Woman begins weaving again.	Why the moon grows and disappears.

FIGURE 3-3

Students are now well equipped to begin drafting their own legends about the moon. The children and the teacher brainstorm possible topics for legends. The following list is one example:
- Why the moon gets smaller
- How the moon was formed
- What causes a halo around the moon?
- Why the moon rises when the sun sets
- How the moon affects the tides
- Why do stars shine?
- How can the moon be visible in the morning?
- Why do coyotes howl at the moon?

After selecting a topic, the students develop the story line. What will be explained? Who will be the characters? What is the setting? How will the problem be introduced? What episodes will be included to solve the problem? Will you include dialogue? How will you start the story? Some students may want to develop story maps or storyboards. Others may choose to put pen to paper and let the words flow.

Our students wrote many legends in their Moon Journals in response to nightly observations. For example, Cleavant began with this brief entry:

> Tonight is a cold night. I came outside and I couldn't see the moon. I was worried because it was 8:00, and the moon still wasn't out. I looked outside one more time, upstairs in the family room window, and finally there it was! I heard crickets chirping. The moon looked like a partly peeled orange. I heard my friend, Pete, shouting for me to come outside and see the moon, so I did and I saw the moon one last time.

Then Cleavant wrote the following legend:

Why Do Crickets Chirp?

> Every five years, a monster named Terrible Tex tries to eat the moon. Five years ago, Terrible Tex arose from his five-year sleep. He had a craving for a nice, juicy moon.
>
> The moon was sleeping and didn't know Terrible Tex was coming. The moon and the crickets were friends. They sang and played games with each other. The crickets saw terrible Tex and warned the moon. They chirped and chirped. Finally, the moon woke up and yawned. As he raised his arms, he hit Terrible Tex into space.

Writing lunar legends will help children connect all the players in nature's nighttime theater. The moon and stars, crickets and birds, facts and fantasies will all partake in the drama described in their Moon Journals.

WRITING INVITATION #13

From Prose to Poetry: Breaking Lines of Prose into a Poem

"I can't write poetry. I can't make my poem rhyme. Does this poem have to have a certain number of lines? How do I make a poem sound like a poem?" Poetry is difficult for children who make statements or ask questions like these. They struggle with trying to fit words and ideas into preconceived notions of correct form. And yet, for other children, poetry is the freest form of written expression. When these students compose a poem, their voices sing out in the lines of their verse. Helping children discover the joy in writing poetry is one of the pleasures of teaching. This invitation explores working with prose, which for some children is easier to write.

When students break sentences into shorter lines, they are often surprised to find a poem emerge. Candace, for example, wrote the first draft of "The Moon of the Never-Ending Seas" in a prose format.

> A full, bright moon is gleaming over the ocean. Powerful waves are crashing like the strong north wind trying to break through a wall of steel! No one is here, just the moon and the stars and the ocean that seems to go on forever.

When Candace first brought this draft to Joni during a writing conference, she wasn't sure how to turn her thoughts into a poem. Together, they worked on creating distinct mental images for the reader. They asked questions and gave answers. What do you see first? The full bright moon. What is this moon like? It's gleaming and (after a pause) shimmering. Where is it? It's hanging over the ocean and the waves just go on forever and ever.

As Candace responded to the questions, Joni jotted down her responses in single lines.

> The full bright moon
> is gleaming and shimmering,
> it's hanging over the ocean
> and the waves just go on and on forever.

They discussed how breaking the sentences up into phrases is like illustrating pages in a picture book. You focus on one image at a time. Joni showed Candace how she developed a poem from a brief observation in her nature journal.

> I saw a hummingbird in my garden. It seemed to be perfectly still and suspended in space. It looked like a helicopter with its little wings whirring away. It turned its head, capturing images, and blended into the jasmine, honeysuckle, and morning glories.

When Joni experimented with turning this entry into a poem, it became

Hummingbird

seemingly still,
suspended in air,
intent.
Like a helicopter hovering,
an eye in the sky,
capturing images
with each turn of its head.
And yet . . .
constantly in motion,
wings fluttering like propellers,
blending in with the honeysuckle,
the morning glories,
the jasmine.

Candace noticed that Joni changed a few words from her original entry and the language switched from matter-of-fact to playful and descriptive. Joni invited Candace to experiment with her own prose and poetry, changing some words or combining ideas until each line of the poem offered the reader the image *she* wanted to communicate. Here is Candace's final draft.

The moon is full and bright
gleaming and shimmering
over the never-ending seas.
Waves crash with forceful power
like the north wind
rushing to break through a wall of steel.
No one is here . . .
just the moon,
the stars,
and the never-ending seas.

When we work with students as they turn prose into poetry, we show them how to insert penciled-in brackets, representing line breaks, into their completed prose. An example follows.

Tonight the crescent moon] grew almost before my eyes.] Leaves are turning colors] and the nights are growing cold.] I welcome fall this year] with its bright colors] cool days] and clear] star-filled] nights.

To encourage our writers to try a variety of possible phrasings, we occasionally select a paragraph from a favorite book. Students are given copies of the passage and are asked to insert brackets that break complete sentences into lines of a found poem. After reproducing several student samples on overhead transparencies, we share them with the whole class during a minilesson. The children consider the effect of the various line breaks.

We practice with additional pieces, including some of our own personal journal entries, a few student selections, and lines of prose found in magazine or newspaper articles. (See Writing Invitation #23: *Found Poems*.) The students learn a valuable lesson: There are many ways to compose poems, the writer can direct the mental images the reader is introduced to, and poetry does not have to start out—or even end up—as perfectly measured rhyming lines.

WRITING INVITATION #14

Draw Me a Story: A Moon Rebus: Recording Observations in Pictures and Words

The idea of using pictures to represent messages is universal. Creating a rebus is a simple way to introduce students to this simple yet meaningful form of communication. The combination of puzzle, challenge, and fun presented in a rebus appeals to students of all ages.

One night Joni wanted to capture the colors of the sunset in her entry. With felt-tip markers, she scribbled in small swatches of color next to certain words in her observation. On this particular night the moon was a thin crescent, like the little tip of a fingernail. She drew a fingertip and a crescent moon to replace these words in her entry. Without consciously setting out to create a rebus, she realized she had one in the making. Joni found she was able to describe, through the little pictures, exactly what she was observing. But most importantly, she was having fun! Starting the entry a second time, she experimented with as many word-to-picture swaps as possible. (See Figure 3-4.)

The following morning the students shared their entries. As usual, Joni presented a selection from her journal after the children read their observations and showed their artwork. She had made an overhead of her rebus entry, coloring in as many pictures as possible with permanent colored markers. The students were delighted! They took turns deciphering different lines from her rebus.

Joni wasn't surprised when the children began to create rebus stories of their own. They flipped back through their journal entries and experimented with transforming some of their words into pictures using colored pencils, markers, pastels, and small cut-outs.

A rebus can become an invitation for further study. On our next visit to the school library, we looked for books with Egyptian hieroglyphics and Native American pictographs. Joni brought in some of the handcarved stamps of Hawaiian pictographs she had purchased during her summer vacation. She thought that it would also be easy to carve pictographs of the moon using erasers and simple carving tools. (See Art Invitation #21: *Handmade Stamps*.)

FIGURE 3-4

A 🌙 📖

Tonight, right after dinner, I ran to my 🚪. I walked outside and stood on the 🏠. It was right before 🌅. A few ☁️ moved across the ⛰️. I was afraid the ☁️s might cover the 🌙! I was 😊 when I discovered the crescent 🌙, resting above a ☁️. It was so delicate; it looked like the edge of a little 🖐️. I 👁️ as it grew brighter in the ✨. Finally, it sank beneath the ➡️. It was so exciting to see the 🌙 again after three nights of no 🌙, only ✨ and ⬛. Maybe you appreciate something more when you miss it. Absence makes the ♡ grow fonder, even for the 🌙. As the night grew darker, more ✨ appeared, shining through the ☁️. I noticed the 🏘️ in my neighborhood, outlined against the deep blue 🌃. I went into my 🏠 to the scene in my 📓.

Creating a rebus is a simple approach to visualization. It helps children "see" their surroundings in new ways, enhancing both their writing and art.

WRITING INVITATION #15

Moon Facts: A Scientific Observation

"All of a sudden we came from darkness into daylight. We were at the moon!" writes astronaut Jim Irwin in *To Rule the Night: The Discovery Voyage of Astronaut Jim Irwin* (1973), his book about the moon mission of Apollo 15. "It hits you just like that. It is the most beautiful sight to look out and see this tremendously large planet. You'd never guess that the moon would be that big, even though you have seen all the pictures. But here you are seeing it with your own eyes for the first time. It is staggering."

For thousands of years myths provided the only answers to people's questions about the moon. Today, thanks to lunar flights manned by scientists like Jim Irwin, we know many facts about the moon.

Looking at the moon through the eyes of a scientist is another perspective open to moon journalists. By the end of the first week, students had many questions to investigate. For example, they wondered why some of their classmates saw the one-day-old crescent moon and others did not. We discovered that due to the time the slender crescent appears, coupled with its low altitude on the horizon, its dim light is very easy to miss.

Scientific study was conducted at school and at home. Moon facts were gathered in a variety of ways. Every morning at breakfast, William found the moonphase chart in the weather section of the newspaper and glued it into his journal. Larissa used her computer's encyclopedia and color printer to produce close up shots of the lunar surface. Then she wrote facts around the border of the pictures. Joshua found moonphase gardening dates in *The Old Farmer's Almanac* and drew a chart. The children got information from books, clipped articles from newspapers, photocopied pictures, wrote notes during classroom discussions, and found facts on the internet and the Weather Channel. They added their scientific discoveries to their Moon Journals. One student's entry described his experiments with a telescope.

Tonight I looked at the moon through my telescope. As I was studying the moon I saw the crater Tycho. I used the Moon Facts in the back of my Moon Journal to help me find other big and little craters. When I got the moon in picture-perfect focus, I told my mom to come out and look through the telescope. I tried to take a picture of the moon. I put my camera right up to the lens of the telescope. In just a few days the moon shall be full. I can't wait for the full moon!

Luke, age 10

After compiling moon facts, Gina invited her sixth grade class to write "how-to" instructions to the moon. First, the students listed a few facts in their journals. Sara's list looked like this:

- 4.5 billion years old
- 238,906 miles from earth
- Earth's only natural satellite
- 27 days, 8 hours to go around earth
- no water, no air, no light of its own
- thousands of craters

Next, students combined their moon facts with a set of playful directions as they instructed their lunar friend on "How to be the Moon." Sara had this advice to give in her poem:

How to be the Moon

To be the moon
you must be four and a half billion years old,
station yourself
238,906 miles from earth,
and be wide—
2,160 miles!
You should take about 28 days
to circle the earth,
and get used to being hot and cold,
for you are 212 degrees in the day
and −320 degrees at night.
Watch out!
You might get dizzy
from going way too fast,
as you orbit the earth
at 2,300 miles per hour.
What a ride!
Don't change a bit,
not for another 3 billion years
and you can be
the perfect moon!

Another student chose a prose format:

Now to be the moon you must, and I mean must, be ready to be old and pretty fat! You also have to be fast and bright. Well, not bright all the time! But you have to be fast enough to get around the earth in twenty-seven days, seven hours, forty-three minutes and eleven and a half seconds. You can't have an extra minute or you'll mess everything up.

And I hope you know how to behave yourself. Let's say some planet comes strollin' along and invites you to come with her to the Crater Crash. Don't go! Trust me, you would go bouncing off into space, mess up the earth's gravity and ruin the tides. Now do you understand how to be the moon?

Sara, age 12

Children can use this same format to write other how-to poems. Topics can include stars, clouds, seasons, rain, crickets, or falling leaves. After they have learned about a subject through scientific research, our students have genuinely enjoyed writing these poems.

WRITING INVITATION #16

Investigating Questions About the Moon: Group Research Projects and Presentations

The moon provides a wonderful inspiration for writing and art, but it also offers equal opportunities for scientific investigation. Short, Harste, and Burke (1996) identified three sources of knowledge that inquirers draw from in their search for answers: personal and social knowing through life experiences; knowledge systems, including history, biology, astronomy, and physics; and sign systems as alternative ways of creating meaning about the world through art, music, movement, language, or mathematics. The Moon Journal experience actively involves students in personal and social knowing on a daily basis, and the invitations to respond through language, art, music, and dance provide multiple opportunities for creating and sharing meaning through various sign systems. Posing and probing questions and using the historical, cultural, and scientific bodies of knowledge available to help us answer our queries plays an equally important part in this study.

When we begin our studies of the moon, we are careful to wait before presenting background research and information to our students. This doesn't mean that we haven't assembled all the books, maps, charts, newspaper and magazine articles that we can find! We purposefully look for a variety of sources, and our students soon learn that many of their questions are still being pondered and researched by scientists. Theories sometimes conflict, and no one book has all the answers. The materials are available in the classroom, but we want the children to discover how to ask questions, make their own observations, and then back up their hypotheses with further study that includes additional observation and research.

We also want students to figure out how to find resources and information outside the classroom. We plan a visit to the school library to look for additional books and CD-ROMs. Many students go on-line via the internet to gather information.

Some children use a telescope to investigate the moon and then compare their findings to what they read about in books.

About a week into the study, when Joni's students had observed several nights of change in the appearance of the moon and in the times and locations of their sightings, they began their second round of queries. The children discovered that many of their original questions had already been answered. For example, on the first day the students wanted to know how much of a difference they would notice in the moon each night. Now, after sketching and describing the moon's early phases, they were able to answer that question. But one of their queries remained unanswered: Why does the moon change every night? Also, a new question was added to the list: After the full moon, will the waning moon follow the same pattern as the waxing moon?

Joni listed her students' new questions on the board, adding additional queries as the cycle continued. Throughout the study the children used reference materials to investigate their questions, and many of their entries reflected their new understandings, as Luke's entry demonstrates (Figure 3-5).

Midway into the cycle Joni asked her students to reconsider all their questions and to cluster them by topic (Figure 3-5). At this point students signed up for particular questions of interest, forming small collaborative research groups. They began with many questions. What are our big questions? How and where can we find our information? What resources are available to us? What role will each person play? Will we always work together? How will we put our information together? How will we present this information to the class? Who will draw, act, and explain what we find? How can we make it interesting? How will we prepare for the presentation? What materials will we need? Where and when will we work?

Some of the student groups met with Joni or parent helpers and explained their ideas. The adults reviewed the process described by the students, and together they mapped out a plan. Other groups did not need this kind of support and were ready to undertake their research on their own. The groups spread out around the room, surrounded by various resource materials. Some children took notes, others flagged specific pages with bookmarks, and a few began sketching. Small groups signed up to use the computer lab or arranged to meet for telescope viewing. When all the information had been gathered, each group decided on its method of presentation.

Short, Harste, and Burke (1996) describe how "presenting increases conscious awareness of the connections that have and could be made, forcing us to push our own thinking as well as push the thinking of our thought collective. By presenting we bring our learning to a new level of knowing. What was intuitive and taken for granted has to be made public and understandable."

The decisions the children made regarding how they would present their knowledge moved the investigation to the next level: creating and sharing meaning through various sign systems (Short, Harste, and Burke, 1996). One group constructed models showing the orbit of the moon. Other children dramatized the

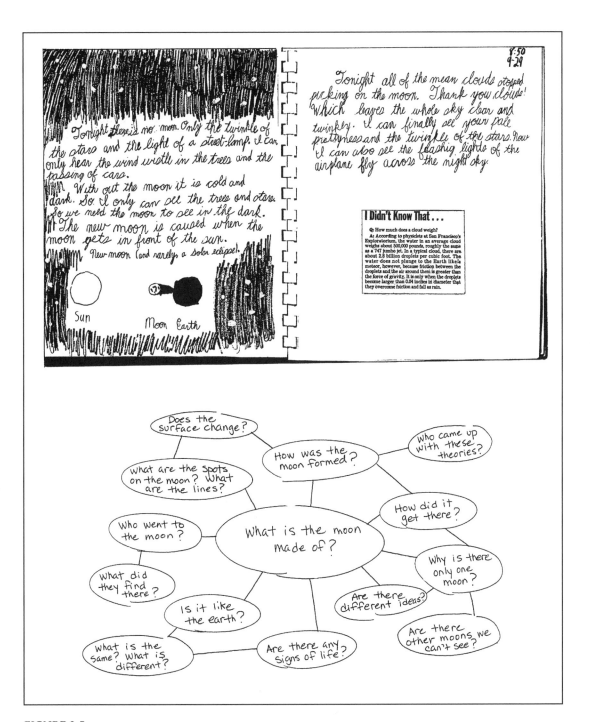

FIGURE 3-5

moon's cycle using an orange, a flashlight, and a globe. Poems were read, songs were sung, and a dialogue between the sun and the moon was dramatized.

We paid attention to how each group went about its research, the different roles students played, and the methods they used in their presentations. The audience responded to each presentation, pointing out what they learned and aspects of the presentation they especially enjoyed. Learning was taking place. But if you asked the students about their research projects, they would begin by describing how much fun they had gathering information and developing their presentations.

As you invite your students to research their questions about the moon, consider experimenting with some of the procedures described in this invitation. The results of student investigations and research projects will be as unique as each phase of the moon—each with their own characteristics, each with their own time to shine.

WRITING INVITATION #17

Moon Mail: Correspondence to and from the Moon

Do you remember how great it was to get mail when you were a child? It didn't happen very often, but when a letter came addressed to you, complete with a canceled stamp and delivered by a person in uniform, it was a special event. It's nice to know, despite telephones, modems, and FAX machines, that some things never change. Our students tell us they love to receive mail. In many homes, sorting these deliveries is a daily family ritual. "I just want to see if I got something," one third grader reported. "My mom and dad are luckier. They get a bunch of stuff every day."

With this love of receiving mail in mind, we developed *Moon Mail*, an invitation that adds letters and postcards to the pages of Moon Journals. We began by asking our students why they thought it was exciting to get mail. They expressed a variety of reasons: "I like a letter from someone I don't get to talk to on the phone very much, like my best friend that moved away" or "I only get to see my cousin when it's summer vacation so I like it if he writes" and "On my birthday and Christmas or days like that I know I'll get lots of cards."

Many students love the fact that they often receive mail unexpectedly. "It's so great finding a surprise in the mailbox. Sometimes you can even get some money from your grandmother," Sebastian, a first grader, said. His classmate Marissa added, "Yeah, and if you get an invitation, you get to go to a birthday party!"

Having discussed the reasons why it's fun to get mail, we turned our attention to the types of things found in mailboxes. The children indicated that letters, postcards, greeting cards, invitations, thank you notes, magazines, small packages, and junk mail are items most frequently sent to them.

The art of written correspondence is the focus of several recent popular books. We introduced two of them to our classes: *Letters from Felix* (1994) by Annette Langen and Constanza Droop and *The Jolly Postman* (1986) by Janet and Allan

Ahlberg. The children especially enjoyed the unusual envelopes and original stamps depicted in the books. We talked about how the authors and illustrators creatively combined letters, greeting cards, invitations, and postcards with mail art in both books.

At this point we narrowed our focus to letters and postcards and spoke briefly about the format of a letter versus that of a postcard. Next we asked, What kind of information do you usually read in letters? How does it contrast from the type of message written on a postcard?

Gina's sixth grade class created two lists on the board detailing the differences between letters and postcards.

Letters

- can be short or long
- are often written on special stationery
- give readers an update/tell what the writer has been doing
- include day-to-day events
- give specific details of recent incidents
- tell how the writer is feeling
- tell what other family members or friends have been doing
- mention things that are happening at school or work
- can discuss the weather
- explain upcoming events or plans
- ask their readers questions: "What are you doing?," "What's new?"
- expect the reader to respond

Postcards

- are short, just a few sentences, getting to the point right away
- sometimes have a funny message
- are usually sent by people who are on a vacation
- usually have a photograph on the front of the card
- give details about a trip
- tell readers about people, customs, food, language, money
- describe places visited, specific sights remembered
- recall special moments on a trip or funny happenings
- sometimes say, "I miss you," "I wish you were here," or "thinking of you"
- tell readers why they would enjoy that vacation spot
- do not expect the reader to respond

Gina invited sixth graders to write Moon Mail. Naturally, the moon was expected to respond!

Dear Mr. Man in the Moon,

I am writing to you because I have some questions. Some kids in my class say that the little part of the moon is God's fingernail but others say it is the

Cheshire Cat's smile. I think that it's your kayak and that the quarter moon is your ship. My mom has been asking me where I want to go for vacation, so I was wondering if we could come and stay in the moon with you. There are three people in my family, my mom, dad, and me. I hope you say yes.

> Your friend,
> Elizabeth

P.S. Please write back!

Dear Elizabeth,

No matter whether the moon is crescent, quarter, or full, it's just my home, but it can be whatever you want it to be. If you want to you can visit, but you may not see me. I will be inside keeping the moonlight. Maybe you can help me with this job. I need a moonbeam helper.

> Your friend,
> The Man in the Moon

Inspired by the books they shared in class, students designed colorful envelope pockets for their letters and glued them into their Moon Journals. (See Art Invitation #19: *Mail Art*.)

Gina's third grade class made lunar postcards. The students imagined they were vacationing on the moon. Using blank postcards made from white cardstock, they drew pictures, created moon stamps, and wrote messages to their family and friends on earth.

William wrote a postcard to his parents.

Dear Mom and Dad,

I'm wearing super-powered moon boots up here. The rocketship felt like it was going 5 mph but it was really going about 355 mph. How is everything down there?

> Love,
> William

Nathaniel wrote a postcard to astronaut Neil Armstrong.

Dear Neil Armstrong,

I know you have been on the moon before and I'm here now. The earth looks tiny from up here. I see a lot of meteors, probably you saw that too when you were here. I'll be down next week. See you on earth.

> Sincerely,
> Nathaniel

After reading this in class, Nathaniel called our attention to the address on the postcard. He said, "I looked up NASA's address. This could really get there!"

Alternate Ideas

1. Make a classbook of moon mail by creating a cover and binding the students' handmade envelopes together (envelopes should be same size). Letters can be tucked into the envelopes after binding.
2. Students can use their moon letters as a springboard for a verse letter, also called a letter poem.

> *Dear Moon*
>
> Dear moon,
> How are you?
> I really liked how
> you turned orange last night.
> It was cool.
> Anyway,
> could you teach me how to change colors too?
>
> *Lindsey, age 11*

WRITING INVITATION #18

Ode to the Moon: Writing and Scoring an Elementary Ode

The moon is a master of surprise. As our students observed the sky throughout the month, they noticed the ever-changing scenes with amazement and delight. Often they'd enter the classroom in the morning saying things like "Did you see how clear the dark part of the moon was last night?" or "The crescent was all the way at the bottom, like a smile!" and "I saw the moon on the way to school. Did you?"

One cloudy winter morning, several children noticed a halo around the full moon. Everyone wanted to discuss their theories on how such a phenomenon occurs. Joshua, a sixth grader, said, "Do you think this is the first time there's ever been a round rainbow or have we just been missing them?"

This student's reflection was not unusual. We have seen it happen repeatedly. In the process of keeping a Moon Journal, something triggers that "aha" moment; a stunning sight, a unique sound, or perhaps an unusual texture causes children to think about what they miss simply because they do not stop to look.

As we watched the children's excitement and new-found awareness appear in the pages of their Moon Journals, we presented *Ode to the Moon* in our writing workshops. Although odes can be written in several forms, we chose to introduce the "elementary" ode to our students. The elementary ode, also called the elemental ode, is a short-lined, free-verse poem and was created by the poet Pablo Neruda. The unique feature of the elementary ode is its subject matter: common, everyday things, often focusing on elements in nature. We thought this to be a good tie-in with the observations the children were writing about in their journals.

Gina's fourth grade class discussed the different ways in which Gary Soto's *Neighborhood Odes* (1992) and Pablo Neruda's *Odes to Opposites* (1995) demonstrate this poetry format. Collin liked the way Gary Soto "picked stuff like fireworks, goats, and shoes to write about." Aneetha said she noticed that "[Soto] starts his odes like a mystery. If you don't look at the title, you're not sure what the poem's going to be about." Aneetha's observation also showed the class that poets too have methods of "hooking" their readers.

Next, the class turned its attention to Pablo Neruda's work. Gina read aloud excerpts from three of Neruda's odes that focus on nature: "Ode to rain," "Ode to fall," and "Ode to clouds." When Gina finished reading she said, "Aneetha told us that Gary Soto begins many of his poems 'like a mystery.' Does Pablo Neruda do the same?" "No, this guy tells you what the poem is about right away," Katie responded. "What are some of Neruda's writing tools?" Gina questioned. Hands went up. Some comments were "He uses the five senses," "There's some good action words," and "He likes colors." Alex said, "It sort of sounds like [Neruda's] talking to someone." "He talks to everything, like the rain and clouds, as if they were people. I like the way he uses the word *you* when he talks to them," Chris added. As they listened to Neruda's odes, the children recognized writing techniques previously taught, including the use of dialogue, personification, and strong verbs. (See Writing Invitation #9: *The Maiden and the Man in the Moon.*) This gave them more ideas to consider when writing their own odes.

The moon, the sky, the seasons, weather conditions, clouds, stars, nocturnal creatures, and all the other subjects in our nightly entries presented many possibilities for odes. Because the students had seen how odes reflect deep feelings and insights in the works of Soto and Neruda, they were ready to make the connection between their own response to the moon and this form of poetry.

The children went through their journals gathering images and observations to use as ideas for their odes. They selected different sentences and phrases, scientific facts, personal reflections, poetic descriptions—anything that struck them with its imagery or emotional impact. Once these were gathered, they selected a topic and played with the short-lined, free-verse format of these poems. (See color insert, Day Twenty-one: "Ode to Stars.")

Ode to Darkness

You hide
my house
in your dark clouds.
You warn me
that it's my bedtime,
time to rest.

At dawn
you run away
and I wait
until dusk
to see you again.
Sometimes you make me
furious
when you scare me,
you with your
black, cold air.
But in the morning,
when you've left
I forgive you.
You've been with the world
and will always be
the only night sky.

Amanda, age 9

Alternate Idea

We told the children that originally odes were sung by choral groups. Some children thus scored their odes (see Writing Invitation #5, *Moon Music*) and others sang them to the tune of a familiar song.

WRITING INVITATION #19

The Unexpected Moon: Describing the Moon You Discover by Surprise

When we look back through the pages of our students' Moon Journals, some of our favorite entries describe unexpected sightings of the moon. Many of us have experienced finding the moon by surprise. Often you discover it in your rearview mirror as you're driving home at night, or through a window when you hastily glance outside. But sometimes you are engaged in an activity when discovering the moon is delightfully unexpected, as Jason's samples demonstrate.

Saturday, September 30th
The moon is out and it's a first-quarter moon. It is 2:30 p.m. and the moon's out really early. I'm surprised it's out this early! I'm at Magic Mountain having fun and I see the moon in the sky. The rollercoaster just climbed to the top and I saw the silhouette of the car with the people waving their arms right in front of the moon! I hear the clicking and clacking of the rollercoaster and then I hear the screams!

Several nights later, Jason found another surprise moon.

> Wednesday, October 4th
> The moon is waxing gibbous tonight. The time is 5:30 p.m. and I am at the park with two of my very best friends and we are playing football. Pete threw me a long bomb and when I looked at the ball, the moon was right beside it! Then I caught the ball and ran to score. I hear the leaves rustling in the trees and the frogs croak in the creek.

Jacki loves to play tennis and practices almost every night. This is the lunar surprise she discovered one evening early in the cycle:

> September 26th, 8:08 p.m.
> While I was playing tennis I happened to look up at the sky. Oooohhhhh, how I wished for my Moon Journal or at least a scrap of paper! It looked as if the sky threw a party to welcome the moon! The mountains put the crescent moon in such a good place it looked like a picture frame!

Rob was eating his ice cream when he happened to look up and was surprised by the moon.

> Today there is a beautiful crescent moon in the sky. I was surprised that I could see the entire moon even though only a little part of it was illuminated and bright. As I stood there eating my ice cream I gazed up and there it was, the beautiful moon that I am describing now! It was a very clear night so I could see many stars and the moon. I found three constellations, the Little Dipper, the Big Dipper, and Orion.

When Pete showed Joni one of his initial journal entries, she didn't know what to make of it at first. He had drawn a rough sketch of some trees and the crescent moon, viewed between the lines of an unusual grid. She asked Pete to explain his entry and he said, "Read what I wrote!" Here is what he had recorded in his journal:

> After a good day of football I looked up in the sky, and I saw the moon! My knee stinged from a cut when I fell on a sharp rock, but when I looked in the sky the pain stopped. My heart beat faster than a race car. I saw the two-day-old moon! It was so exciting I even told my friend Peter Gomez. "That was awesome," I said to myself.

Now Joni understood; Pete sketched exactly what he saw as he looked up at the moon above the trees in the park while wearing his football helmet! The grid he sketched was the part of the face mask he needed to look through while gazing at the moon. (See Figure 3-6.)

FIGURE 3-6

Joni's students asked her if she had ever been surprised by the moon. She read them an entry she had written a few nights earlier that described a visit to her daughter at the university.

> Jeff and I drove up the coast to Santa Barbara. It was unusual for us to make the trip on a school night, but it was Kylie's birthday! We wanted to surprise her by taking her out for a special dinner. This was the night of the full moon and all evening I searched for it, hoping to see it rise over the ocean. The moon was hidden behind the gentle peaks of the coastal range. A teasing glow occasionally emerged.
>
> As we pulled around the corner into the campus I happened to glance over my shoulder at the open land surrounding the lagoon. There it was: the full moon at the head of a zigzagging trail of clouds. The clouds were illuminated and seemed to flow from the gleaming moon itself, like a celestial river. I remember catching my breath and asking Jeff to slow down so I could press this scene into my mind to paint later. By the time we reached Kylie's apartment the clouds had shifted well below the moon, but I will always remember the river of clouds and connect this mental picture with my daughter's twentieth birthday.

After sharing the written observation, Joni wrote this poem as her students watched:

> A cloud trail
> zigzagged across the sky last night
> like a meandering river
> whose source was the rising moon—
> full, white and gleaming.
> A tiara of stars
> encircled the skyscape
> with shining brilliance.

Later that day, during art studio time, Luke illustrated his teacher's poem using oil and chalk pastels. He captured the movement of the sky with Van Gogh–like broad strokes and swirls of color. It became a picture Joni cherished, along with the memory of a special time spent with her daughter.

When describing an unexpected moon in your journal, be sure to record the setting or circumstances in detail. What were you doing before you discovered the moon? What was your point of view? What did the moon and its surroundings look like? What were you thinking when you first saw it? What will you remember? In your entry, see if you can capture the surprise you experienced when you first discovered the moon. Later, you can pick out a few lines of your entry to explore through poetry or art.

WRITING INVITATION #20

Who Am I? Using Personification to Give Voice to the Moon

The moon has a long history of personification. In virtually every culture, dating from prehistoric times to the present, people have given the moon various attributes and powers. The moon has been called many names, including The Great Mother, Luna, The Eternal One, Roong, The Old Woman Who Never Dies, Moon-Chief, White Goddess, Shepherd of the Stars, Aah, Goddess of Storms, White Face, and The Queen of Life and Death.

The moon has been held responsible for creation, fertility, tides, farming, time, nature, love, reason, wisdom, death, magic, sorcery, and lunacy. And these are just a few of the items on the moon's list of diverse tasks!

Anyone as busy as this celestial body must have a lot to say. *Who Am I?* invites students to give voice to the lunar face. Through the use of personification, the children can present the moon's point of view in the pages of their Moon Journals!

We introduced this invitation to our classes by sharing stories and articles that gave examples of the moon's history among different peoples of the world. *Moonscapes: A Celebration of Lunar Astronomy, Magic, Legend, and Lore* (1991) by Rosemary Ellen Guiley and *Mysteries of the Moon* (1992) by Patricia Haddock contained a variety of tales. Other material was gathered from encyclopedias, historical references, and books on the ancient folklore and mythology of Egyptian, Greek, Roman, Native American, African, Latin, Asian, and Hawaiian cultures. Additionally, we read two children's books and one book series: *Moontellers: Myths of The Moon from Around The World* (1995) by Lynn Moroney, *Thirteen Moons on Turtle's Back: A Native American Year of Moons* (1992) by Joseph Bruchac and Jonathan London and the *Thirteen Moon* series (1992) by Jean Craighead George.

After hearing lunar tales and other moon names, the children were asked to imagine the voice of their favorite moon. We asked, What would the moon tell you if it could talk? (See Writing Invitation #9: *The Maiden and the Man in the Moon*.) One of Gina's classes brainstormed this list of questions before writing:

How old is the moon?
How does it feel about its job?
What is its job description?
What tasks does the moon do all night?
Who gave the moon its job?
How does it feel about people on earth?
Does it have emotions? Does it feel happy, sad, concerned, angry, tired, lonely?
What is the sound of its voice?
What are some events or stories the moon might tell?
What is the moon's day like?
What are its plans for the future?

As the students imagined the moon's answers to these questions, their poems developed. Many of our students used the simple format of beginning each line of their poems with the words *I am.*

A fourth grader's poem, "I Am the Moon," is an example of this formatting:

I Am the Moon

I am the moon,
I am the night-light outside your window,
I am the gleam of an orange harvest,
I am the face you see at night,
I am the sly smirk of the Cheshire Cat,
I am the yellow beam lighting your path,
I am the spooky shadows in ghost stories,
I am a round chunk of Bleu Cheese,
I am the glowing reassurance that you are not alone,
I am the moon.

Kimberly

Sometimes students like to think of a specific moon name and all of the attributes that can be associated with that name. It can be a name given to the moon by another culture or a name the writer makes up. The words *I am* can begin each line, or the phrase can be used merely as an opening or closing line. These following poems were written by sixth grade students:

Shepherd of the Stars

I am the shepherd of the stars.
I work in a pasture of gleaming black grass,
I carry a staff made of moonbeams,
I tend a twinkling flock,
I guard my herd from black holes,
I watch them frolic in the Milky Way,
I shake the stardust from their wool,
I wash their coats until they sparkle,
I provide deep craters for them to sleep in,
I nourish their young until their light is strong,
I search for better grazing galaxies,
I am the shepherd of stars.

Joshua

Goddess of Storms

I am the Goddess of Storms.
I am the deep, heavy clouds.
I am the pounding rain.
I am the raging winds.
I am the crashing waves.
I am the one who creates horrifying hurricanes.

I am the keeper of terrifying lightning and thunder.
I am the Goddess of Storms.
I am the moon.

> *Bryan*

WRITING INVITATION #21

A Calendar of Moons: Naming the Seasonal Moons

When children keep Moon Journals they notice more than the moon. The entries in their journals describe both sky and earth. Are tree leaves budding or falling? Is the sun setting earlier this month, or later? Is the moon covered with rain clouds in April, or reflected on January's snow? Do they hear summer's insects, or the silence of December? Each month's moon is a representation of the seasonal changes that characterize nature's cycle.

Native Americans used the moon to mark time, cycles, and seasons. By naming the moon, they identified monthly reference points for events in their lives. For example, a child may have been born during the Hunter's Moon, or a tribe may have planned to move during the Budding Moon. In *Thirteen Moons on Turtle's Back: A Native American Year of Moons* (1992), Bruchac and London have chosen one moon story from each of thirteen different Native American tribal nations. The moon stories are told as seasonal prose poems, accompanied by Thomas Locker's beautiful illustrations. In another picture book, *Dancing Moons* by Nancy Wood with paintings by Frank Howell (1995), the author describes the Native American "twelve great paths of the moon." Poems, meditations, and paintings reflect the patterns and characteristics of each month and season.

As the end of the twenty-eight day cycle approached, we set out to name *our* moon. The children reviewed the pages of illustrations, sketches, poems, and observations in their journals. Some students selected random phrases that best described the seasonal characteristics of the moon. Others chose to focus on descriptions of a specific night.

Next, we composed a cumulative list poem. (See Writing Invitation #6: *Lunar List Poems.*) We began by clustering words and phrases that children selected from their journals. Some of the suggestions included the following:

fog and mist
illumination
wispy gray clouds
burnt umber leaves
rushing wind

We experimented with changing the single words into more specific descriptive phrases.

fog: *like a blanket over the hills*
sunsets: *colors spilled across watercolor paper*
leaves: *crumbly and crackled*

By arranging and connecting these phrases together to describe the moon cycle, we composed our naming poems. The final step was to experiment with names or titles for our particular moon. Often the name was embedded in the lines of the piece, as Kelly's poem demonstrates.

Moon of the Dark Night

The whistle of the wind sounds winter's alarm.
Now the animals burrow,
and their sheltered caves protect them
from the downy quilts of snow
that tumble down from the sky
like an eagle diving down for its prey.
Nights grow darker
and the owls with their yellow eyes
sound the noises
reminding all that night has taken over
like a hawk spreading open its wings
pulling a blanket of darkness across the earth
blocking us from the light of the burning sun.
Wolves stare up into the nighttime sky.
Only sparkles of stars and a round golden moon are the guides—
a pathway of light.

Another example of this technique is Christy's poem, "The Moon of Shining Dust."

The Moon of Shining Dust

The clouds are covering the glowing moon.
The air is rushing, cold.
The quilt of fog plays peekaboo
with the crescent moon that illuminates the mist
like shining dust.
The colors of the sky are indigo,
smoky gray and midnight black.
The hills are silhouetted against the night
like waves in a sea of sky.
The coyotes call and call . . .
on this night of mystery.

After writing their poems, the children selected an art medium that would allow them to depict their seasonal moon. Several students chose watercolors for tumbling leaves, and others worked with pastels to capture mist and fog. After they illustrated their own poems, some students tried illustrating the poem of one of their classmates, as Thomas Locker did for Bruchac and London. Each child contributed to a class anthology of naming poems, adding illustrations to accompany each written piece.

If you work with young children, try keeping a running list of phrases from their nightly entries or dictated descriptions. Use these words and phrases as a word bank throughout the moon study and especially when you and your students experiment with a naming poem for the moon.

WRITING INVITATION #22

Random Collage Poem: Combining Printed Text with Image

The *Random Collage Poem* is a combined writing and art invitation. It is an opportunity for you and your students to play with words and visual imagery. Essentially, this invitation meshes the artistry of collage with the creation of a found poem. Our students experimented with this invitation in groups during Moon Journal studio time. As always, they had the option of including a random collage poem of their own in their Moon Journals.

First, the materials needed for the project were collected. A note was sent home with our students, requesting parents to gather old magazines, sales catalogs, and any other printed material containing advertisements or words in large print. We also asked for scraps of wrapping and tissue papers. These scraps would be added to the hand-painted papers in our classroom "treasure" box. (See Art Invitation #11: *Handpainted Papers*.)

After accumulating supplies for about a week, we were ready to begin. The students formed into groups of four or five. Each group had a stack of magazines, catalogs, colorful papers, an 11" × 17" poster board, scissors, and glue sticks. We asked the children to look through the printed material and cut or tear out interesting words or phrases. The students' text selections were based on content and/or graphic appeal. Single words—especially verbs, articles, and conjunctions—were also assembled. Some groups tore out moon- or night-related pictures.

Then the groups spread everything out in front of them. This allowed each group member to view the assortment of material easily. We told the children that a poem was waiting to be discovered somewhere within their collection of words and phrases. They were asked to play with different text arrangements until that hidden poem was found.

Each group was responsible for writing one poem dealing with any subject that was appropriate for a Moon Journal. Students selected topics such as the moon, night, dreams, stars, rain, clouds, and even bats. While writing their poems, groups sometimes needed extra words. Students were encouraged to trade text with classmates or form words by gluing single letters together.

After completing their poems, the groups collaged the text, the colored papers, and other magazine images onto the poster board. Most of the children thought it was easier to glue the papers and pictures down first and then add the words. Poems were shared aloud and then displayed together on our Art Gallery bulletin board.

There are many ways to create a random collage poem. Exploring and experimenting with the juxtaposition of words and images is the purpose of this invitation. (See Color Plate 7.) The random collage poems below were written by two groups of fifth graders.

Bats

Bats
hang on in caves.
Bats
search for
insects.
They feed on
wildlife.
Bats
are
tough enough
to survive
in the night!

Brett, Jeff, Johnny, Jonathan, Nicholas

Night

Sacred time.
Imagine
Rediscovering a forgotten
Paradise.
A land of
Diamonds in the dust.
There's no other
Street of dreams
Stretching around
the
World.

Jessica, Kristen, Lynn, Nyssa, Sara

WRITING INVITATION #23

Found Poems: Writing a Poem with Text Found in Moon Journals

A found poem is composed of text "found" in various settings. In Writing Invitation #22: *Random Collage Poem*, text was cut from nonpoetic material such as sales catalogs, magazine advertisements, or newspaper headlines and put into a poetry format. In this invitation, students write a found poem using words, sentences, or phrases selected from their own Moon Journal entries.

We introduced this invitation toward the end of our twenty-eight day project. This maximized the number and type of journal entries that could be used. It also provided an opportunity for the children to review their accomplishments and to see their growth as writers as they searched for their favorite words from their journals.

Our students chose passages from any type of journal entry. They were not limited to words that already "sounded poetic." We encouraged them to make selections from different genre: scientific facts, naturalistic observations, letters, research material, personal reflections, and, of course, other poems.

The process was simple. The students created a list of found words, phrases, and sentences. Next they moved their list elements around, adding and subtracting words, until they were satisfied with the arrangement. Finally the children rewrote their text in a poetry format. (See Writing Invitation #13: *From Prose to Poetry.*)

> Tonight I saw the full moon
> And stars
> A thousand little sparks and lightning bolts
> Like diamonds, rubies and gems.
> The fiddler played
> And I started dancing
> Faster and faster
> With little brown moths
> Circling tall gray street lamps.
>
> *Larissa, age 9*

> Moon,
> Lightning of the sky,
> Tending all,
> Bringing joy.
> Night heaven,
> A place to plan
> my dreams.
> When I was little
> I would call to the fairies.
> But now,
> I almost always wish
> For the moon
> Right outside my window.
>
> *Melissa, age 12*

> Full moon,
> Super-powered spotlight

> in the sky.
> Goes round and round
> and never, ever ends.
> I'll continue watching it
> forever.
>
> *William, age 9*

Found Poems invite children to work with poetry in new ways. Gathering, combining, and rearranging words and phrases help children gain insight into the real work of poets.

WRITING INVITATION #24

Phases of My Life, Phases of the Moon: Writing and Telling Life Stories in Words and Pictures

In their Moon Journals, students record the waxing and waning moon as it passes through the phases of its cycle. They watch it grow slowly from the thinnest crescent to its full glory and then gradually diminish back to a delicate sliver of light. In Writing Invitation #27: *Moon Cycle, Life Cycle*, young writers compare the lunar cycle to other cycles in nature.

In this invitation, students record the phases of their own lives through brief memoirs, captions, quotes from family members, pictures, photographs, paintings, sketches, and collages. Words and pictures are combined to create a whimsical mixed-media accordion book that compares the phases of the moon with the phases of each child's life.

We began this project by reviewing the lunar phases with our students and making thumbnail sketches of the growing and shrinking moon on scrap paper. Together, students and the teacher recorded the name of each phase: new moon, crescent, waxing crescent, quarter, waxing gibbous, full moon, waning gibbous, quarter moon, waning crescent, and crescent.

Next, we invited the children to think about their own lives and the "phases" they had personally experienced. We gave our students one 12" × 18" piece of newsprint that was folded into eighths. The little boxes created a continuous "lifeline," with each segment representing a phase in each child's life. As a prewriting activity, we recorded on the board as many phases as we could recall: infancy, the crawling stage, toddler days, preschool, kindergarten, and so on. These phases were generic and easy to list.

The activity became more interesting as we thought of phases that were unique to individual children. For example, Josh went through an "I-Won't-Touch-Sand-at-the-Beach" phase when he was about eighteen months old, and an "I-Won't-Wear-Shirts-with-Collars" phase when he was three. Other students added their personal phases to the cluster: I-Will-Only-Wear-My-Bunny-Slippers, I-Love-

Bananas, I-Want-to-Be-a-Power-Ranger, I-Want-to-Have-a-Puppy, I-Am-a-Balle-rina, Mom-and-Dad-Read-Aloud-to-Me, and I-Love-to-Play-Soccer. As teachers, we demonstrated samples of our own phases and told the stories that lay beneath each phase title.

At this point we invited our students to ask parents, grandparents, and older brothers and sisters to help them remember some of their personal phases from younger years. The children took their blank, folded pages home, filling them in with titles for the phases, quotes from family members, short stories, captions, and drawings. Talking to family members and looking through photo albums helped fill in details from periods when the children were too young to remember certain events. Many children gathered photographs to help them represent each phase.

When the papers and materials came back to school, we were ready to create our "Phases of My Life" accordion books. The pages the students filled in at home were first drafts; now we were ready to revise and edit the captions and stories.

To create the books, we cut 12" × 18" construction paper into 6" × 18" halves. We folded the long strips into quarters and attached the two folded strips together with clear tape. By using the front and back of the attached papers, each child had a sixteen-page book.

In every other section the children drew a picture of the eight phases of the moon, beginning with the new moon. Underneath each moon shape the students wrote the name of a phase in their life, and then described the phase with words and pictures. We did not end the sequence of phases with the current stages the children were experiencing, but added some phases projected into the future. The full moon represented who the children thought they would be at age twenty-five, and the waning moon indicated phases they would experience as they continued to mature. The children enjoyed predicting their occupations, the location of their homes, the composition of their families, and their hobbies and interests. Some of Gina's first grade students wrote about the phases in their lives:

> The Grabbing-Fingers Phase: "When I was around one I used to grab fingers. I wouldn't let go until someone pulled their finger away. My mom told me."
>
> *Camille*

> The Dalmatian Phase: "I had a phase that I was a Dalmatian at Halloween for three years. I have little, medium, and big costumes in my drawer. I have a hat with ears. I put black spots on my face. Last Halloween I was finally not a Dalmatian."
>
> *Nicholas*

> The Roller Blading Phase: "I am going through a roller blading phase. I really like to skate at the beach. I know how to go fast."
>
> *Casey*

The Dating Phase: "When I am a teenager I will date a lot of boys. When I am 19 we'll do stuff like go to lunch and eat hamburgers and milk shakes. I'll stay on the phone too."

Marissa

The Listen-to-My-Kids-Complain Phase: "When I am a mother I will listen to complaining all the time. All my kids will be saying: He hit me. No, I didn't! Yes, you did. No, I didn't! I'm telling Mom on you! And I'll have to listen to this forever. I know because I complained all the time when I was little."

Jessica

The Old Phase: "I will be sitting down all day when I am 62. I'll be an old geezer and play cards with my friends. I'll watch football every Saturday."

Matthew

You and your students will decide how you want to approach this writing and art invitation. There are many options. Students can cluster their phases and write one particular memoir or create a photojournal of snapshots and captions representing many phases. Some children may decide to create a time line of their phases, with simple sketched illustrations and short captions. The accordion book is only one example of this project that combines words, pictures, and personal reflections.

This activity is an ideal closure project because it combines many of the techniques previously introduced in both the writing and art invitations, and it encourages students to reflect on the changes they have experienced in their lives as a natural part of growing older.

WRITING INVITATION #25

Nighttime Rituals: Recording a Family Story

The moon's twenty-eight day show is a scripted performance. The month-long ritual is always the same: The moon grows full, then shrinks. However, our Moon Journal observations verify that this predictable cycle is anything but a humdrum string of nights. Radiant crescents, star-filled skies, swirling clouds, mysterious moonshadows, and rainbows after dark show the splendor that lies within the routine of the lunar orbit.

Many children think of their day as a routine sequence of events. They get up, get dressed, get on the bus, go to school, go to soccer practice, come home, do homework, eat dinner, and go to bed. When asked, "What did you do today?" a typical reply is "Nothing" or "I don't remember." Most adults can empathize. We all have those days that seem featureless. It's easy to do when many activities and tasks are done repeatedly. One day can feel like the mirror image of the day before. But just as we learn to recognize the multitude of surprises in the moon's predictable orbit, we can also come to appreciate the small treasures that lay hidden within our own daily cycle.

Nighttime Rituals is an invitation to the children to pay attention to a meaningful, yet often overlooked, segment of the day: the close. We asked our students, "What are the things you do each night before going to sleep?" For weeks our journal keepers had been busy observing events going on outside their windows; now it was time to think about the family rituals happening inside.

Initially our students did not recall the particulars. They said things like, "I just go to bed" or "I read and then fall asleep." Going to bed, reading, and falling asleep are obvious examples of nightly activities, but we were after a more detailed account.

To jog the children's memories, we suggested that they make a time line that included everything they normally did between dinner and falling asleep. What were the predictable things that happen every night? Times and events were recorded.

Lindsey's time line looked like this:

6:00 dinner
6:30 dessert
6:45 shower
7:00 put on pajamas
7:10 unload dishwasher
7:30 brush teeth
7:40 journal and read
8:15 get ready for bed
8:20 ask Dad what to dream about
8:30 go to bed
9:00 (around) fall asleep

The list provided a way for Lindsey to recall the events that occur in her home every night. Now she was ready to "step into the scene" and develop her story. This was the second part of her entry:

> "Put on your head gear. Brush your teeth. Hurry up. Go to bed, now! If I have to come up those stairs—" These are the things I hear every night while my brothers and I get ready for bed. It gets a little frantic. But then my mom and dad come and tuck me in and kiss me good night.
>
> Then I ask my dad what I should dream about. We started playing that game when I was little because I dream a lot. Every night I ask, "What to dream about, Dad?" Sometimes he tells me to dream about what I'll be when I grow up, like an artist. One night he thought I should dream about a weird family vacation. I really did have that dream! A lot of times I dream about a perfect house or owning a horse.

Then I get under the blankets and turn off the light and I pretend I'm an imaginary person. I think about the things that happened during the day and I put them into my fantasy.

Sometimes I think about who I like and who I don't like. Somewhere in between all this thinking I fall asleep.

Lindsey

A third grader following the same process wrote:

I have dinner at 6:30 p.m. After that I go out and look at the moon. I draw a picture and write. When I finish my journal I have a snack. I go upstairs and brush my teeth. Next I get into bed and make sure my alarm is on. Then I ask my mom to turn on the fan. Then I get hugs and kisses from Mom and Dad and a hug from Alicia.

Jennifer

Lindsey and Jennifer have recorded important family stories. It's the little things that happen to children every day that shape who they are and who they will become. Although our students may not recognize the significance of bed-time reading, planning dreams, reviewing the day, a parent's nightly hug, or drawing the moon, we hope that it will become apparent to them in the years ahead. Calling attention to life's landscape is something we as teachers and parents need to do for our children.

WRITING INVITATION #26

Moon Memoirs: Turning Moon Memories into Moon Memoirs

As the moon makes its pilgrimage across the sky month after month, we too continue on our own journeys. The memorabilia of our travels come in the form of life stories. Each new moon marks the end and the beginning of a unique collection of personal remembrances. Discovering, sharing, and recognizing the importance of these stories is the way we come to know ourselves and each other.

Clarissa Pinkola Estes, in *Women Who Run with the Wolves* (1992), writes, "Once, we lived by these cycles and seasons year after year, and they lived in us. They calmed us, danced us, shook us, reassured us. . . ." What are the memories that you have gathered in the cycles and seasons of your life? What are the stories that live in you?

A single memory can provide a writer with a solid foundation for a journal entry, story, poem, essay, article, or even an entire novel. *Moon Memoirs* invites journalists to use the present moon to trigger a memory about a past moon. The remembrance is then turned into a memoir. There have already been many moons in the life of even the youngest school-aged child: winter moons, summer moons, moons of sadness and celebration, learning moons, vacation moons, moons over sporting events, new-friend moons, moons for growing and creating, moons for standing still.

Keep in mind these rich memories are not always about life's major milestones; more often they involve a commonplace incident that was somehow noteworthy to the writer. Every moon comes with a story. Can you remember a moon that was significant in your life?

Begin your moon memoir by quietly observing the moon. Do this without interruption for several minutes. Now "go beyond" the scene in front of you. Sometimes your thoughts carry you off to a seemingly unrelated experience. Does this scene remind you of another night? Is there a color, a sound, an element in the setting that brings to mind a previous occasion? Look for the patterns of light or shadow created by the moon and stars. What do they remind you of? How does the sky and landscape make you feel? Calm, peaceful, cold, optimistic, frightened, artistic? When was the last time you were in this mood? Let your thoughts wander. Jot down whatever comes to mind. See if you can make a connection between the present moon and a past moon.

Gina gave this example to her sixth grade class: "One night while moon gazing you hear a mockingbird's song. As you are listening, you are reminded of Marea, your friend who loves birds. You remember the hike the two of you went on in Sycamore Canyon during wildflower season. It was in the early morning and the moon and sun shared the sky at the same time. The moon has led you to your story. Tell us about your friend and her birds, or maybe share the story of your hike. Perhaps your journal entry might be titled 'Marea's Moon' or 'The Bird Who Sang About Wildflowers.' Jump into the flow of your memories, thoughts, and reflections. See where they take you."

One of Gina's sixth graders saw the moon resting with some pine trees. The scene led her to thoughts of a family vacation spent in the mountains.

Pine Trees

I see pine trees growing around my block. The moon is sitting on top of one. Pine trees have scents that I love. They clear my mind and give off one of my favorite fragrances. Some pine trees grow really tall. The one I'm looking at seems tall enough to touch the moon! This view reminds me of the winter of 1994 when my family went to my grandparents' house in the mountains for Christmas.

I love staying with my grandparents. I love it when I wake up in the morning, especially when I'm awakened by Sammy and Little Girl, my grandparents' dogs. I love it when I walk downstairs and see everyone in their robes, cozy with a cup of coffee, talking to each other. I love how my grandparents have a stove they put wood in to keep warm. I love knowing that my grandpa cut that wood. I love being there.

Jessica

When we work with the primary grades we introduce *Moon Memoirs* a little differently. Sometimes younger children have difficulty recalling past incidents. "I don't remember anything" is a response we often hear at first. We reassure our authors that memory is a writing tool that has to be developed; like anything else, the more you practice, the better you become. It's as if you're telling your brain, "My memories are important to me, so don't forget them. I have plans to use them later."

To prime the children's writing pumps and release a flow of memories, we write a simple list poem first and then follow with the memoir. We begin by talking about the moon's cycle so that the children can figure out their ages in months instead of years. This gives them an idea of how many moon cycles there have been in their lives. We point out that many things have happened between the time of their first full moon and the present. (See Writing Invitation #24: *Phases of My Life, Phases of the Moon.*) Students imagine what they might have been doing under a full moon at one, two, or four years of age. They recall incidents that happened last year, then last month.

Next, we invite them to create a list of memories in a poetry format. The children begin each line with *I remember.* The last sentence is a memory about a moon from their past.

Dylan, a second grade writer, came up with this list poem:

My Memories

I remember having no hair.
I remember falling down when I tried to walk.
I remember hating applesauce.
I remember crying on my three-year-old birthday because my sister blew
  out the candles before I could.
I remember being scared of Charlie the dog.
I remember putting syrup in snow and eating it with a spoon.
I remember playing on a different playground at a new school.
I remember the moon when we were camping.

The children then take their moon memory and "write off of it," turning it into a memoir. This was Dylan's moon memoir journal entry:

I remember seeing the moon in the forest. We were camping with a campfire. The moon was shining and it was a full moon. There was a reflection of it on the water. When the wind made waves on the water the moon changed back and forth. It reminded me of a flip book. We slept on the floor in our trailer. When we woke up the sun was shining through our trailer windows. I could smell the fresh air and I thought about going home. But I remember that camping trip because it was lots of fun.

WRITING INVITATION #27

Moon Cycle, Life Cycle: Life Lessons from the Lunar Cycle

The lunar cycle begins with a gestation period: the night of the new moon. In our first entries we frequently describe the moonless night sky and anticipate its first appearance. We imagine what the moon will look like, we estimate what time it will arrive in the evening sky, and we wonder where we will be when it first appears. With great excitement, the children discover the delicate waxing crescent moon, the first moon to be recorded in their journals. In a sense, this first sighting is the moon's birthday or the day of its arrival in our lives. We may have seen the moon many times before, but *this* moon is *our* moon, and we claim ownership by observing it carefully, sketching and writing, as we watch it grow.

The Moon Journalist records the growing moon in the same way parents record the growth of a child in a baby book. The students supply the "photographs" or illustrations along with captions and written descriptions. We watch the moon reach its prime on the night of the full moon. A difference, however, is that we know exactly how long the lifetime, or complete cycle, of this moon will be. After we celebrate its night of full glory we watch it slowly wane until it finally disappears.

The children are always sad and somewhat disappointed when the cycle is completed. Their journals are filled with beautiful descriptions, celestial drama, and personal reflections. Events from their own lives are intermingled with their lunar observations. Our students know a new moon will arrive again within a few nights, but *their* moon is gone, their journals pages are complete, and this adventure is over. Even though it will be the same moon in the sky going through a new cycle, the season will be changing, the weather conditions will be different, the events in the children's individual lives will alter. Their fellow moongazers may not be there with them in the same way again. The conclusion of this study is bittersweet; it is a good time for both personal reflection and community discussion.

We often begin by looking back through the pages of our journals. We reread our initial questions about the moon and our "I Wonder" poems. We discuss the parallels between waiting for the moon to appear and waiting for a new baby to be born. Inevitably, the disappearance of the moon is compared to the end of a life. Questions help the children reflect. Will you remember your moon? Can you think back to the nights when you watched the moon with your mom or dad, a brother, sister, or friend? How did you say good-bye to the moon in your journal? Do you remember grandparents and people you have loved that have passed away? Do they live on in your memory?

At this point in the discussion, the children invariably begin to tell their stories of grandparents, sometimes parents, friends, and even special pets who have died, but whom they remember with love. During the years that our students have kept Moon Journals, three children experienced the loss of a parent, and family members of many children have been seriously ill. Death is not a topic that is part of our standard curriculum, although it certainly is a part of our students' lives. For this reason we initiate this discussion, and we often begin by inviting the children to hear some of our personal stories.

Joni began one conversation with her students by sharing several of her family photo albums. The children laughed when they looked at her baby pictures, and enjoyed thumbing through the pages of her childhood photos. She showed them her wedding album and the pictures of when she was expecting her first child. Her students loved looking at the baby books of Joni's two children, watching them change and grow into young adults.

She showed the children a current picture of her daughter who is now in college and away from home for the first time. She explained that even though she is happy and excited for her daughter, she still misses her very much. She also shared photographs of her mother and talked about how sad she was when her mom passed away. She told stories of happy times with her mother that she will always remember. Finally, she shared a poem that she drafted and revised in one of her last Moon Journal entries. (See Figure 3-7.)

Some of Joni's fifth grade students chose to sketch or write their own entries comparing the moon's monthly journey to other life cycles.

> Ms. Moon, I enjoyed the phase I spent with you. Your cycle reminds me of the cycle of a rose. At first the rose bush is bare, nothing on it except leaves, like the night of a new moon when there is nothing in the sky but stars. Then a tiny bud appears on the bush, just like a tiny crescent moon. Bit by bit the rose petals open, petal by petal, like the waxing gibbous moon. After the time of full glory, petal by petal, the rose withers away as the moon wanes away, sliver by sliver.
>
> Moon, you are a lot like me. You are growing and changing, too. My grandpa says I am growing quickly and I think you are growing quickly! He likes to watch me and I like to watch you.

In addition to the life cycle comparisons, some of the children wrote memoirs and poems about special people in their lives. Sean wrote a poem dedicated to his grandparents.

I Just Believe

Are my grandparents the moon?
Are they the white glowing ball—
Will they come back soon?
Yes, I just believe.
Will they come to me in a dream?

FIGURE 3-7

Do they still love me?
Yes, I just believe.
Was I born to keep their memory alive?
Am I a part of them?
Do they watch me?
Yes, and I just believe.
Do I love them?
Do they love me?
Yes, I will always love them,
And they will always love me.
This I just believe.

Maturity is something that takes time, that grows slowly as children experience both sadness and celebrations. It can't be rushed. There are new moons to observe and new chapters in life to be experienced. Throughout our lives, reflection and celebration help us realize our promise and potential.

WRITING INVITATION #28

Farewell to the Moon: Final Reflections After Completing the Cycle

Keeping a Moon Journal helped me to learn
That the moon's monthly cycle will always turn.
The moon's shape, color and size
Will compare with a flower in someone's eyes.
Just hold your finger up to the moon—
Your finger and your heart will light up soon.
If you look up, high in the sky,
You'll see the moon floating by.
In that minute you will forever see
That it changes your heart temporarily.
My appreciation has changed a lot,
In the glow of moonlight, it's gotten caught!
By the light of the moon, by the shine of a star,
It will walk in my heart, from near to far.

Crystal, age 10

For twenty-eight days the students have watched the moon change, gradually growing rounder and then slowly diminishing until it slips away, marking the end of the Moon Journal cycle. As the moon changed, the children changed too. By inviting students to make discoveries in writing and art as they chronicle their discoveries about the moon, the teacher observes a cycle of growth in the children.

The teacher knows what the children may not consciously recognize at first: Their journals are portfolios that give evidence of growth over time. Student folders are filled with rough sketches and drafts, scraps of inspiration, and bursts of creativity. The journal pages record a journey in both improvisation and patient observation. In a classroom community in which metacognition is as much a part of inquiry and learning as the work in writing and art, the invitation to reflect is critical. The student, not just the teacher, is able to look back and trace his or her growth as artist, writer, naturalist, researcher, and thinker. Other factors, perhaps not as obvious but equally important, are by-products of this study as well. The children develop patience, curiosity, and a willingness to take risks; they learn to improvise, apply skills and techniques, and ask questions.

Reflection occurs throughout the Moon Journal study, not just in the final entry. From day to day students become aware of the expanding repertoire of techniques they use to create journal entries. Likewise, the teacher asks process questions on a daily basis. The end of the cycle, however, provides a good opportunity to look back and consider growth over time and the cumulative effect of a studio environment.

There are many ways to begin this process. The first year we had our students meet with partners and slowly turn through the pages of their journals, pointing out favorite entries, new techniques, and successes in art and writing. Many of the children attached Post-it notes to certain pages, describing their thoughts about the entries. The usual procedures for portfolio assessment were employed in this review of the Moon Journals.

The following year we tried a different approach. Because the children had enjoyed writing moon mail (Writing Invitation #17: *Moon Mail*), it seemed a natural extension to include a final letter to the moon, filled with their reflections and conscious statements of growth.

We asked the students questions as they turned through their journal pages and shared comments with their classmates. The questions were asked *conversationally*, amid whole-group and small-group discussions. These are some of the questions we asked:

- What different types of writing did you experiment with in your journal? Letters? Rhyming poems? Free verse? Observations? Lists? Recorded conversations? Questions? Memoirs? Legends? Rebus stories?
- Which writing selections were the most challenging? The most fun? The most satisfying? Why?
- Did you learn or apply any particular writing techniques, such as Show Not Tell (Caplan, 1984), or personification? Did you play with metaphors and similes, comparisons, repetition for effect, and so on? Can you find examples of your use of these techniques?
- Did you learn or apply any particular writing conventions? Did some poems require certain forms?
- Is there a written entry you would like to revise? Why? What would you change about the piece?
- Is there a particular piece you might want to develop? Which one? Why?
- Is there a piece you might like to approach using another "sign system" (Short, Harste, and Burke, 1996) like art, music, drama, or dance? Which one? What do you have in mind?
- Which art media did you use in your journal? Which media did you enjoy the most? Why? Which media challenged you the most? Why?
- Which of your art entries are the most satisfying or the least satisfying? Why?
- Which entries demonstrate that you took a risk?
- Which entries were inspired by another classmate or artist?
- What will you remember the most about this project?
- What did you learn about the moon? What questions did you have? Which ones were answered? What questions do you still have?
- What did you learn about yourself? Have you changed? How? Why?

Our students thought about these questions several times during the final week of the project. Sometimes one question led to an extended discussion; at other times several related questions were addressed together. We encouraged the children to take their journals home and share them with their parents. Some mothers and fathers added their own reflections to their children's journals. Jason's mother slipped this message, written to the moon and to her son, into his Moon Journal:

> You've been there all my life,
> I've grown up looking at your light,
> But never before have I realized
> how much you resemble a child.
> For with each passing night you change,
> As does a little boy or girl,
> And with each change something grows,
> To be seen, awed at, and treasured forever.
>   by Charlene Levy
> P.S. Thank you, Jason, for allowing me to share my thoughts in your beautiful journal.
> Love, Mom

The following day the children were ready to write their final reflective letters to the moon. The moon had become almost a personal friend, and we knew many of the children were sad about ending the cycle. These letters, incorporated into the journal, would help bring closure to the study.

> Dear Moon,
>   I like the way you can change shapes. I drew a picture of you when you were full. I colored it in with yellow markers. I used a crayon to make spots. Now I know that you have phases and I do too.
>   Love, Jessica, age 6

> Dear Mr. Moon,
>   I really enjoyed sharing all of my Moon Journal time with you. How is your earth journal coming along?
>   When I kept my Moon Journal I felt like I was making magic. I felt like all my worries disappeared, and do you know what? For those moments, they did! When I was working on my Moon Journal things popped into my mind before I even had time to think about them. I felt like I was soaring and that no one could stop me.
>   I learned many things in my Moon Journal. I know now why you change shape and color. I think you are like a flower in some ways because at first you are like a seed just about to start growing, then you are like a bud about to bloom into a beautiful creation, after that you become a radiant flower, then you are finished and start to die, but a while later you are resilient and bounce back.

When I kept a Moon Journal I looked at Ms. Nature and you in a different way than I did before. Before I started the journal I thought you guys were beautiful, but I did not really care. When I started keeping my Moon Journal I really started respecting you and Ms. Nature more. I thought you guys were two of the most beautiful things in the world.

I loved being able to write down whatever came into my mind about you. It made me feel free, confident, and brave. I loved drawing what I saw exactly how I saw it. It made me think about and understand things better. I also loved to try out new things and new ways of making art. I really like using pastels the best, because I can make mist and fog and clouds with them. I like blending the colors with a tissue until it looks just right.

I love being able to gaze at your reflection on the water. I love your moonbeams. I wrote poems about you when you shine on the ocean and make the waves turn gold.

Well, Mr. Moon, I have to go! I'll see you tonight! I will always look for you!

Your friend,
Candy, age 11

Dear Man in the Moon,

I have watched you every single night from my backyard. Sometimes I did it with my dad. My mom thought I was going to get cold because I stayed outside for so long so she brought sweaters all the time. I noticed a lot of things that I never did before. I was surprised how quickly the moon phases happen and that you are in a different spot in the sky every night. I wrote my favorite Moon Journal story on Halloween. The moon was full and it was pretty spooky. I also like finding stuff in the newspaper to put in my journal.

Even when it's quiet outside there are lots of noises. I listened to crickets, coyotes, barking dogs and airplanes. I recognized the shapes of plants in the field behind my house, even when it was totally dark. When you were full you were like a giant spotlight in the sky. It was almost as bright as day. I will keep watching you forever.

Love,
Will, age 8

A fifth grader wrote her final reflection as a poem.

Finale

On this final page,
I look at the sky as a giant stage.
The moon, clouds and stars are the players I see,

each day brings a new set, a new beauty.
No night is the set ever the same,
Is it any wonder the sky has such fame?
We gaze at its beauty, applaud with our hands,
as we on earth remain loyal fans.

Alyson, age 10

Dear Mr. Moon,

I have learned so much about you that I now feel very close to you. You have great wonders and possibilities, and I never really knew you until I did my Moon Journal. I especially loved drawing pictures of you! I learned lots of things about you and here are just a few: You don't *really* change shape, the sun just reflects off of you in different ways and so we see a little bit more of you every day and then a little bit less until you are gone again. I know the names of all your phases, too!

My Moon Journal was a passport to the sky. I got to draw you as you grew and as you got smaller. I got to put down my feelings and thoughts. I'm glad that you always come back.

Keeping a Moon Journal made me appreciate nature and its beauty. I just remember, before I started my Moon Journal, I would look up at you and say, "Oh, there's the moon." But now I get very excited when you come out. I remember when my dad and I bought a telescope and set it up to look straight at the beaming full moon. I looked through the telescope and you filled up the whole looking space! The round edges of the telescope were illuminated by you and it even hurt my eyes! The craters were digging into the moon like a shovel digging sand. It was amazing!

I also liked watching to see what shape you were going to appear in each night. When you were a crescent, sometimes you looked like the smile of a Cheshire cat!

I feel really good, sort of like a sense of relief, when I see you out in the sky. You are always there, shining down on me, and it gives me a good feeling. I watch for you until you appear and I say, "There it is! The moon is back!" I feel very special to have all my knowledge about you and to be able to use it. I tell lots of people about you.

I learned lots of different techniques so I can draw and create you in my journal. My favorite art entry is my tissue paper collage. I liked tearing just the right shape, and painting the right colors on the tissue paper. I put the torn tissues wherever I wanted them to go. I could blend colors when I put one color over another. I am really proud of my collage and I think I will frame it.

I even used things from home and made new things to put in my jounal. I have things from my house, outside and school all mixed in together.

My favorite phase of the moon is the full moon because then the star has arrived! The show can start now. You appeared. I just think that you are beautiful and I love to look at you. I know I always will.

Love,
Megan, age 11

Reflection is an important part of the process, and when you and your students look back through the pages of your Moon Journals, we think you will find the story of a relationship with nature, as well as the record of your growth in writing and art.

Destinations

I asked the Censor
why he had returned,
Unannounced,
like the gas meter man
or the boy on the bike that
goes door-to-door selling religion.
A fellow traveler weighted with
baggage
following the course of my
excursions.
We'd booked tickets
to the same destinations before,
midnight meetings on bridges
he convinced me not to cross,
rendezvous on roads
that suddenly seemed narrow,
the voyages in balloon baskets
that never left the ground.

I asked the Censor
why he had returned.
When we journey together
I loose the path between
my shadow and the morning sun,
the seeds stay sleeping in the soil,
and I forget to water the birch trees.
"I cannot share this night," I said.
The moonlight carries
ladles of ocher
I must pour,
the owl is humming a tune
I know the words to,
the seeds need watering
and I see the path between
my shadow and the morning sun.

Gina Rester-Zodrow

Chapter Four

The Art Invitations

If it were possible, we'd invite each of you to our homes. We'd sit around the kitchen table and share all twenty-eight Art Invitations. In fact, the kitchen table is precisely where many of our art ideas begin.

In her book *The Artist's Way* (1992), Julia Cameron encourages the planning of an "artist date" when the artist-in-you is "taken out, pampered, and listened to." We like to make artists' dates with each other. We set times to meet with all our paints, pencils, and papers. Sometimes we have pictures that we've cut out of magazines, interesting greeting cards, or a page from our seed journals with a new idea for an art project. We spread our supplies out on the table and begin to play, to experiment with art.

Neither of us are professional artists with formal art training. However, we both delight in the process of art and, often but certainly not always, we are pleased with the product. We have learned various techniques by trying them again and again, putting them aside, learning from the attempts that did not work, and celebrating those that did.

Our first choice would be to share these Art Invitations with you in an unstructured, relaxed environment with your favorite music playing in the background. But since that isn't possible we'd like you to keep that kitchen table idea in mind. We encourage you to create a comfortable place as you experiment with these techniques yourself and when you share them with your students.

Each Art Invitation has step-by-step instructions, but these are not meant to lock you or your students into specific end products. Rather, they are here to provide a starting point. The artwork in the sample Moon Journal color insert and the figures in this chapter help illustrate each technique. The first time you try a particular Art Invitation, you may find yourself reading the instructions carefully and producing a piece that looks similar to the model. Once you have a feel for the technique you can begin to have fun. Experiment. Use a heavier or lighter application of the medium you have selected. Try completely different colors, change the setting, or move the design elements around to create a new composition.

After you and your students have explored a number of Art Invitations, you may want to combine techniques and materials. Consider collaging hand-painted papers over an acrylic background, splattering paint over pastels, or tearing a watercolor landscape into strips and weaving it back together. Mix art and writing composition modes and allow image and text to become one combined piece. You will soon begin to play with art techniques in your mind as you observe the night sky. Without paints, you will splatter stars; without paper, you will tear out leaves and collage a tree; without pastels, you will rub in the crescent moon. When you finally sit down with your journal, you will know just how to express what you saw in your mind.

We can all remember a time when we've looked at our completed art work and said with disappointment, "It doesn't look the way it's supposed to. It's all wrong." The voice of that personal censor is unforgiving. It doesn't remind you that art is a process—a personal journey where there are no mistakes, just surprises. At first you may have to silence your internal censor as you discover its voice cropping up, telling you perhaps to avoid bold colors, to use symmetry in all your projects, or to resist abstract creations. "Don't, shouldn't, too much, not enough"—these are words and phrases to watch out for and resist. "Relax, try it, play, have fun, experiment"—these are words to use frequently. Try to approach the empty paper and the jars of paint with the excitement and confidence of a kindergarten child standing before an easel. Think of the sky as a canvas, and make a date to paint by moonlight.

ART INVITATION #1

Pencil Sketching: Recording Nature's Details in Simple Pencil Drawings

Pencil sketching is a core component of the Moon Journal art process. Portable, easy-to-manage materials—a pencil and paper—make it possible for journalists to record their immediate response to the environment. This simple medium encourages children to "see" the details around them. With the eyes of an artist, students come to notice a world of lines, shapes, spatial relationships, textures, and values. Over time the children learn to use these design elements to speak a new visual language. Their pictures become like words that capture the feeling of the experience.

Like a brief journal observation or written snippet, a simple pencil sketch often becomes a seed that grows into a pen-and-ink drawing, a watercolor painting, a collage, or some other mixed-media piece. (See Writing Invitation #3: *Growing Poems from Seeds.*) When used in this manner, pencil sketches are an important preliminary planning medium whereby the young artist is able to block in basic shapes, proportions, and composition. Not all pencil sketches are transformed into another piece of art; some are beautifully complete within themselves. Most student Moon Journals are filled with them.

The value of pencil sketching does not begin and end with art. We have found that drawing is an excellent prewriting activity as well. For example, as the young artist sketches the details of a tree trunk, the writer-within thinks of the words *bark*, *peeling*, *rough*, *sap*, *ants*, and *maple*. We encourage our students to be aware of this dual process and to jot down written notes next to their completed sketches.

Artist and writer Jim Arnosky, in his book *Sketching Outdoors in Autumn* (1988a), writes about the art of pencil sketching. "In setting out to do these outdoor sketches, I followed my own hunting instincts, hoping they would put me on the track of an autumn beyond the spectacular show of colorful leaves: a pencil sketcher's season, with interesting lines, sharp contrasts, and a variety of tones. . . . The autumn I was hunting had to be tracked and stalked before it could be captured." Pencil sketches are often the purest record of the Moon Journalist's season.

Materials

- drawing pencil (HB, B, or 2B)
- Moon Journal or blank drawing paper
- eraser (white vinyl erasers are gentle on paper surfaces)

Process

1. Look at the scene and select only a portion of it to draw. You might choose a single subject, a cluster of objects, or a section of the landscape. Over the course of keeping your Moon Journal, consider a variety of subjects. Try sketching expansive scenes or close-ups: distant mountains or a dandelion's head, a grove of trees or a curled leaf, a row of rooftops or a single window, a cloud-filled sky or the full moon.
2. Some artists like to begin by drawing a border on their paper. This serves as a frame for the sketch and helps with composition. Usually borders are rectangular in shape, but square or circular borders make interesting variations. Using this type of framing is a personal preference. See what works best for you.
3. If you are drawing more than one subject, notice how the objects in the scene compare to each other in size. Do they overlap at any point? Sometimes foreground objects appear larger than distant objects and are drawn in the lower portion of the picture. Background objects usually seem smaller and are drawn in the upper portion of the picture.
4. Take a few moments to look carefully at what you have selected to draw. You might want to close your eyes and visualize it in your mind.
5. Block in the overall shapes. Sketch the basic outlines and forms (Figure 4-1A).
6. Add line detail to the sketch. Go "into" the shapes. Consider line variety (curved, straight, thick, and thin lines), texture, and patterns (Figure 4-1B).
7. Then define values. Values show the lightness or darkness of objects in the scene. Dark areas are usually the easiest to see. Consider adding these accents first (Figure 4-1C).

FIGURE 4-1

ART INVITATION #2

Pen-and-Ink Drawings: Contour Drawings and Field Studies in Pen and Ink

The pen-and-ink medium was first introduced to our classes through "blind" contour drawing. Contour drawing defines an object's shape and border. It is done very slowly as the artist carefully observes the edge of an object, drawing it without looking at the paper. The goal is not to create an accurate image of the object; in fact, the artist's pen lines may not even resemble the object.

Contour drawing is an exercise in concentration and "seeing." As Betty Edwards points out in her book *Drawing on the Right Side of the Brain* (1979), "in pure contour drawing, it is the quality of the marks and their character that we care about. The marks, these living hieroglyphs, are records of perceptions." After experimenting with blind contour several times, students try looking back and forth from the objects to their papers. We remind them that artists spend most of their time observing their subjects rather than the marks on their sketch pads.

A second aspect of our children's pen-and-ink experience involved field studies. A series of nature walks provided different opportunities for quick sketches and written observation. Three books provided examples of artists' work in an outdoor setting: *Sketching Outdoors in Summer* (1988b) and *Sketching Outdoors in Autumn* (1988a) by Jim Arnosky and *The Sierra Club Guide to Sketching in Nature* (1990) by Cathy Johnson.

Materials

- paper
- journal
- black ink pen (There are many types of pens to choose from, such as ballpoint, felt-tipped, technical, rolling ball, fountain, and brush pens. Each one produces a different line quality but all are suitable for this invitation.)
- masking tape

Blind Contour Drawing Process

1. Select a small natural object to sketch, such as a leaf, flower, seed pod, or rock.
2. Place it on a table or drawing board.
3. Tape your paper to your work area so that it will not slide while you are drawing.
4. Pick a spot along the edge of the object—it doesn't matter where you begin. Put the tip of your pen on your paper. Let your eyes creep along the contour of the object. As you do this, very slowly draw what you see. Do this without looking at the paper or your hand. Your eyes should never leave the subject. After you've completed the outside boundary, go "inside" the object and

FIGURE 4-2

"blind" contour drawing of oak leaf

A.

Kansas
Storm clouds fill the sky. angry moss green gray, purple. Corn & wheat still in the field moon resting on a barn

B.

2/4
10:10
It's chilly out—sweater weather. The sky is filled with moving clouds, not thick fog, but clouds that look like old quilt batting—torn, pulled apart, frayed in places.

Hundreds of delicate lines. Use the blood leaf pulse. Use extra-fine tip.

The oak tree is casting moon shadows. Bright enough to see the fallen leaves and acorns.

Bubbled texture. Multicolored acorn cups; browns, reds, burnt orange. Some are black.

Squirrel snack.

C.

observe those contours. Just let your hand and pen move along with your eyes (Figure 4-2A).

Field Study Process

1. Select several items in nature and do a series of pen-and-ink drawings on one sheet of your journal. Focus on the lines, shapes, and values in your subjects. Drawings can be randomly placed on the paper (see Figure 4-2B) or sketched inside frames (Figure 4-2C).
2. Write field notes next to each drawing. Your notes might include personal feelings and reactions, the physical qualities of the subjects, or perhaps ideas for future artwork in another medium.

Alternate Idea

Cut out a section of a brown paper bag and use it for a pen-and-ink drawing. The black-on-brown image can later be glued into your Moon Journal.

ART INVITATION #3

Watercolor Wash Backgrounds: Painting a Watercolor Graded Wash

When we look at the night sky we see that it is darkest directly overhead and gets lighter toward the horizon. A basic watercolor technique called a graded wash is one way to depict the sky's dark-to-light tonal change. This invitation demonstrates a simple method for producing this gradual effect. You will also notice that we have used it as the first step in other Art Invitations in this book. A graded wash makes a dynamic background for almost any project.

Each time we use this medium, we remind our students that watercolor is beautiful but unpredictable. Sometimes unplanned things happen as the paint flows over the wet paper. Fortunately, even irregular washes with streaking and uneven color distribution can make beautiful skies and clouds.

Materials

- watercolor pan paints (lid can be used as a mixing palette)
- watercolor paper, precut to fit Moon Journal
- flat 1" brush
- masking tape
- rigid board, such as Masonite or plywood (larger than paper size)
- container with water
- newspaper or drop cloths

FIGURE 4-3

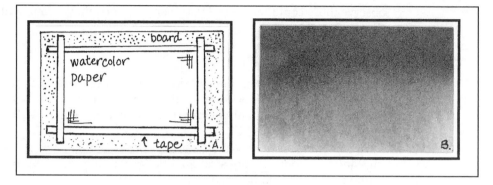

Process

1. Cover work area with newspaper or drop cloth.
2. Securely tape all four edges of the watercolor paper onto the board. It should look like a "frame" of tape (Figure 4-3A).
3. Select one paint color for the wash. Wet paint with several drops of water. Wait about a minute for the water to be absorbed into the paint. Dip the brush into the pan of fluid paint, then dab the paint onto your palette. Repeat this step until you have a lot of paint on your palette to work with. It is important not to run out of pigment during the wash procedure.
4. Tip the board at a slight angle. This can be done by resting one edge of the board on a book, wood block, or other similar object. The raised end should be away from you.
5. Wet the entire paper using a clean brush and clear water. Note: The wet paper may buckle but it will flatten out as it dries.
6. Load the brush with paint from your palette.
7. Working from left to right, paint a horizontal stripe of color straight across the top of the entire paper.
8. Moving down the page, paint a second stripe of color that slightly overlaps the first.
9. Dip the brush in water and paint a third and fourth stripe. You will notice that the addition of water lightens the color.
10. Continue adding more water to the paint for each successive brushstroke. Paint stripe after stripe, each slightly overlapping, until you reach the bottom of the page.
11. The overlapping strokes, the angle of the board, and the wet paper allow the paint stripes to merge. No bands of color should be apparent. The result is an evenly graded wash that gradually moves from dark to medium to light (see Figure 4-3B and graded background sky in Color Plate 1). Note: Laying a graded wash takes some practice. Your students need to work smoothly but quickly down the paper before it dries.
12. Carefully remove the masking tape after the paper is flat and dry.

ART INVITATION #4

Swirling Watercolor Sky: Using Wet-into-Wet Watercolor Techniques

Moon Journalists soon discover that there are many colors in the night sky. Dropping watercolor pigment onto a piece of wet watercolor paper allows colors to blend and diffuse. By tilting the surface of the board the watercolor paper is taped to, the artist can create swirling colors in a night sky. The moon can be incorporated into artwork by masking the shape of the moon before applying water and paints, painting on top of the dried watercolor background, or by gluing a cutout of the moon onto the background of the watercolor sky. See Color Plate 5 (the sky background) and Color Plate 4 (the leaf background) for color samples of this technique.

Materials

- a piece of watercolor paper, taped to a board
- watercolors
- container of clear water
- watercolor brush
- table salt (optional)
- masking fluid (optional)
- 2"-wide masking tape (optional)
- opaque paint (optional)
- cutout moon and/or stars (optional)

Basic Process

1. Tape a piece of watercolor paper to a board (Figure 4-4A).
2. With a wide brush, cover the watercolor paper with clear water. The paper should be totally wet, but avoid creating puddles.
3. Load the brush with a color of your choice and "drop" the pigment onto the paper by touching the brush tip to the wet paper (Figure 4-4B).
4. Clean the brush in a container of water. Dip the clean, wet brush into the next color of your choice.
5. Drop the second color onto the still-wet paper.
6. Pick up the board and tilt it, blending and swirling the two colors (Figure 4-4C).
7. Clean the brush in the water container. Dip the clean brush into the next color of choice. You may want to create the third color in your mixing tray by combining the first two colors or by mixing a lighter or darker value of the first or second colors, or you may choose a contrasting color that will add interest and dimension.
8. Drop the third color onto the still-wet paper, tilt the board, and swirl or blend the colors.

FIGURE 4-4

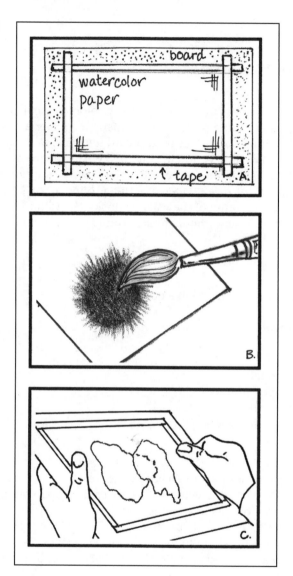

9. As long as the paper is wet, it is safe to drop in more color(s) if you choose.
10. Right before the paper dries (but while is still has a shine), you may choose to sprinkle some table salt onto the damp paper. The salt will absorb some of the pigment, creating a "starry" effect in the colors. (See Art Invitation #6: *Salt Stars and Clouds*.) Do not brush the salt off until the paper is completely dry.

Process Option #1: Creating a Masked Moon in the Sky Before Applying the Watercolor Background

1. With a pencil, *lightly* draw the shape of the moon on a piece of dry watercolor paper.
2. Use an old paint brush to cover the moon shape completely with masking fluid. Clean the brush immediately to remove all traces of the fluid.
3. When the fluid is dry, follow steps 1 through 10 of the basic process.
4. When the paper is completely dry, gently rub off the masking fluid (revealing the shape of the moon).
5. Paint over the white moon with a pale blue or yellow wash (optional).

Process Option #2: Alternative Masking Method (Using Masking Tape)

1. Peel off a piece of 2"-wide, paint-grade masking tape. Lightly adhere the strip of tape to a piece of waxed paper. Draw the shape of the moon on the piece of masking tape and cut it out. Lift the moon-shaped mask off of the waxed paper.
2. Decide on a pleasing location, and adhere the moon-shaped mask to the watercolor paper.
3. Follow steps 1 through 10 of the basic process.
4. When the paper is dry, gently lift off the masking tape (revealing the shape of the moon).
5. Paint over the white moon with a pale blue or yellow wash (optional). See Color Plate 5 (the moon) for a sample of this technique.

Process Option #3: Adding the Moon to the Painted Sky (Alternative to Masking in Advance)

1. Follow steps 1 through 10 of the basic process.
2. When the watercolor paper is dry, paint a moon in the sky using an opaque paint such as acrylic or tempera.
3. Another option is to glue a cutout moon and/or stars onto the watercolor paper. See Color Plate 8 (the moon) and Color Plate 9 (the moon) for samples of this approach.

ART INVITATION #5

Splattered Stars: Using a Toothbrush to Create Splattered Stars in a Night Sky

The Milky Way and other galaxies are easy to represent in a Moon Journal by using a common tool: a toothbrush. Artists can choose from among many media that can be applied by a toothbrush. Masking fluid, opaque watercolors, gouache, acrylic, and tempera paints are effective media to use when creating splattered stars in the night sky. See Color Plate 1 (the stars in the sky) and Color Plate 11 (the birch trees) for samples of these techniques.

Materials

- watercolor paper taped to a board
- dark construction background paper (optional)
- toothbrush
- paints (opaque watercolors, gouache, acrylic, or tempera paint)
- masking fluid (optional)
- paintbrush
- container of water
- 1" masking tape

Process Option #1: Creating Splattered Stars with Masking Fluid

1. Cover your table with newspaper. This can be a messy project!
2. Tape a piece of watercolor paper to a board (Figure 4-5A).
3. Dip an old toothbrush into a small container of masking fluid.
4. Use your forefinger to flick the bristles of the toothbrush quickly. The masking fluid will splatter across the watercolor paper (Figure 4-5B). Practice on scrap paper first. The splatters should be fine; avoid thick blobs. Allow the masking fluid to dry.
5. When the fluid is dry, paint over the splatters with your brush (Figure 4-5C). You may want to paint on dry paper, or you may choose to wet the paper first. Use either wet-into-wet or graded-wash techniques; cover your paper with color (see Art Invitations #3: *Watercolor Wash Backgrounds* and #4: *Swirling Watercolor Sky*).
6. When the watercolor is completely dry, lightly rub away the masking fluid splatters with your fingers. The white splatter marks that are now exposed will stand out against the darker colors of the painted night sky—a galaxy of stars!

FIGURE 4-5

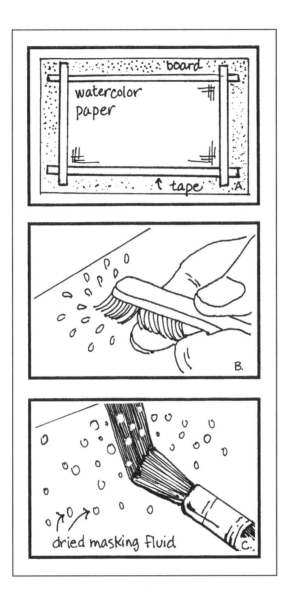

7. For a softer effect, brush a very light wash of palest blue over the stars (optional).

Process Option #2: Adding Paint-Splattered Stars to a Dark Background Paper

1. Select a piece of dark construction paper. Position it on a table that has been covered with newspaper.
2. Dip a toothbrush into paint (options include opaque white watercolors, gouache, and acrylic or tempera paints). Make sure the paint is not too thick.
3. Drag your forefinger across the bristles of the toothbrush. The paint will splatter onto the paper. Practice on scrap paper first until you learn how to achieve splatters that simulate stars in the sky. The spray should be fine; avoid large blobs.
4. Let the splatters dry. You now have a galaxy of stars! You may want to paint or glue a moon in the sky and add the silhouettes of houses, trees, or figures in the foreground.

ART INVITATION #6

Salt Stars and Clouds: Dropping Salt into Watercolors

Although the moon is the leading actor of a Moon Journal, stars and clouds play important supporting roles. Dropping salt into watercolors can create the effect of delicate misty clouds and/or galaxies of stars. See Color Plate 5 for a sample of this invitation.

Materials

- a piece of watercolor paper, taped to a board
- watercolors
- container of clear water
- watercolor brush
- table salt

Process

1. Tape a piece of watercolor paper to a board with masking tape. (See Art Invitation #3: *Watercolor Wash Backgrounds*, Figure 4-3A, for illustrated instructions.)
2. With a wide brush, cover the watercolor paper with clear water. The paper should be totally wet, but avoid creating puddles.
3. Dip a wide brush into the watercolor pigment of your choice. Create a straight or graded wash (Art Invitation #3: *Watercolor Wash Backgrounds*), or drop colors onto

the wet paper in a random design (Art Invitation #4: *Swirling Watercolor Sky*). Let your observations of the night sky guide your choices for color application.

4. After you have applied the colors to your wet paper, wait until the paper has *almost* dried. The paper should still be slightly wet and the shine of the watercolors should still be visible.
5. Sprinkle some table salt onto your paper wherever you want to create the effect of clouds or stars.
6. Watch the salt start to absorb some of the pigment. Allow the paper to dry completely.
7. Gently brush the salt from the dry paper. You will discover stars and clouds in the watercolor sky!

Creating a Masked Moon in the Starry Sky (Option)

1. Peel off a piece of 2"-wide, paint-grade masking tape. Lightly adhere the strip of tape to a piece of waxed paper. Draw the shape of the moon on the piece of masking tape and cut it out. Lift the moon-shaped mask off the waxed paper.
2. Decide on a pleasing location, and adhere the moon-shaped mask to the watercolor paper.
3. Follow steps 1 through 7 of the basic process.
4. When the paper is completely dry, gently lift off the masking tape (revealing the shape of the moon).
5. Paint over the white moon with a pale blue or yellow wash (optional).
6. Using a wide, flat watercolor brush, add the silhouette of buildings or landscape shapes in the foreground.

ART INVITATION #7

Bubble Prints: Texture Prints Made with Soap Bubbles

Bubble prints are easy and fun to create. They make stunning sunsets, dazzling stars, colorful clouds, or textured moons (see the blue and purple bubble-print sky in Color Plate 9). At least one child in every class says it reminds him or her of "making milk bubbles." A first grader remarked, "My mom gets mad at me when I do this at restaurants." Needless to say, this is one of our students' favorite invitations.

We usually break our class into small groups of four or five. Each group's workstation has three or more colors of bubble mix, one cookie sheet, a straw for each child, and lots of paper. (When working with young children we cut a couple of tiny holes in the straws. This allows the children to blow air out of the straws but not drink the bubble mix.)

Materials

- white construction paper
- plastic straws
- cookie sheets (with sides)
- acrylic paint, tempera paint, or food color
- dishwashing liquid soap
- water
- small jars or containers
- newspaper or drop cloths

Process

1. Cover work areas with newspaper or drop cloth.
2. Make the bubble mix in the small containers using half dishwashing soap, half water, and a few teaspoons of paint or food color. Stir gently. Add more food color or paint until you are satisfied with color intensity. Repeat the process until you have at least three different colors of bubble mix per workstation. (Groups can trade colors.)
3. Place one jar of bubble mix on the cookie sheet. Put a straw into the bubble mix and blow gently. Let the bubbles flow over the edge of the container (see Figure 4-6). Remove the straw. Lightly place the paper on top of the bubbles. The bubbles leave a colored print as they pop. Put the straw back into the bubble mix and continue the process until you have filled the page with as many prints as desired. Note: If groups use one color at a time, bubble mix can be poured back into the container from the cookie sheet.

FIGURE 4-6

Day One

It is a dark night, but the sky isn't just black! I see blue, some black, and magenta. There are thin gray clouds that look like smoke from a chimney. There's no moon tonight. Only stars are shining. I wonder where the moon is? Maybe he's on vacation.

Alex, age 9

Color Plate 1

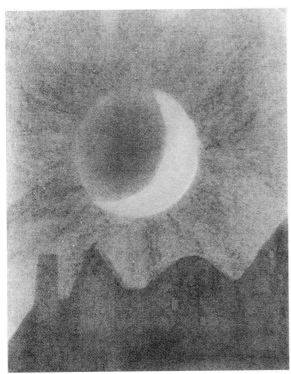

Day Three

Nights are getting darker,
days are getting shorter,
and misty, pearl-colored clouds
are covering the beautiful sky
like a blanket.
Trees are dropping their leaves,
animals are singing good-bye songs,
and the ground is covered
with a rug of red, purple, and gold.

Andy, age 10

Color Plate 2

Day Seven

My cat is wandering around the house. Owls are hooting and crickets are chirping under the moon. The cars are honking. Night bats are hanging upside down. The ants are going down their hole and a jet is rushing by.

Eric, age 7

When I was little like a sliver moon I was in The-Preschool-Phase. When I was in preschool I was a crazy driver. One day I was driving a plastic car and it had bad brakes. I didn't stop for the red light and I hit a boy in the leg!

   When I was a little older, about five, I went through the Roller-Skate-Phase. Every time my sister went roller skating I'd say, "Can I go? Can I go?" She'd say, "OK, put on your skates." So that's how I learned to skate.

Anthony, age 6

Color Plate 3

Day Eight

Silent Leaves

The mornings are cold.
I see clouds resting on my neighbor's roof top.
The sun tries hard,
and peers through the fog
the way I clear off a steamy window
in my grandpa's car,
with my hand.
I see the
tree's
leaves
up so
high . . .
one is
falling
down,
down
down.
When it
touches the
ground
you don't
hear a
sound—
it is silent.
It is like
the moon,
moving so
quietly in
the sky,
whispering
all the time
to the sun.
And now it
is gone.
It was only
a dream,
a quiet and
peaceful
dream.

*Robbie, age
10*

Color Plate 4

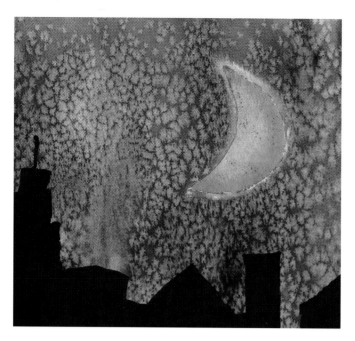

Day Nine

Shhh . . .
The sky is like a movie
Moving all the time.
Changing every minute,
Moving like a mime.
The sky changes
in mysterious ways
and you never know
what's going to happen.
So shhh . . .
and watch
the mysterious sky above.

Lindsay, age 11

Color Plate 5

Day Twelve

Plains of Snow

In the east, dark clouds
are moving southwest
through an ocean of
indigo-colored sky.
Rabbits, created with
God's paintbrush
and fluffy white lambs
are running across their
pasture of blue.
Illuminated leaves of
clouds
and two gray squirrels
run across heavenly
plains of snow . . .
Clouds.

Kassondra, age 10

Color Plate 6

Day Fourteen

I see the misty sky with the moon's white glow behind it. It's very foggy so I can just make out the silhouettes of the trees. The soft wind is blowing through their branches and I can hear the rustling of the leaves. The moon's still gleaming and bringing some light into the world. It's a very glamorous sight. It would be worth staying up all night to watch. I can hear the silent night. I understand the message the moon is giving me.

I feel very lightweight, like I could fly. I just want to fall asleep, now. When I wake up the moon will be gone. But I'll just wait for tomorrow night so I can see it again.

Lindsey, age 12

Full Moon Night!

Move clouds!
Move now!
The full moon is here!
Move clouds!
Move clouds!
The moon's a full sphere!
Move clouds!
Move clouds!
Tonight's the night!
Move clouds!
Move clouds!
The moon's so bright!
It's a full moon night!

Sheila, age 10

Color Plate 7

Day Fifteen

Day Eighteen

Day Twenty-one

Ode to Stars

You are bright,
shining,
sparkling.
You are the earrings
of the night.
You catch
my eye,
You lead
my way,
You are sun's
children.
I feel
you close to me,
even though
you're so far away.
You comfort me
when night
creeps up
on me.
I can't
count you,
but I can
count on you
protecting
and guarding me
from the dark night.

Katherine, age 9

Color Plate 10

Day Twenty-eight

Dear Mr. Moon,
  I have learned so much about you that I now feel very close to you . . . My Moon Journal was a passport to the sky. I got to draw you as you grew and as you got smaller. I got to put down my feelings and thoughts. I'm glad that you always come back . . . I feel really good, sort of like a sense of relief, when I see you out in the sky. You are always there, shining down on me. I watch for you until you appear and I say, "There it is! The moon is back!" . . . I think that you are beautiful and I love to look at you. I know I always will.

Megan, age 11

Color Plate 11

4. Consider using other colors. Multiple-colored bubble prints can be made on the same sheet of paper. For example, a sunset can be created on one sheet of paper by using red, orange, and yellow overlapping bubble prints.
5. Dry thoroughly.
6. Cut prints into different shapes or use for collage. (The bubble print sky in Color Plate 9 was collaged with oil pastel textured papers.)

ART INVITATION #8

Simple Stenciled Shapes: Making Images from Precut Designs

Adding the moon, stars, buildings, and background foliage to a painting or illustration is greatly simplified through the use of handmade stencils. Young artists can draw the shapes, cut them out, and use them over and over again. Various textures can be created using pastel rubbings and sponge-and-splatter painting techniques. For examples of the stenciled shapes, refer to
- Color Plate 4 (the stenciled leaf shapes)
- Color Plate 11 (the crescent moon)
- Writing Invitation #27: *Moon Cycle, Life Cycle*, Figure 3-7 (the sponged images of the lunar phases)

Materials

- cardstock, index cards, or construction paper
- sheets of mylar or clear transparency film (optional)
- scissors or craft knife (older students)
- pencil
- paper
- Options: pastels, tissues, cotton swabs, cut-up sponges, old toothbrush, rubber stamp inks

Process

1. Draw the shape you will use for the stencil.
2. Make a small hole in the center of the shape with the tip of the scissors. Carefully cut out the shape (Figure 4-7A). Teachers of younger children may want to cut the initial opening for the students. Set aside the cutout shape. The remaining paper with the missing shape is the stencil.
3. Position the stencil on the background paper (Figure 4-7B). Fill in the cutout area with pastels, paint, or inks. Consider these options:
   a. For a soft effect, rub the side of a chalk pastel on a sheet of scrap paper. Pick up the pastel chalk dust with a piece of tissue. Carefully rub the pastel dust into the cutout area with the tissue (Figure 4-7C).

b. For a textured effect, dip a piece of sponge into some tempera or acrylic paints. With the stencil in place, fill in the cutout area with the sponge. Press lightly, and change colors to create a layered, dimensional effect (Figure 4-7D).

c. For a brushstroked texture, take a stencil brush and dip the flat surface of the bristles into acrylic paint. Dab the stencil brush onto a damp paper towel to remove any excess paint. Place the stencil on the background paper and apply the paint in circular motions over the cutout area (Figure 4-7E).

d. For a splattered effect, dip an old toothbrush into watercolor paints or watered-down tempera paint. Position the stencil on the background paper. Use newsprint to cover all of the exposed paper; only the cutout area of the stencil should be left exposed. Brush your forefinger over the toothbrush. The splattered paint will fill in the cutout area (Figure 4-7F). Note: Use

FIGURE 4-7

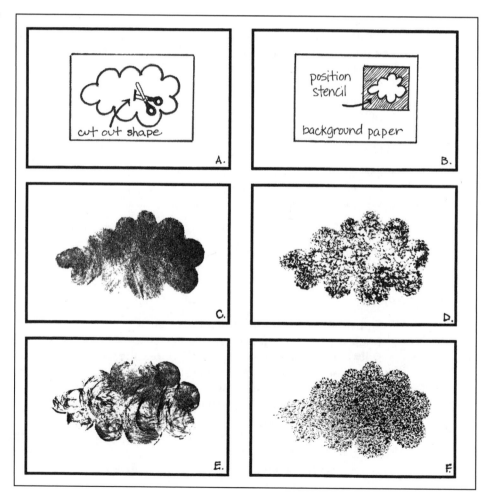

opaque paints (white or light yellow tempera or gouache) to stencil a pale moon on top of a darker background.

ART INVITATION #9

The Masked Moon: Using Masking Techniques to Create Shapes with Pastels

Masking techniques allow artists to create clean-edged, well-defined shapes. When you create a mask, you "hide" an area and prevent it from being covered with pastels or paints. Student artists can use the masking techniques described in this invitation to help them create images of the moon in its various phases. (See Color Plate 2 for a sample of this technique.)

Materials

- a piece of construction paper, cardstock, or acetate for the mask
- scissors or craft knife
- drawing or construction paper for the background
- newsprint
- soft pastels or chalks
- tissues
- acrylic paints and/or stamp pads (optional)

Process

1. Cover your work space with newsprint.
2. Decide if you will create your masks out of construction paper or acetate. Acetate works well if you plan to use paints or stamp pads.
3. Draw two circles of the same size (about 3" in diameter) on construction paper, cardstock, or acetate. Inside one of the circles, draw a crescent moon shape (Figure 4-8A).
4. Using scissors or a craft knife, cut out the shapes as shown in Figure 4-8B. The cutout circle is called mask A. The paper with the missing circle is called mask B. The paper with the crescent moon shape is called mask C.
5. Lay mask A (the full moon circle) in position on your construction paper (Figure 4-8C).
6. Using the pastel you have selected to depict the night sky, lay down a solid swatch of color on your scrap paper. Rub the side of the pastel, rather than the tip, against the paper. This will allow you to create a thick, soft layer of color. If your sky contains more than one color, use additional pastels and follow the same procedure (Figure 4-8D).
7. Crumple up a tissue and dab it in the pastel swatch of color. The tissue should pick up the chalk or pastel "dust."

FIGURE 4-8

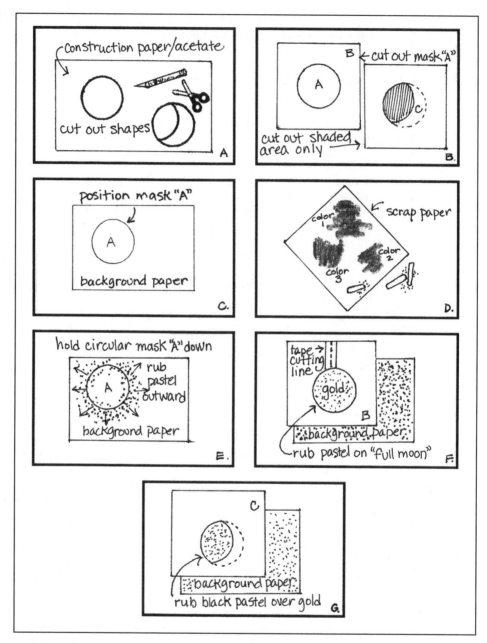

8. With one hand, hold the mask of the full moon firmly in place on your paper.
9. With your other hand, rub the pastel-covered tissue over the mask and onto
    the surrounding paper. Start rubbing in the center of the circular mask and

move outward in straight, even strokes as though you were creating sun rays (Figure 4-8E).

10. Repeat this procedure to create other colors in your sky. Use a clean tissue for each color.
11. Remove circular mask A. You will see a pastel-created night sky surrounding a blank, white "full moon" circle.
12. Take mask B and carefully place it around the blank, white "full moon" circle. (If you used scissors to cut the circle shape, tape the mask together along the cutting line.) Rub some gold or yellow chalk pastel onto a piece of scrap paper and pick up some of this pastel dust with a clean tissue. Using circular strokes, rub the gold or yellow color inside the blank, white "full moon" shape (Figure 4-8F).
13. Lift mask B and your full moon should now be yellow or gold. If you want to portray a full moon, stop at this point. If you want to create a crescent moon, continue.
14. Place crescent moon–shaped mask C over the gold moon (Figure 4-8G).
15. Rub some black or gray chalk pastel onto a piece of scrap paper and pick up some of this pastel dust with a clean tissue. Carefully rub a small amount of the black or gray color into the exposed area of the gold full moon.
16. Lift mask C, and you will have a gold crescent moon shining in the night sky. See Color Plate 2 for a sample of this invitation.

Alternate Idea

For a different look, consider using acrylics or stamp pad ink instead of pastels when applying the color. The acrylic paint or the stamp pad ink can be dabbed in with a small sponge.

ART INVITATION #10

Moonlit Silhouettes: Landscape Silhouettes Made from Handmade Stencils

As students illustrate their Moon Journals with pictures of the night sky, they often include a representation of the landscape and/or setting. Because the observations are usually made during or after sunset, the environmental surroundings are often depicted as being silhouetted against the heavens. The darkened shapes of a variety of natural and man-made settings are easy to make when students learn to create their own stencils. The process is very similar to that described in Art Invitation #9: *The Masked Moon.* See Color Plate 1 (the roofline) and Color Plate 2 (the houses below the moon) for samples of this technique.

FIGURE 4-9

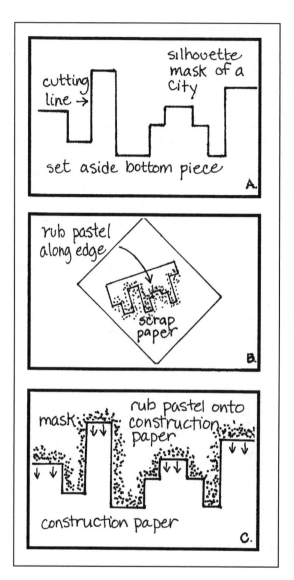

Materials

- scissors
- a piece of construction paper, cardstock, or acetate for the stencil
- construction paper for the background
- chalk pastels
- pencil
- ruler
- scrap paper

Process

1. Decide on what you will represent in your silhouette. A cityscape? A forest? Trees in your backyard? The roofline of your neighborhood? Mountains?
2. Draw the silhouette line on a piece of construction paper or cardstock. If you are drawing buildings, it might help to use a ruler.
3. Carefully cut the silhouette line with your scissors. Set aside the bottom piece. Only the top section will be used. This is called the "silhouette mask" (Figure 4-9A).
4. Place the silhouette mask on a large piece of scrap paper. With the side of a chalk pastel, rub heavy strokes of color along the edge of the silhouette mask (Figure 4-9B).
5. Take the pastel-covered silhouette mask off the scrap paper and place it on your construction paper. Note: In place of construction paper, you could use a graded wash, handpainted paper, or splattered paper for a background.
6. With a clean tissue, gently rub the pastel chalk off the silhouette mask and onto the background paper with downward strokes (Figure 4-9C).
7. Carefully lift the silhouette mask from the background paper. You should now see the silhouetted image against the sky. You may want to spray the pastel covered area of your paper with a fixative.

ART INVITATION #11

Handpainted Papers: Painting Designs and Textures

Handpainted papers are prepared by applying tempera or acrylic paints to papers using paintbrushes, toothbrushes, sponges, or other household items. Many well-known artists and illustrators use handpainted papers to create bright, highly textured artwork. You may want to share the work of Eric Carle, Leo Lionni, and Ezra Jack Keats with your students in preparation for this Art Invitation. Handpainted papers can be done individually or by a group of students working together to create "community" papers.

Community papers can be put into a classroom "treasure" box and used by everyone. These papers can be cut or torn and used as celestial bodies, landscape shapes, collage elements, or textured backgrounds. (See Color Plates 3 and 7 for ways in which handpainted papers can be used.) Don't forget to put all the left-over scraps back into the treasure box!

Materials

- white and colored tissue paper
- white and colored construction paper
- tempera or acrylic paints in various colors
- paintbrushes, toothbrushes, household sponges (can be cut into squares, triangles, and circles)
- other items for texture (such as widetooth combs, netting, small carpet squares, needlepoint canvas, bottle caps, and tree twigs, among others)
- scissors
- glue
- water for rinsing brushes
- butcher paper or painter's plastic dropcloth
- construction paper precut to a size slightly smaller than the page size of your Moon Journal

Process

1. Cover your work area with butcher paper or dropcloth.
2. Set out paperplate palettes of warm and cool colors.
3. Get a single sheet of tissue paper or construction paper to paint on.
4. Use the paintbrush or sponge attached to a clothespin holder to paint random lines, curves, or squiggles. Don't try to make it "look like" anything, just have fun experimenting with the paint.
5. Add a layer of texture by dabbing patterns with dry sponges.
6. Splatter paint with the toothbrush (dip brush into paint and use forefinger to pull back the bristles).
7. Use the other items you have gathered, such a combs and netting, to create various textures.
8. Let the textured paper dry.
9. Take a sheet of construction paper that is slightly smaller than the page size of your Moon Journal. Paint a night sky with large, sweeping strokes of blue or gray paint. Tip: If you are using two colors and you don't want them to blend together, wait until the first one is almost dry before applying the second. Alternate idea: Use an unpainted sheet of blue, gray, or black construction paper for the background "sky" paper.
10. Take your dry handpainted paper and cut out a variety of clouds, moon, stars, or landscape shapes.

11. Glue shapes onto your background sky paper.
12. Completed artwork will be added to your Moon Journal to accompany a written entry.

ART INVITATION #12

Painted Paper Landscapes: Depicting the Environment with Handpainted Papers

Students can create imaginary landscapes with handpainted papers. (See Art Invitation #11: *Handpainted Papers*.) Simple forms representing the moon, stars, trees, hills, fields, rocks, or flowers are cut or torn from the paper and assembled into a composition. (See Color Plate 3 for a sample of this technique; note the color, size, and spatial relationships of the landscape elements.) In these fanciful images, students abandon realism and give nature a new look with brightly colored textures, exaggerated proportions, and expressive shapes. Stars may be growing in a meadow, a flower might be the size of a house, and the moon may be spotted with purple.

Materials

- cardstock precut to fit into the Moon Journal
- handpainted papers
- scissors
- glue

Process

1. Draw a quick pencil sketch of the scene. (See Art Invitation: #1, *Pencil Sketching*.)
2. Select several pieces of handpainted paper. Think about color variation and textural design. Remember that you are creating an abstract piece of art. The colors you select do not have to match those found in the real scene.
3. Look carefully at the basic shapes in your pencil sketch. Decide if you will alter the proportions of the elements in your scene. Cut and/or tear these shapes out of the handpainted papers.
4. Lay all of the landscape elements on the cardstock. Experiment with different compositions: overlap shapes, vary the textures that are next to each other, alternate your *cut* edges with your *torn* edges, change spatial relationships, and/or combine different colors. Make several arrangements before gluing the pieces onto cardstock.
5. Landscapes can be embellished with oil pastel or paint. (See the moon and the hills in Color Plate 9 for a sample of oil pastel and watercolor resist papers.)

ART INVITATION #13

Tissue Paper Collage: Exploring Color and Texture with Tissue Paper

Tissue paper collage can be used in Moon Journals to create abstract landscapes and skyscapes. This approach to collage differs from other types of collage methods because the papers are transparent. We have found that this is a good introduction to the collage medium because it heightens our students' awareness of the colors, textures, and spatial relationships of the elements in their artwork.

We began this art project by asking our students to select a pencil sketch from their journals. Next, the children converted the objects in their sketches into simple shapes. For example, some students turned clouds into ovals, trees into a series of rectangles, and mountains into a pattern of "Ss." Others simply tore thick and thin paper strips.

Color choices were carefully made. The children tried to include a range of dark, medium, and light values. Overlapping and layering papers produced a richly colored, textured surface. Additional texture was created by using fingertips to wrinkle the wet tissues slightly after they were placed on the support. Finally, the dry collages were embellished with other media. (See Color Plate 8 for a sample of this technique.)

Materials

- support material (heavyweight, background paper)
- white, black, and colored tissue paper (solid or patterned)
- white glue
- small plastic container
- washi or Japanese rice papers (optional)
- watercolors, acrylic paints, oil pastels (optional)
- newspaper

Process

1. Cover your work area with newspaper.
2. Pour a few ounces of glue into the container and dilute with a little water. Blend well.
3. Stain some of your white tissue paper, washi or rice papers with watercolors and hang to dry (optional).
4. Tear or cut strips and shapes from different colored papers, including the painted papers. Consider making a few long strips that will extend the full width of your support paper. It is important to vary size and color.
5. Do several trial placements of elements. You may want to arrange the largest shapes first and then add the smaller ones. Final composition can be lightly traced so that you know where to glue papers.

6. Tissue papers can be adhered to the support paper in three ways:
   - glue is brushed onto the support and dry papers are placed onto the wet surface
   - glue is brushed onto the papers and wet papers are placed onto the dry surface
   - papers are dipped into the glue and placed onto the dry surface

Be careful that puddles of glue do not form on your support; remove excess glue with a brush.

8. Tissue papers can be embellished with oil pastels, acrylic paints, or watercolors when the collage has dried.

Alternate Idea

The support paper can be painted with a watercolor wash before applying the tissue papers.

ART INVITATION #14

Mixed-Media Collage: Collage Materials and Techniques

Artists approach collage in different ways. Some collages are unplanned and arranged with minimal organization; shapes are randomly attached to a paper or board. However, most collage artists use standard elements of design, color, texture, shape, value, form, line, and space during the building of the piece. Fortunately, collage materials are easily arranged and manipulated, so young artists can explore many possible compositions before making the final decision to glue their shapes down to the paper support.

The first step in collage work is to gather interesting raw materials. It's half the fun of this invitation. We asked our students to become pack rats for a week or so and fill their treasure troves (shoe boxes) with papers, found materials, items from nature, and other scraps. With the help of their parents, the children scavenged drawers, closets, garages, attics, backyards, and even wastebaskets in search of papers and materials. In class, we sorted, labeled, and arranged these items. Then the children used these materials in school and at home for nightly Moon Journal art entries. (See Color Plate 7.)

In many ways, collage is like poetry without words. Just as poets gather and weave together words and phrases, collagists collect and layer an array of materials. Collage is a process of personal discovery, filled with communication and expression.

Materials

- support material (heavyweight paper or posterboard)
- colorful papers, such as construction paper, origami paper, or handpainted papers (Art Invitation #11: *Handpainted Papers*)

- found papers, such as gift wrap, handmade papers, magazine pictures, photographs, packaging labels, handwritten text, canceled postage stamps, photocopies, computer images, postcards, paper bags, maps, newspapers, or metallic foils
- items from nature, such as feathers, grass, pressed flowers, or leaves (See Art Invitation #22: *Signs of the Season.*)
- fabric scraps, yarn or string, cotton
- glitter, sequins
- paint, oil pastels, markers, colored pencils, or crayons
- scissors
- plastic container
- white glue
- water
- stirring stick or spoon

Process

1. Cut support paper or board to size of journal.
2. Put a couple ounces of glue in the plastic container. Mix in water a little at a time until you get a "soupy" consistency.
3. Cut or tear different colored papers into a variety of shapes: big and small, free-form and geometric. Arrange shapes on your support paper. Consider overlapping or clustering some of the elements while allowing other shapes to stand alone. Note: If you are creating an abstract landscape, natural elements such as trees, mountains, and the moon can be reduced into simple shapes.
4. Next, add materials such as pressed leaves, fabric scraps, yarn, or printed text. (See Writing Invitation #22: *Random Collage Poem.*)
5. Arrange and rearrange elements until you are satisfied with the overall design. Think about creating contrasts through color, shape, texture, and value that will bring interest to the piece.
6. Glue the papers and other materials in place. (Glue can be applied with fingers or a brush.) Sometimes it's easier to adhere the larger shapes and materials down before attaching the smaller elements.
7. After the glue dries, collage can be enriched with numerous materials, including glitter, sequins, pencils, paint, oil pastels, markers, and/or crayons.

ART INVITATION #15

Crayon Resist: A Mixed-Media Technique Using Wax Crayons and Watercolor Paint

Crayons are a readily available art medium in most classrooms. They are simple to use at school and easily slipped into a backpack for home use. Most children are very comfortable with crayons and it is often their medium of choice. However, many young artists are unaware of a crayon's versatility. Through color blending, textural experimentation, and variation in pressure, children can produce a wide range of visually interesting images. When watercolor paints are applied over the finished drawing, the waxy crayon *resists* the water-based pigments, thereby adding another colorful dimension to the artwork.

We recommend that several layers of newspaper or newsprint be placed under the drawing paper. This soft underlayer will allow students to apply color with heavy pressure, thereby achieving maximum color intensity when desired.

Students should explore crayon application techniques early in the course of keeping Moon Journals. This type of experimentation gives them lots of choices for nightly illustrations. This invitation explores wax-resist technique, but simple crayon drawings of any type make beautiful journal entries.

Materials

- crayons
- heavy drawing paper or construction paper (white, beige, yellow)
- newspaper (or newsprint)
- pan or tube watercolor (Dark colors like black, blue, or purple create dramatic nighttime scenes.)
- water
- spray bottle or dropper
- paint brush

Preliminary Experimentation

Color Blending.   First, use the primary colors, red, yellow, and blue to experiment with color blending. Select two primary crayons—perhaps, yellow and red—and crayon in two patches of color side by side. Overlap the patches in the center. The two blended colors will produce a third optically mixed color. (See Figure 4-10A.) In this example, the red and yellow overlapped area will appear orange. How does the blended orange differ from an orange crayon? Do the same experiment again but this time vary the pressure as the crayon is applied. Compare the color intensity of a light pressure versus a heavy pressure. Now try these same experiments with other colors.

Creating Texture.   Interesting textures can be created by using the different surface areas of the crayon: sharpened tip, flat side, or rounded end. Capture other types of surface texture by crayoning lines, squiggles, dots, or cross-hatching within specific areas of the drawing. (See Figure 4-10B.) Try placing a textured surface, such as sandpaper, tile, or netting, under the paper before drawing.

Process

1. Precut paper to fit the journal.
2. Place several layers of newspaper or newsprint under the drawing paper.

FIGURE 4-10

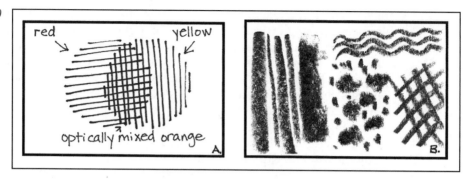

3. Sketch a preliminary line drawing in yellow chalk or light crayon. (We suggest that pencils not be used for initial designing. Fine pencil lines are hard to fill in with the thick tip of a crayon.)

4. Color the drawing using a heavy pressure. A bold approach to color and texture at this stage will ensure a visually interesting end product. Remember that crayons applied too lightly may be covered over when paint is applied.

5. Leave several areas of the picture uncolored. This will allow places for the paint to saturate the paper. For example, if drawing the night sky, you might choose to color in the stars and the moon and leave the rest of the sky untouched. If black watercolor is applied, the star and moon shapes will resist the paint but the rest of the sky will be black.

6. When crayon application is completed, paint the entire surface of the paper with watercolor. Note: If using pan watercolors, wet the paint with water from a spray bottle or dropper a few minutes before applying. This allows maximum color intensity.

7. Dry the pictures and glue them into the Moon Journals.

Alternate Idea

Oil pastels can be used in place of crayons. (See the moon and the mountains in Color Plate 9 for a sample of the resist technique.)

ART INVITATION #16

The Picture Window: Creating a Composition Within a Lift-up Window Frame

Moon Journalists often view the night sky through their windows. The moldings of a window create a frame for nature's composition, and students can create lift-up acetate windows to frame their paintings or drawings of the moon. This art experience offers children an opportunity to play with design elements and to make compositional choices within a given frame. Should the moon be positioned high or low in the night sky? Should it be placed to the right, left, or center of the frame? Will the addition of stars add interest and/or balance to the composition?

When creating this piece, it is best not to adhere any cutout shapes to the background paper until the design is viewed through the oversheet (the window) and the artist has made satisfying compositional decisions. See Color Plate 9 for a sample of this project.

Materials

- scissors
- ruler
- soft-lead pencil
- background paper for the night sky, cut to the size of a Moon Journal page
- a sheet of clear acetate (or overhead transparency film)
- cutouts of the moon and/or stars, clouds, rooftops, trees, hills, and so on
- a piece of black construction paper (1" longer than the background paper, but with the same width)

Additional Materials for Younger Children (See Process Step 5 Below)

Precut six strips of black construction paper for use when gluing together a window frame:
- three ¾"-wide strips (a little longer than the length of the background paper)
- three ¾"-wide strips (a little longer than the width of the background paper)

Process

1. Cut out a piece of paper that will be used for the background, or the night sky. Options include construction paper, painted paper, tissue-paper collage, bubble prints (Art Invitation #7: *Bubble Prints*), or handpainted papers (Art Invitation #11: *Handpainted Papers*).
2. Cut a piece of black construction paper that is one inch longer than the background paper. The width should be the same as the background paper (Figure 4-11A).
3. With a soft-lead pencil and a ruler, draw four panes of glass within a window frame on the black construction paper.
4. Carefully cut out the four rectangular frames. With the point of a pair of scissors, cut a small hole in the center of a pane. Cut to the edge of the pane and then cut out the entire opening. Repeat with the other panes (Figure 4-11B).
5. An option for younger students is to create the frame out of six precut strips of black paper. Arrange, cut, and glue the strips together to create the window frame on the background paper. Trim away the excess ends of the strips (Figure 4-11C).

6. The piece of clear acetate should be slightly larger than the entire paned area but smaller than the entire top cover sheet (the window). Tape the acetate to the back of the cut black construction paper or the paper strips, creating the "glass" in the window.

7. Lay the window on top of the background paper. Decide where the moon, stars, and other shaped cutouts should be placed. Play with compositional elements. Where will the focal point be? What shape will you make the moon? How many stars will you include? The teacher may want to create a large demonstration piece with assorted cutouts. Let the students play with moving the pieces around and covering the background with the window pane. After watching the teacher and other students design the demonstration piece, individual students can then work on their own through-the-window compositions.

8. When each artist has decided on the design, cutouts can be glued in place or shapes can be painted on the background paper.

9. Fold over the top of the "window" (it is 1" longer than the background paper) and glue it to the back of the background paper. The window can now be easily lifted or "opened" (Figure 4-11D).

10. Glue the entire piece (background sheet and lift-up window) into the Moon Journal.

FIGURE 4-11

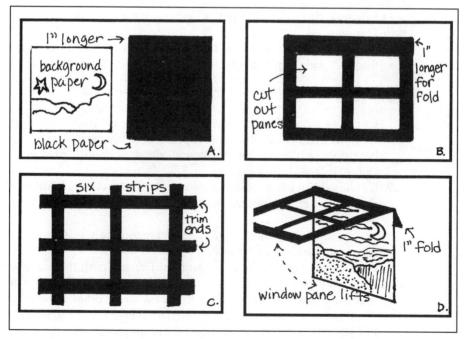

ART INVITATION #17

Oil Pastel Expressions: Oil Pastel Application Techniques

The rich, bold colors of oil pastels are well suited for depicting dramatic night scenes. Oil pastels are similar to wax crayons but usually have more pigment and flexibility. Because of their soft and pliant nature, they can provide thick layers of colors. Color blending and the textural techniques described in Art Invitation #15: *Crayon Resist* are also appropriate with oil pastels. We use two additional methods of oil pastel applications in our classes: textural rubbings, also called "frottage," and a color-scraping process known as "sgraffito." (These two techniques were used to produce the textured papers for the moon and the hillside landscape in Color Plate 9.)

Pastels and embellishments can be used throughout Moon Journals and are referred to in several Art Invitations. (See Art Invitations #13: *Tissue Paper Collage*; #14: *Mixed-Media Collage*; #15: *Crayon Resist*; and #18: *The Moon in Motion*.)

Materials

- oil pastels
- smooth, white paper
- colored construction paper
- scraping instrument, such as a metal nail file, wide screwdriver, or sharp twig
- watercolors
- newspaper

Frottage Process

1. Find several textured surfaces. Fabrics (such as burlap), walls, floor tiles, metal grids, wood, leaves, and tree bark are just a few possibilities.
2. Peel the wrappers off the oil pastels.
3. Place a piece of paper over a textured surface.
4. Gently rub the side of the pastel across the paper. (See Figure 4-12A for a sample tile rubbing.)
5. Now move the paper to another angle and rub again. Many patterns can be created by shifting paper positions. (See Figure 4-12B.)
6. To create a color overlay, select a different color and apply it to the same paper.
7. A different effect can be achieved by painting a watercolor wash over your rubbing. (See Art Invitation #15: *Crayon Resist* for an explanation of this technique.) All the areas of your paper that are not covered by pastel will absorb the paint.
8. The textural rubbing process can be used in several ways.
   - Use your rubbing as a background paper. Take a sharpened black pastel and make a simple line drawing over the textured markings.

- Tear or cut the rubbing for use as textured collage paper.
- Use it as part of a paper weaving. (See Art Invitation #25: *Paper Weaving*.)
- Create a landscape or skyscape by rubbing bands of colors across your paper. For example, rub one textured surface with green pastel to create a hillside, then move your paper to another surface and rub with blue pastel to depict the sky.

Sgraffito Process

1. Place several layers of newspaper over your work area and lay your paper on top.
2. Select one or more light-colored oil pastels. Using firm pressure, apply an even layer of colors over the entire paper surface. (Remember that you are not drawing a picture at this point. Simply lay down various color patches. Some artists like to plan their color locations; others rub random swatches.)
3. Now cover the light pastels completely with a layer of black pastel. When you are finished you should have an even black tone over the entire paper.
4. Using your scraping tool, carefully "draw" a picture by scratching away the black pastel. (You can make a preliminary sketch on the black overlayer with a sharp white pencil.) Make sure you do not tear your paper. As you remove the black pastel, you will reveal the underlayer of light pastels. (See Figure 4-12C.)
5. Think about ways to create line, texture, and pattern in your image. (See Figure 4-12D.) Sometimes it is easier to scrape a line drawing first and then add texture and pattern.

FIGURE 4-12

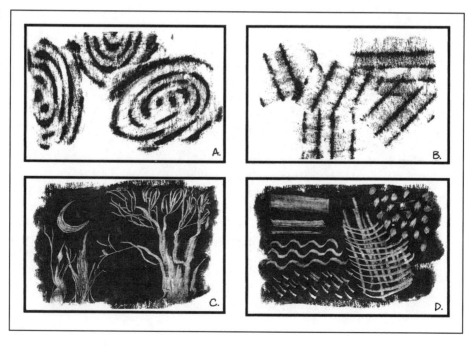

Alternate Idea

Cover light-colored construction paper with a layer of black pastel and scrape through to reveal the paper color.

ART INVITATION #18

The Moon in Motion: Van Gogh's *Starry Night:* Creating Movement in the Sky and Learning About Composition

As any Moon Journalist soon learns, the night sky is often filled with movement. Clouds float, mist swirls, and stars and constellations wind their way across the heavens. The moon itself rises in the east and sets in the west, gliding across the sky on its nightly journey. In his painting *Starry Night*, Vincent Van Gogh captured the movement of the sky in glorious colors. A wave of clouds, pinwheel stars, and a vibrant waning crescent moon are surrounded by circular lines of yellow, gold, and sea green. This invitation offers young artists an opportunity to examine composition and to create their own moon-in-motion masterpieces using crayons or pastels.

Materials

- a print or copy of Vincent Van Gogh's painting *Starry Night*
- oil pastels, chalk pastels, or crayons
- colored construction paper (We suggest black, gray, or navy blue.)

Process

1. Begin this lesson by showing the students a print of Van Gogh's *Starry Night*. (See Figure 4-13A for a sketch of this piece.) Look at it carefully for a few moments. Consider asking the following questions: How does this painting make you feel? Which part of the painting captures your eye first? What do you think is going on in the painting? What art medium do you think Van Gogh used? What is the setting of this painting? What colors do you see? Are they warm, cool, or both? What is in the foreground? The background? Where is the horizon line? What surprises you about this painting? What is special about this painting?
2. After giving the students a chance to make their own discoveries and form their own impressions, begin the guided lesson. Ask these questions: What do you think the focal point is? How does Van Gogh invite you to enter his painting? Many children point out the bright crescent moon in the right-hand corner, and other children point to the tall cypress trees. They notice that the eye is drawn to one image and then travels around the painting as it notices other colors and shapes.
3. Ask: Are either of these images (the moon and the tree) in the center of the painting? Would the painting be as interesting if they were? (Cover half of the

painting with construction paper.) How do you feel about the painting now? Is it as interesting? Why or why not? Discuss focal point, balance, and composition (the thoughtful placement of images in the painting).

4. Next, talk about how Van Gogh represented his images. Children often comment on the line strokes, the blended colors, and the highly textural quality of the piece. How do these lines produce a sense of movement?

5. Invite the children to look at the individual shapes in this painting and to practice sketching them on their scratch papers in Van Gogh's style. For example, have the children draw a star, a tree, a cloud, and a moon. They are not to put the composition together yet.

6. Next, have each child look carefully at the placement of the horizon line. Ask: Is the horizon line in the middle of the page? About three-fourths of the way down the page? Is it drawn straight across the page? How would you draw this first line? Have one of the children come up to the board and sketch a horizon line, and then ask the other children to sketch in a horizon line across their piece of scratch paper.

7. Next, ask the students to block in the basic compositional elements of the piece on their scratch paper. Most children sketch in the cypress tree, the swirling clouds, the crescent moon, and the stars. Remind them to look carefully at the hills in Van Gogh's painting, noticing how they overlap and give the painting depth and dimension. Add hills to the scratch paper compositions (Figure 4-13B).

8. Now the children are ready to begin their color versions of *Starry Night*. Media options include crayons, chalk, and oil pastels. Students may experiment with these materials until they decide on the medium that will produce the effect they desire.

9. Offer the students black, navy blue, brown, purple, or gray construction paper as possible choices for the background. After the children select their papers, they can depict the horizon line with their crayons or pastels and then begin to add the other compositional elements. Some students make thick, bold lines and others use delicate, thin strokes to portray the movement in the sky. Encourage a variety of approaches.

FIGURE 4-13

10. The students continue to create their pictures by sketching in the crescent moon, the swirling clouds, the centers of the stars, the cypress tree, and the village (Figure 4-13A).
11. Colors are gradually added and layered, producing richly blended effects. Encourage the students to use lines and strokes to fill in their shapes. As they work, the children make decisions on how to achieve the right colors for the cypress tree, the clouds, and the hills.
12. Display the completed pictures to create a *Starry Night* gallery. Point out various approaches and discuss how different children produced interesting effects. Students might enjoy writing poems to accompany their artwork. (See Writing Invitation #7: *Similes by Starlight* or Writing Invitation #11: *Colors of the Night*.)

Alternate Idea

If the students use crayons or oil pastels on white paper, they can go over the finished drawings with black watercolor or diluted black tempera paints to create the night sky background. (See Art Invitation #15: *Crayon Resist* for complete directions for this process.)

ART INVITATION #19

Mail Art: Designing Envelopes and Postcards

Mail Art adds handmade envelopes and picture postcards to the Moon Journals. Letters to and from the moon, and postcards with messages and stamps provide memories of the students' lunar travels. (This is introduced in conjunction with Writing Invitation #17: *Moon Mail.*)

Materials

- pencil
- scissors
- colored paper (Light colors work best.)
- white cardstock
- glue
- an envelope (smaller than the size of a Moon Journal page)
- a "real" postcard
- one or more of the following: felt-tip markers, black pen, colored pencils, crayons, stickers, rubber stamps, and stamp pad

Process for Envelope Art

1. Carefully open the glued seams of an envelope and unfold it. This shape will be the template for your handmade envelope. (See Figure 4-14A.)
2. Take the template and trace the envelope shape onto colored paper. Cut along this line.

3. Fold the paper cutout into an envelope using the original envelope as a model.
4. Glue the seams together. Do not to let glue seep into the envelope's pocket.
5. Decorate the back or "flap" side of the envelope using black pen, felt-tip markers, colored pencils, crayons, stickers, and/or rubber stamps.
6. Glue the "front" side of the envelope to a journal page. (See 4-14B.) Put moon mail inside it.

Alternate Idea

Envelopes can be made from wrapping paper, handpainted paper, photocopied moon pictures, or many other materials.

Process for Postcard Art

1. Cut cardstock to the size of a postcard, approximately 4" × 6".
2. Using a "real" postcard as a model, draw in the design elements found on the back of the blank card: the center dividing line, the address lines, the stamp box, and so forth.
3. Design a stamp on a separate sheet of paper using felt-tip markers or colored pencils. Cut out the stamp and glue it into the postcard's stamp box. Cancellation marks can be drawn over the stamp with the black pen. (See Color Plate 1.)
4. Write a message and the complete address section.
5. Glue the postcard into the journal.

FIGURE 4-14

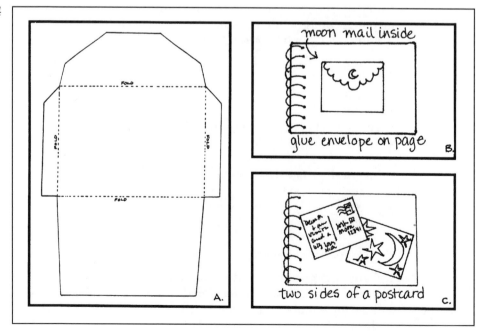

Alternate Idea

Give each student two 4" × 6" pieces of cardstock. These pieces represent the front and back of a single postcard. A picture is drawn on the "front" piece. The "back" piece can be filled in as described above. Glue both "sides" of the postcard onto one journal page. (See Figure 4-14C.)

ART INVITATION #20

Matisse Cutouts: Making Collages from Cutouts and Silhouettes

In Henri Matisse's *Icare*, the black silhouette of a human form is contrasted against a background of deep blue. Bright yellow starlike shapes surround the figure and a single spot of red catches the eye and the mind. The children wonder if the figure is dancing or suffering. Although the images in this piece are strikingly simple, they create a strong impression on the viewer.

In their Moon Journals children create colored pictures of the moon in the night sky. At first many students are surprised to discover that the sky isn't always black; in fact, it is often indigo blue. Dark-colored rooftops and trees are contrasted against the colored sky. In this invitation, students create their own collages using Matisse's colors: a deep blue background, a black silhouette, yellow cutouts, and a spot of red. The artist plays with design elements and makes compositional decisions. What will be in the foreground? The background? Will there be symmetry or purposeful asymmetry? Using elements found in Matisse's work, student-artists experiment with the possibilities of creating collages of the moon in the night sky. (See Figure 4-15D.)

Materials

- a print of Matisse's *Icare*
- a teacher-created construction paper version of *Icare* (Do not glue the figure or stars to the background paper.)
- black, deep blue, yellow, and red construction paper
- glue
- scissors
- pencil

Process

Note: Before beginning this lesson, the teacher should prepare a construction paper version of *Icare*. You will need a dark blue background and cutouts of the black figure, the yellow stars, and the red dot. Do not glue these design elements in place. (See Figure 4-15A for a sketch of *Icare*.)

FIGURE 4-15

1. Show students a print of Henri Matisse's *Icare*, and ask several open-ended questions: What colors do you notice? What do you think is the focal point? What do you think is going on in this piece? What about the figure? How do you think it feels? What do you think the yellow shapes are? The red spot? Does this piece have a message? What might it be?

2. Place the cutout of the black figure on the blue background paper in the same position as it is seen in *Icare*. Ask the students to compare your composition to Matisse's work. One by one, add the yellow star cutouts and ask the children to notice what happens when this color is contrasted against the blue and black. Discuss how the colors seem to "pop out," adding contrast, excitement, and dimension.

3. Invite the children to cut out different figures and shapes from black construction paper. Options include the silhouettes of houses, trees, tall buildings, cars, animals, and human figures. (See Figure 4-15B for samples.) In addition, they should cut moon and star shapes from yellow construction paper, and a single red design element.

4. Arrange the cutout pieces on navy blue background paper. (See Figure 4-15C for a sample.) While looking at this figure, imagine that the background paper is blue, the silhouetted buildings are black, and the moon, stars, and windows are yellow. One of the windows is red. This is just one possible approach. Each student will design a unique composition using the shapes he or she has created.

5. In small groups the students respond to the designs and experiment with moving their shapes around on the background paper. The discussions within the groups focus on balance, design, contrast, color, and effect. The students enjoy hearing the impressions and comments of their friends, but they know the final compositional decisions will be up to them.

6. When the children are satisfied with their designs, have them glue the collage pieces in place. An instant exhibition is created on the desktops.

ART INVITATION #21

Handmade Stamps: Printmaking with Common Materials

Handmade stamps can produce one simple image like the crescent moon, or they can be used to create an entire landscape. This important and flexible medium lends itself to experimentation with color, shape, pattern, and texture. It also provides an opportunity for students to investigate and practice basic design principles.

A handprint is an example of a stamping process that we are all familiar with. Like hands, many articles can be made into stamps without changing them at all: leaves, flowers, pencil erasers, cookie cutters, and crunched paper. Other stamps can be created by cutting or carving common materials, including vegetables, sponges, and styrofoam. (See Figure 4-16.) In all instances, the stamp's surface image is transferred to paper using paint or ink and simple printmaking techniques.

We used stamps in our Moon Journals in a number of ways. For example, a series of cutout eraser stamps, sponge stamps, or potato prints depicted the moon's phases. These images were stamped into the students' journals day by day to

FIGURE 4-16

mark the passage of the moon's cycle. The children also used stamps on page borders, collage, handpainted papers, envelopes, and postcards.

Materials for All Stamp Projects

- paints (acrylic or tempera)
- plastic or foam meat tray
- printing inks (optional)
- stamp pads (optional)
- flat paint brushes
- brayer or small roller (optional)
- water container
- heavy paper
- paper towels
- newspaper or drop cloths

Materials for Vegetable Prints

- vegetables with interesting shapes, such as celery, carrots, broccoli, cauliflower, mushrooms, and string beans
- kitchen knife
- craft knife

Preparation. Cut each vegetable lengthwise or widthwise with a kitchen knife. Potatoes are especially versatile. Slice them in half for ovals and circles, or use a craft knife to carve shapes into their surface. Dab the surface of the vegetable on a paper towel to absorb excess moisture before applying ink or paint.

Materials for Sponge Prints

- household sponges and/or compressed sponges (available in sheets through art or school supply companies and at many craft stores)
- scissors

Preparation. Cut sponges into various shapes, such as moon, cloud, and stars. Note: Compressed sponges come in flat sheets and will expand into form when moistened with water.

Materials for Styrofoam Prints

- styrofoam pieces at least 1" thick
- craft knife
- pencil

Preparation. Draw a shape on a styrofoam block. The pencil line will serve as a guide for cutting. Using the craft knife, cut into the block about ½" all the way around the shape. Cut away the negative shape (the excess styrofoam that surrounds the shape you plan to use for the print).

Materials for Cardboard Cutout Prints

- thick cardboard and/or corrugated board
- craft knife or scissors
- pencil

Preparation. Draw a shape on cardboard. If you are using a craft knife, you can cut the design out of the center of the cardboard and create a positive and negative image. Stripping the paper backing off of one side of the corrugated board creates a textured stamp.

Materials for Eraser Stamps

- plastic erasers
- craft knife
- ballpoint pen

Preparation. Draw a simple shape on the wide surface of an eraser with a ball point pen. Cut away the negative shape with the craft knife. (This should be done by older students or adults.) Note: The round tips of pencil erasers or rectangular ends of plastic erasers make fun designs too.

Materials for Rubber Stamps

- thin sheet of rubber, approximately ¹⁄₁₆" to ¼" thick (Rubber printing blocks are available through many art and school supply companies. Often this material is adhesive-backed and simply requires cutting, peeling, and sticking.)
- wooden blocks about 1" thick or heavy cardboard
- wood glue
- hard rubber brayer (optional)
- Speedball linoleum cutter (optional)
- waterbase block printing ink (optional)
- scissors or craft knife

Preparation.   Draw one or more shapes on the rubber sheet. Cut out with scissors or the craft knife. Arrange shapes on wooden blocks or cardboard, and mount with adhesive backing or wood glue. (Several shapes can be mounted on one block for more complex designs.)

Alternate Idea

Older students can use linoleum cutters to carve fine lines, details, and textures within the shapes. Use the brayer to apply ink or paint to the surface of the rubber stamp.

Process for All Stamp Projects

1. Cover all work areas with newspaper or drop cloths.
2. Fold several paper towels together and place them in a plastic or foam meat tray.
3. Pour paint onto the paper towel pad.
4. Spread the paint into the paper pad with a brush or brayer. Your pad should be moist and saturated but not runny.
5. Dab your stamp on the pad. Cover the stamp's surface with an even layer of paint.
6. Press the stamp firmly onto a sheet of paper.
7. Carefully lift the stamp off the page.
8. Experiment with different colors, random or linear patterns, and overlapping images. Stamping on colored papers is another option.

Alternate Idea

Apply paint or ink to stamps with brush, brayer, or commercial stamping pad.

ART INVITATION #22

Signs of the Season: Creating Nature's Collages with Pressed Leaves, Flowers, and Prints

Keeping a Moon Journal is an invitation to interact with nature. The journalist notices more than the moon and often records the signs of the various seasons. Leaves and flowers are primary players in any nature journal. A traditional method of preserving nature's flora is to use pressing techniques. After about a week of pressing, the colors and delicate textures of leaves, flowers, and grasses are captured and frozen in time. The artist can use the pressed materials to create nature collages in a journal or to embellish written entries. In addition, the actual fresh leaves can be used to create leaf prints and splatter designs. For examples of these techniques, see Color Plate 4.

Pressing Flowers and Leaves

Materials

- leaves and flowers
- old telephone book
- white paper towels
- heavy books or objects to place on top of the phone book
- background paper for collage
- glue

Process

1. Collect leaves and/or flowers for pressing.
2. Open a telephone book to a page that is near the center of the book. Place a white piece of paper towel on top of the page. Carefully arrange a few leaves and flowers on top of the paper towel. Avoid overlapping specimens.
3. Cover the leaves and flowers with another piece of paper towel. Carefully close the telephone book.
4. Place a few heavy books or objects on top of the telephone book. Do not disturb the book for five to seven days.
5. Remove the books or weighted object(s) and carefully open the telephone book. Gently remove the top paper towel. The leaves and flowers are pressed and ready to use for collage.
6. Carefully apply glue to the back of the pressed flower or leaf. (You may want to use an old paint brush to apply the glue.) Use the glue sparingly. Lightly press the object in place onto the background paper.

Note: Many craft books recommend the use of a flower press and acid-free paper for pressing. Although these materials produce excellent results, we have found that an old telephone book and paper towels work effectively for classroom use and are inexpensive and readily available.

Leaf Prints

Materials

- fresh or pressed leaves (Look for strong leaves that will produce interesting shapes and textures.)
- tempera or acrylic paints
- waterbased printing inks (optional)
- brayer
- newsprint
- construction paper
- foam or plastic meat trays
- paper towels

Process

1. To apply paint to the leaf and create the print, brush paint or waterbased printing ink onto the leaf using a brush (Figure 4-17A) or a brayer (Figure 4-17B). Paint the side that reveals the most veins.
2. Place the leaf, paint-side down, on a piece of construction paper.
3. Press the leaf gently with your fingers. (See Figure 4-17C for a sample of leaf print created by finger pressing.)
4. Option: Cover the painted leaf with a sheet of newsprint. Roll over the leaf with a clean brayer. (See Figure 4-17D for a sample of a leaf print created with a brayer.)
5. Carefully lift the leaf off the construction paper. Make more prints using different colors and shapes, if you choose. When the prints have dried, the paper is ready to be cut to size and glued into the Moon Journal.

Splattered Leaves

Materials

- leaves
- watercolor, tempera, or acrylic paints
- old toothbrush
- newsprint or scrap paper
- construction paper
- container of water
- newspaper

Process

1. Spread newspaper on a table. Cover a large area for this fun but messy project!
2. Mix watercolor, tempera, or acrylic paint with water. The paint solution should be runny.

3. Lay a sheet of construction paper (white or colored) on the newspaper. Arrange the leaves on top of the construction paper.
4. Dip the toothbrush into the paint solution. Hold it over a piece of scrap paper. Using your forefinger, quickly flick the bristles of the toothbrush. The paint will splatter onto paper (Figure 4-17E). Try to avoid creating large splotches of paint. (This can happen if the paint is too thick or too runny.)
5. Splatter the paint over and around the leaves that you arranged on the construction paper. Change colors if you choose.
6. Keep the leaves and paper in place until the paint has dried. Then remove the leaves and see the leaf shapes created by the splattered paint (Figure 4-17F). The paper is now ready to be cut to size and glued into the Moon Journal.

FIGURE 4-17

Color Lifting Using Leaf Stencils

Materials

- leaf stencil (See Art Invitation #8: *Simple Stenciled Shapes* for instructions on stencil making.)
- watercolor paper
- watercolor paints and brush
- tissues or a natural sponge (Elephant ear sponges work well.)

Process

1. Drop watercolor paint onto wet watercolor paper. (See Art Invitation #4: *Swirling Watercolor Sky.*)
2. When the watercolor paper is nearly dry, place a leaf stencil on top of it.
3. Using a slightly damp tissue or a natural sponge (such as an elephant ear sponge), gently rub out or "lift out" the watercolor pigment you dropped onto your paper. There will still be color within the stencil shape, but it will be lighter than the background.
4. When you remove the stencil, the outline of the leaf should be apparent. Option: Embellish the design with torn Japanese rice paper, tissue paper, pastels, or paints. See Color Plate 4 for a sample of this technique.

ART INVITATION #23

The Moon of the Birch Trees: Creating Birch Trees Using a Variety of Watercolor Techniques

The rising moon glimpsed through the delicate limbs of birch trees has been celebrated by poets and painters. This invitation allows the artist to use many of the techniques described in this book, including masking, creating a graded wash, toothbrush splattering, and stamping. It introduces the young artist to a new technique of using a cut-up credit card to create textured bark on the birch trees. Artist Michelle Safer designed and simplified the procedures of this invitation for students. See Color Plate 11 for a completed sample of this art invitation.

Materials

- watercolor paper, taped to a board
- masking tape
- flat watercolor brush
- old toothbrush
- old credit card cut in half

- watercolors
- mixing tray or palette
- container of water
- masking fluid (optional)
- handcarved stamp of the moon or stencil of the moon (optional)

Process

1. Tape a piece of watercolor paper to a board (Figure 4-18A).
2. Tear masking tape to form the trunks of the birch trees and adhere them to the paper. Consider varying the groupings. Some can be straight, others slightly curved. Add a few smaller and thinner pieces of tape (coming out of the larger trunks) to create additional limbs. Leave space at the top of the page or between the trees for the rising moon (Figure 4-18B). Option: Older students may want to apply a light toothbrush splatter of masking fluid around the masking tape birch trunks. (See Art Invitation #5: *Splattered Stars* for the basic procedures of this technique.) Allow the masking fluid to dry completely.
3. Brush clear water across the watercolor paper and the masked trees.
4. Dip a watercolor brush into the color(s) you select to represent the evening sky and paint a graded wash across the top two-thirds of the page. (See Art Invitation #3: *Watercolor Wash Backgrounds*.) Allow the wash to dry completely.
5. Mix a palette of colors in the mixing tray that you will use for the background foliage (birch leaves). Which season of the year do you want to represent? Choose red, orange, gold, brown, or even mauve for fall; yellow and green for spring; deeper green for summer, and so on. Be sure to choose colors of different values and intensities; this will create dimension, depth, and contrast in your painting.
6. Dip the toothbrush into the watercolor pigment. Since you will be splattering over the color of the night sky, be sure your pigment is strong and vivid. Brush your forefinger over the bristles and lightly splatter the paint around the masked birch trunks (Figure 4-18C). (See Art Invitation #5: *Splattered Stars*.)
7. Mix some colors for the foreground of your painting and lightly splatter them onto the piece of watercolor paper. Try to use a gentle touch for this splattering; the foreground should not dominate the painting. Option: After you have splattered the colors with the toothbrush, lightly mist the paper with a *fine* clear water spray. This will blend and diffuse the colors. Allow the paint and water to dry completely.
8. Carefully peel off the masking tape. The white trunks of the birch trees will be revealed.
9. Pick up the credit card that has been cut in half. Dip the straight edge into brownish-black watercolors. Starting at the outer edge of the birch trunk, carefully drag the credit card across the white space (Figure 4-18D). Irregular lines will add texture and create the impression of birch bark.

FIGURE 4-18

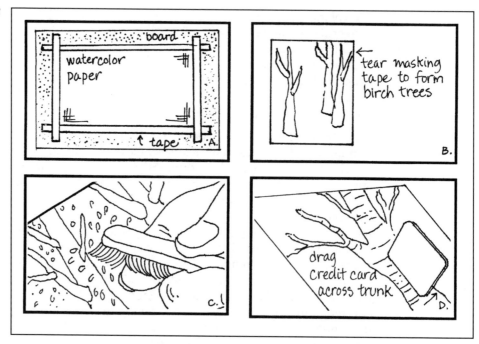

10. Using the toothbrush, *lightly* splatter some additional color over the trunks in just a few places to soften the edges.

11. Decide on the placement of the moon. Using a stencil (Art Invitation #8: *Simple Stenciled Shapes*) or a rubber stamp (Art Invitation #21: *Handmade Stamps*), add a moon to your painting. Opaque stamping ink (white or parchment yellow) or paint can be used to create a moon that will stand out against the sky.

12. When your painting is dry, mat it on a piece of construction paper. Choose a color that picks up one of the colors in your painting.

Note: This Art Invitation coordinates well with Writing Invitation #21: *A Calendar of Moons.*

ART INVITATION #24

Monoprints of the Moon: Printing Painted Designs onto Paper

A monoprint (literally, "one print") is a one-of-a-kind original. This type of print sometimes has a soft, slightly blurred texture that offers the artist an interesting choice for creating a specific feel and/or look. The basic shapes of the moon and stars and the silhouettes of hills, trees, and buildings work well in the classroom when creating simple monoprints with inexpensive materials. See Color Plate 10 for a sample of this invitation.

Materials

- a smooth linoleum square, a cookie sheet with sides, or a piece of Plexiglas
- paper
- thick tempera or acrylic paints
- waterbased printing inks (optional)
- paintbrush
- soft brayer
- hard brayer (or the back of your hand)
- cardstock or construction paper
- scissors

Process

1. Paint a picture on the linoleum, cookie sheet, or Plexiglas (Figure 4-19A). Make sure the paint is not too thick. Remember, any unpainted area will appear white on the paper.
2. Lay a sheet of construction paper on top of the painting. Gently press down over the surface of the paper with a brayer, your fingers, or the back of your hand, being careful not to smudge the paint underneath.
3. Gently peel the paper off the painted surface, and examine your print!

Monoprint Options

1. Although a true monoprint is one of a kind, artists sometimes make "ghost" prints of the original painting if enough paint is left on the surface. Simply repeat the process described above in steps two and three. The "ghost" print will be paler and more subdued.
2. To "paint" the background without using a brush, roll a soft brayer in waterbased printing ink or paints. Test the consistency of the ink or paint on a piece of scrap paper. Roll the brayer loaded with ink or paint across the cookie sheet or Plexiglas (Figure 4-19B). This will produce an evenly colored background. Using a 1" soft brayer loaded with paint, you can produce interesting effects: rainbow arches in various colors, stripes, mountain peaks, and so on.
3. To create distinct shapes (such as the moon and stars) in your print, draw the designs on cardstock or construction paper and cut them out. Position the cutouts on top of the painted background (Figure 4-19C). Place the clean print paper on top of the painted surface, gently rub the paper with your hand or a hard brayer, and lift the page. Distinct white shapes will be evident wherever the cutouts are placed (Figure 4-19D). When the print has dried, you may choose to add tint to the white spaces with soft pastels, colored pencils, or other media.

FIGURE 4-19

4. When working with young children, consider the following simplified process:
   a. Pour tempera paint into a container and add flour (a mixture of three parts paint and one part flour).
   b. Turn over a large cookie sheet or plastic tray. Spread the paint over the surface of the tray with a piece of cardboard.
   c. Use a finger to "draw" thick lines and create a picture of the moon (Figure 4-19E). If thin lines are desired, use a pencil or ballpoint pen.
   d. Lay a piece of paper over the paint and smooth it out with the back of your hands. Take hold of the top corners of the paper and lift it off. Enjoy your print!

ART INVITATION #25

Paper Weaving: Weaving Techniques Using Paper Strips of Text and Image

In this Art Invitation, paper strips with words and images are woven together to form one piece of art. In the process, the text and picture are no longer seen as separate entities but rather as an interwoven whole.

Many artists and writers have combined visual images with the written word in their artwork. Examples of this can be seen in museum collections, art books, diaries, and journals. To illustrate this we shared selections from the following books with our classes: *The Amazing Paper Cuttings of Hans Christian Anderson* (1994) by Beth Wagner Brust and *The Writer's Drawing Book* (1995) edited by Kate Pullinger and Julian Rothenstein.

Materials

- 2 pieces of paper cut into 2½" × 5" sections
- art materials of choice: pastels, watercolor, felt-tip markers, crayons, or other media
- 1 sheet of scrap paper
- scissors
- ruler
- fine-tip pen
- pencil
- masking tape
- glue stick

Process

1. Using the ruler and pencil, draw four parallel lines, ½" apart, along the 5" length of both papers. This will divide each paper into five long, narrow segments.
2. Select a poem that you have written. Using a fine-tip pen, write the words of the poem between the pencil lines on one piece of your paper. It's not important that the poem be written in poetry format; just try to fill the paper completely with text. (See Figure 4-20A.)The words are being used as a visual image in this art piece, not as a poem that is meant to be read.
3. Take the second sheet of lined paper and place it on your work area. Position the lines vertically. Now flip the paper over and draw or paint an illustration of your poem. (Make sure the lines on the back remain in the vertical position.) Try to fill the entire page with color and images. (See Figure 4-20B.)
4. Cut each paper into five strips using your pencil lines as guides. Stack the paper strips in order as you cut. Keep the poem strips separate from the illustration strips.

5. Tear off two 3" pieces and one 7" piece of masking tape. Place the long piece of tape on your work area, sticky side up. Tape down the ends with the two smaller pieces.

6. Tack the top ends of the illustration strips to the tape, leaving a little space between them. (See Figure 4-20C.) You will see your picture forming again. Be sure the strips are in order.

7. Beginning with the first line of your poem and continuing in line order, loosely weave the poetry strips over and under the illustration strips. (See Figure 4-20D.)

8. Tear off another 5" piece of masking tape and run it along the bottom edge of the illustration strips to hold the completed weaving in place.

9. Remove the 3" strips of masking tape. Carefully flip the weaving over and place it on the scrap paper.

10. Apply glue to the back of the strips.

11. Press a blank Moon Journal page onto the sticky surface.

12. Carefully remove the masking tape from the weaving. Glue down any loose ends. (See Color Plate 6 for a sample of this invitation.)

Alternate Ideas

- Paint the poetry paper with pale watercolors before writing the text.
- Cut strips in varying widths.

FIGURE 4-20

- Tear strips to create irregular edges.
- Weave an asymmetrical pattern with your paper strips.
- Write the complete poem in your Moon Journal under or around the weaving.

ART INVITATION #26

Decorative Borders: Ideas for Framing and Embellishing Moon Journal Entries

Drawing a decorative border around a written journal entry is a colorful way to frame the piece. Ideas for border designs are everywhere: greeting cards, stationery, sales catalogs, magazines, art books, and picture books. Our classes collected samples from these materials in advance to use as ideas.

Borders, simple or elaborate, can be composed of pure line work or can include small drawings, stickers, or stamped images. (See Art Invitation #21: *Handmade Stamps.*) Some decorative borders are enhanced with the words of a poem, a sentence from an observation, or a portion of a rebus. (See Writing Invitation #14: *Draw Me A Story: A Moon Rebus.*)

Materials

- black fine-tip pen
- felt-tipped markers
- colored pencils
- rubber stamps
- small stickers
- ruler

Process

1. Experiment with different lines: thick and thin, straight and wavy, continuous and broken. Do this with each of your drawing materials. Different pens and pencils produce a range of marks. For example, a broad felt-tipped marker can be pulled on its edge to create a thin line or on its wide surface to create a thick stroke. (See Figure 4-21A.)
2. Borders can be drawn freehand or with a ruler. If you choose to use a ruler, take a sharp pencil and draw a faint line around the area you wish to frame. Use this line as a guide to draw in the border design.
3. Sometimes it's helpful to complete the line design first, leaving spaces for images, and then to go back and draw, stamp, or glue in the pictures.
4. Pictures can be drawn anywhere: the four corners, the top and bottom horizontal positions, the right and left vertical positions, or randomly around the border. (See Figure 4-21B for samples of several borders.)

FIGURE 4-21

5. Instead of lines, your frame might be composed of a string of stars, a vine of
   leaves, a trail of paw prints, or wisps of clouds. (See Figure 4-21C.)

ART INVITATION #27

Ornamental Stitching: Producing Texture and Pattern Using String and Decorative Threads

Simple stitched shapes can become part of any mixed-media art piece. Ornamental stitching, with its decorative threads, strings, and yarn, is a way for students to add texture, pattern, and visual interest to their Moon Journals. Linear shapes such as stars are the simplest patterns for stitching, but curved images like the moon and clouds can be stitched as well.

There are many ways to embellish artwork with stitched images: Gold star patterns can be sewn into watercolor skies, a full moon made with yarn can add a three-dimensional image to a collage, or a vine of green threads can produce a decorative border around a written journal entry. With a little planning, entire pictures can be made using this technique. (See the spider and web in Figure 4-23.)

Materials

- string, yarn, embroidery floss, or metallic threads
- needle, sized to fit selected thread (for older students)
- masking tape
- scissors and craft knife
- pencil and ruler
- art materials of choice for decorating cardstock
- cardstock precut to a size slightly smaller than the size of your Moon Journal

Process

The following steps describe how to stitch star patterns, but the same instructions can be adapted for other shapes.

1. Decorate cardstock with paints, pencils, paper, or collage. This will be used as your background.
2. Decide where the stars are going to be sewn.
3. Use a ruler and pencil to draw star patterns. (See Figure 4-22A.)
4. For younger students, prepunch both ends of each line segment with a paper punch or craft knife. (See Figure 4-22B.) Older students will be able to pierce these holes themselves with their needles.

FIGURE 4-22

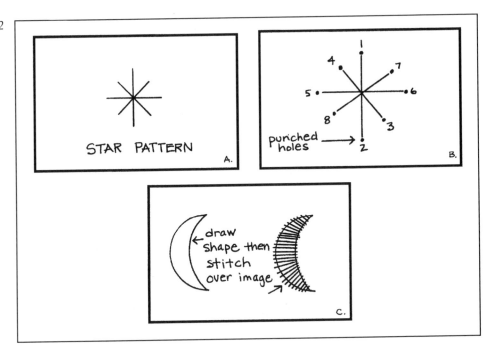

5. Thread needles with floss or thread. The size and quantity of stars will determine the length. Teachers can wrap masking tape around the end of the yarn
   for younger students so the yarn itself can be used like a needle.
6. The first stitch starts at the end of the line segment marked as hole 1 in the star
   pattern. (See Figure 4-22B.) Beginning on the underside of the cardstock, carefully push the needle up through the surface (or the yarn through the pre-
   punched hole). Leave a tail of thread and tape it to the underside of the
   cardstock.
7. Next, push the needle through the end of the line segment marked as hole 2.
   Stitch the remainder of the star in the order indicated. As you are stitching
   make sure that the needle holes are not too close together or the paper will tear.
   Thread tension should not bow the paper.
8. Trim and tape the end of the thread or yarn when finished.
9. Other patterns and shapes can be designed and sewn in the same way. (See Figure 4-22C.)

FIGURE 4-23

Alternate Idea

The spider web in Figure 4-23 was drawn first and then stitched using gold metallic thread. A series of side-by-side stitches was used to form the spider's body. The moon, a crescent-shaped piece of metal, was sewn on last.

ART INVITATION #28

Putting It All Together: Moon Journal Binding Techniques

A blank book holds the promise of exciting things to come, so we begin our Moon Journal project by inviting our students to explore bookmaking techniques. We found that the children benefit from being a part of this process from the beginning. The Moon Journals are special before the first word or image adorns a single page because our young artists and writers have created these books themselves.

There are many ways to make a Moon Journal. The simplest method is to purchase a spiral notebook, composition book, spiral-bound sketchpad, or blank journal. Your students can design a new cover and adhere it to the existing one. Other pages, such as the preface page, can be decorated and attached. (Paper quality is not an important consideration since many of the art entries will be done on heavyweight paper and glued into the book.)

If you choose not to purchase a premade journal, you have many handmade book options. Books such as *Cover to Cover: Creative Techniques for Making Beautiful Books, Journals, and Albums* (1995) by Shereen LaPlantz and *Step-by-Step: Making Books* (1994) by Charlotte Stowell can give you several ideas for format variations. This invitation explains three binding techniques: comb binding, ring binding, and Japanese stab binding. (Figure 4-24 shows a photograph of these bindings.)

Comb Binding Technique

Note: This binding method requires a plastic-binding machine. If your school does not own this piece of equipment, many copying and printing stores have them available.

Materials (per Journal)

- 2 sheets of cardstock or medium-weight art paper for front and back covers
- at least 35 sheets of paper, such as photocopier or typing paper
- plastic-binding comb—½" diameter (available at office supply stores)

Process

1. Precut text papers to 7" × 8½" or other desired size. Coverstock should overhang papers by ⅛" on three sides. (Papers should be flush with the spine.)

FIGURE 4-24

2. Covers can be decorated and laminated before binding.
3. Photocopy and precut any material you want to add to your students' journals.
4. Follow the manufacturer's directions for machine usage. Bind along the 8½" spine.

Ring Binding Technique

Materials (per Journal)

- 2 sheets of cardstock or medium-weight art paper for front and back covers
- at least 35 sheets of paper, such as photocopier or typing paper
- two metal rings (available at office supply stores)
- hole punch
- pencil
- ruler
- spring clip or other clamp

Process

1. Precut text papers to 7" × 9½" or other desired size. Coverstock should overhang the papers by ⅛" on three sides. (Papers will be flush on the spine.)
2. Covers can be decorated and laminated before binding.
3. Photocopy and precut any material you want to add to your students' journals.
4. Stack text papers between the coverstock and clip them together.
5. Measure and mark the positions for two holes along the 7" spine of the journal. (The holes should be ¾" in from the spine.)
6. Punch holes through the entire journal.
7. Bind with metal rings. Note: Some metal rings need to be opened with pliers, others can be opened and closed by hand; either will work.

Japanese Stab Binding

Note: This binding method makes a beautiful finished product but does not allow students to add or remove pages from their Moon Journals without unstitching the spine. We prepunch the holes in the cover and paper, as described below, and use rings or 1½" plated brass fasteners while the students are keeping their journals. When the Moon Journals are completed, they are ready to be permanently bound.

Materials (per Journal)

- 2 sheets of cardstock or medium-weight art paper for front and back covers
- at least 35 sheets of paper, such as photocopier or typing paper
- upholsterers' thread, thin ribbon, or cording (The length should be about 3½ times the height of the journal.)
- #18 needle or a needle with an eye large enough to accommodate the ribbon or cording

- decorative beads and feathers (optional)
- hole punch
- ruler
- pencil
- spring clip or clamp

Process

1. Precut text papers to 7" × 8½" or other desired size. Coverstock should over-hang papers by ⅛" on three sides. (Papers will be flush with the spine.)
2. Covers can be decorated and laminated before binding.
3. Photocopy and precut any material you want to add to your students' journals.
4. Stack text papers between the coverstock and clip them together.
5. Measure and mark positions for four holes along the 8½" spine of the journal. (The holes should be ⅜" in from the spine. The #1 hole is ½" down from the top edge of the journal and the #4 hole is ½" up from the bottom edge. Holes #2 and #3 are evenly spaced in between.)
6. Punch holes through all the journal pages. Make sure the holes are aligned.
7. Thread your needle.
8. With the front cover facing you, go through the #2 hole to the back cover. Leave a 5" tail of thread in the front. (See Figure 4-25A.) Be sure that this tail does not get tangled in the stitches as you proceed.
9. Wrap the thread around the spine at the #2 hole. Go through the #2 hole to the back (Figure 4-25B).
10. Enter the #3 hole from the back. Go through to the front.
11. Wrap the thread around the spine at the #3 hole (Figure 4-25C). Go through the #3 hole from the back to the front.
12. Enter the #4 hole from the front (Figure 4-25D). Go through to the back.
13. Wrap the thread around the spine at the #4 hole (Figure 4-25E). Go through the #4 hole to the back.
14. Wrap the thread around the bottom edge at the #4 hole (Figure 4-25F). Go through the #4 hole to the back.
15. Enter the #3 hole from the back. Go through to the front. (Figure 4-25G shows the path of the thread in steps 15 through 18.)
16. Enter the #2 hole from the front. Go through it to the back.
17. Enter the #1 hole from the back. Go through it to the front.
18. Wrap the thread around the spine at the #1 hole. Go through it to the front.
19. Wrap the thread around the top edge of the journal (Figure 4-25H). Go through the #1 hole to the front.
20. Take the 5" tail (from step 8 above) and knot it with the remaining thread. The knot should be tied at the #2 hole (Figure 4-25I). Trim both threads so they are the same length.
21. The journal binding is now complete. Figure 4-25I shows the finished front view and Figure 4-25J shows the completed back view.
22. Decorate the thread tails with beads and feathers, if desired.

FIGURE 4-25

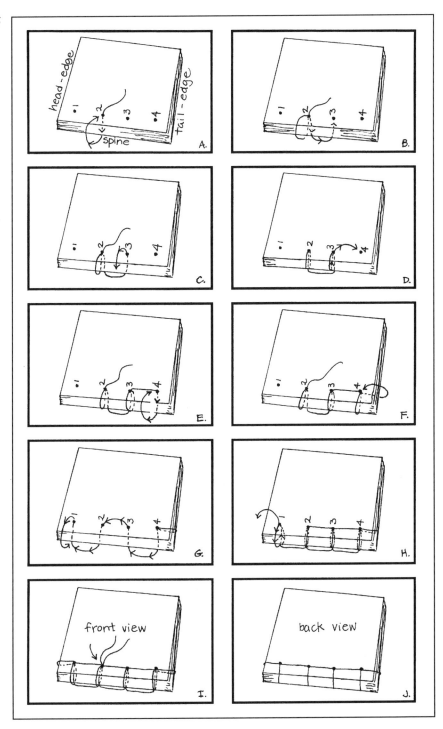

The Moon Is a Seamstress

piecing together patches of life.
Months, seasons, years—
the cycles are woven into a well-worn fabric.
Waxing hopes
and waning passions
are seamed together
with moonbeam threads,
connecting us
who look upon her,
you, in your place,
I, in mine.
We catch our breath—
a needle of silver light
stitches us together
in momentary wonder.

Joni Chancer

Chapter Five

A Final Invitation to the Teacher: Keeping a Moon Journal of Your Own

Frank Smith (1992) describes a view of learning that is "social rather than solitary, and can best be summarized in seven familiar words: we learn from the company we keep." Learning, he writes, "is vicarious; it is not a consequence of instruction and practice but of demonstration and collaboration. We learn from the people who interest us. . . . That is what effective teachers do: they demonstrate what can be done (and their own attitude toward what can be done), and they help others to do it. They make newcomers members of the clubs to which they themselves already belong."

Attitude, enthusiasm, discovery, and passion—students know the real thing when they see it. Nancie Atwell's book *In the Middle* (1987) described "dining room conversations" about favorite books that offered teachers an invitation to connect with students at a genuine level of engagement, to look them in the eye, and to say, "Yes, I loved that book too." She demonstrated how to talk to children and young adults, not just as students in a class, but as readers who care about things that really matter, as fellow members of the club.

Karen Ernst's book *Picturing Learning* (1994) described a studio workshop in which the teacher and children learn together about art and writing through conversations that are not limited to words. Composition and, in a broader sense, meaning-making occur in visual and verbal language. Her book is filled with sketches, line drawings, and personal journal entries that describe what she has learned about art, writing, and children. Her students know her as an artist and a writer, and she demonstrates on a daily basis not just what artists do with various materials but also the kinds of things they notice, the way they look at the world, and the way they make their own choices.

Atwell and Ernst are examples of the effective teacher described by Frank Smith. The children in their classes "learn by the company they keep." In the same way, a teacher who keeps a personal Moon Journal extends a genuine invitation to students: Learn in collaboration with me; watch me as I experiment, as I learn, and as I grow; read me your poem and I will read you mine; help me figure out a way to represent what we both saw in the sky last night.

192

In our workshops for teachers, when we describe the use of Moon Journals in the classroom, we often tell the following story to underscore the importance of teacher participation in this process.

> Imagine traveling in the southwestern desert. This is a new environment for you. It is filled with stories, but your road maps won't tell you how to find the hidden treasures of the land. A guide meets you in a jeep and takes you out into the landscape. She pulls off the dirt road and together you hike up a trail. She shows you a bush that seems ordinary until you crumble a leaf between your fingers and release the strong scent of sage. Down on the ground are unusual insects, crawling near a wildflower at the base of some rocks. Etched into the cliff are symbols, and when you look carefully you discover a story written by weather, movements of the earth, and people who lived thousands of years ago. Each strip of color tells its own tale and offers a chapter of natural and human history. Your day is spent learning to read by using your senses. You thank the guide at the end of the day for bringing you this revelation, but she knows that all she did was help you see in a different way. You made your own discoveries. You will never walk this land in the same way again.

To be the guide that walks with students—to be the company they keep in the process of learning about art, writing, and the natural world—requires more than map reading. The guide needs to know how to read the land and the best spots to take new visitors. This is knowledge that can be learned only through personal experience and by walking through a region many times in different seasons. Both the night sky and a child's backyard offer new worlds to students.

A teacher who observes the dark night of the new moon, who sees hundreds of stars splattered across an indigo sky, and who notices wispy clouds trailing over the rooftops of the neighborhood will know many things. As he makes a sketch in a journal or on a piece of scrap paper, that teacher will be wondering how best to represent the scene: watercolors splattered across a page, cutout silhouettes, soft rubbings of pastels, or delicate tissue paper collage. The experience will begin the process of planning for the next day's possibilities.

In her book *Living Between the Lines* (1991), Lucy Calkins describes an important result of keeping personal notebooks along with the students: "If we keep notebooks, we will expect and welcome diversity. We will soon come to know, in a deep-seated way, that there are variations in how and why writers keep notebooks. Some people always write in sentences and paragraphs; others often include lists and sketches. Some people do most of their writing in jotted notes as they carry their notebook about with them, and others write mostly at their desks during a predictable period each day. . . . In the end, it will be the diversity in our classrooms rather than our minilessons and conferences that extends what we and our students do in our notebooks."

A teacher who sketches and writes about the moon on the back of a napkin one night, who makes an entry directly into the Moon Journal on another evening, and who then sits at the kitchen table painting the scene in watercolors to add to the journal later on will understand the eclectic nature of this process. The teacher's experiments with different art media and writing forms will demonstrate new and diverse possibilities to students and will convey the message that there is no "right" way to follow the moon.

As thoughts are recorded in the teacher's journal, at the same time the students are making their own observations and a connection is made that transcends any planned lesson. When students walk through the classroom door in the morning with excitement in their eyes and ask their teacher, "Did you see the moon last night? Did you write about it in your journal? How did you draw the moon?" that teacher can do more than simply talk about what he observed. He can show the children his experiments in art, or she can read the students her prose and poetry. When the teacher and students discover together nuances of color, light, shadow, and sound with eyes and ears that become attuned to wonder and appreciation, they become fellow members of a club whose initiation is the ritual of watching the moon.

The Writing and Art Invitations in this book include descriptions of our personal experiments in keeping a Moon Journal. They are offered as examples of how teacher *and* student observations became the catalyst for minilessons and demonstrations. We realize that, without the personal experience of composing entries along with our students, this project could easily have floundered. Instead of responding to questions and observations that arose naturally from the nightly journal experience, we might have preplanned a unit that did not build upon the actual conditions of a particular time and place.

For example, not long ago the full moon rose in the early evening. Instead of its usual parchment-yellow color, it was bright orange—rivaling the setting sun in both hue and intensity. We all wondered, Is that *really* the *moon?* Looking hugely sinister, it caused several children to comment that they thought the moon would "gobble up the landscape like a monster from space." It cast a strange light across the entire sky, and clouds turned from white and pink to tangerine and pumpkin yellow. One child wrote, "It looked like a comic book drawing!"

The prose, poetry, and art entries of that night could not have been predicted or preplanned. The phenomenon itself generated experiments in watercolor and pastel, simile and metaphor, and scientific inquiry investigating the reasons for the unusual appearance of the moon. Because we had witnessed the phenomenon ourselves as journalists and teachers, we were prepared to set the stage for the classroom improvisations of the following day. We could plan for surprises.

We have shared our Moon Journals with colleagues and friends throughout the country. Through electronic-mail, telephone calls, and letters we have enjoyed the surprises and discoveries of comparing entries from many different locations. The following examples were not written for the purposes of this book. They are observations and reflections that were written because the authors of these entries shared a common interest in watching the moon. In some cases, East Coast and West Coast observations were made on the same evening, often within minutes of each other, as part of electronic mail conversations. Although drawings were not sent via computer, these teacher-writers did record their observations in sketch books as well. We share these entries as examples of the discoveries, possibilities, and pleasures of keeping personal Moon Journals.

One winter evening in New Hampshire, teacher-writer Linda Rief sat at her desk. In an e-mail message she described what she saw as she glanced up.

> Tonight the moon is bright white. I wonder if cold affects her color. It's about seventeen degrees out. She is almost full. Like a chipmunk she looks like she stuffed acorns in her cheeks, but only on one side. Small fingers of an oak branch trace across her face as I try to see her out my office window.

In a journal entry from two years earlier, Linda had recorded another moon spied through a different window.

> As I sit in an airplane bound for New Hampshire, I watch in wonder as we approach the moon, a crescent that rides the sky, and for the first time that I've ever noticed I'm parallel with her, looking her in the eye.

We shared another message from Linda with our students in southern California on a February day that felt like summer:

> It is snowing again this morning. We watched four deer amble through our back woods, one clearing a patch, and hunching down on the ground. They have all wandered off now, looking for food in the frozen ground. The moon is nowhere to be found. Hiding. Perhaps this snow is moon flakes, slivering off to tell us she's still there.

Linda's message became the inspiration for watercolor moons with swirling skies filled with moon flakes. It was a winter gift to thirty West Coast children. (See Color Plate 5 for a student sample.)

Students know that their teacher keeps a Moon Journal too, and the sharing of teacher-written entries provides working demonstrations of a work-in-progress and a poem-in-process. Gwen Dawson, a second grade teacher in Santa Barbara, wrote the following poem:

> Moonlight over water
> silver liquid
> waves and ripples

like luminous silk
smooth and calm
peaceful light
more gentle than the sun.

"Peaceful light, luminous silk, silver liquid"—this was verbal dessert that became part of the vocabulary treasure box of seven- and eight-year-old writers.

From Pennsylvania, teacher-writer Pat O'Brien e-mailed an ode to a favorite tree in her backyard. Her poem describes much more than the tulip tree of her dedication.

To the Tulip Tree

Smeary sunrises and sunsets
Backlight the horizon, your limbs
Frame the faces of the moon
Lightning shatters
Rain pelts
Snow blankets
The sun sustains us all and
You and I witness
But I know you see more.
Did you grieve as the birch fell
Asleep forever in the mud?
In your wildest imagination, did you
Envision fences enclosing
Backyards
And the municipal swimming pool
Where your kin once thrived?
Is it sorrowful to survive them?
Do you whisper ancient tales when the wind
Calls you to rustle
Do bedtime stories nestle in your
Bark
Veined and rutted as a country road
Traveled by cicadas in late summer
As they drone their rounds.
Do you sing in the rain?
When I leave
Will your branches
Wave
To a woman who met you for coffee
And asked too many questions
As you root into the earth

And branch
And breathe into
The deep night sky.

Susan Whisenand, a colleague who lives on a cliff overlooking the Pacific Ocean, described a morning moon.

I saw the moon this morning before dawn. It was surrounded in cerulean blue and faintly cast over in mist. A foggy sky left a soft edge around the surface; everything was blurry. The sun was on the rise in the east as I looked to the west. It was 6:15 a.m. I was out for my morning walk. Remnants of rain, puddles, and lots of mud were in our path. The dogs loved it . . . I waded my way through it and my soul was restored.

Teacher-writer Maureen Barbieri of Maine described a full summer moon. Her observations took her back in time to another place, another moon, and remembered emotions.

Late at night
when the moon hangs
low and round,
so bright
it keeps me
listening.
Gentle roll of surf
solace
so often,
but times like this
tug, lure
irascible seduction.
Late at night
nights like this
we are thirteen
again, shy and awkward.
I smear mustard on
the yellow poodle
you've won for me.
We stammer wrong words,
without ever a touch,
sending sly messages
with our eyes
all the while
our hearts
racing like

the ferris wheel
carrying us fast, high
and far
from the ordinary days
of our Catholic school lives,
fast as time,
high as hope,
far as the moon
hanging in the sky,
showering the sea
with light, and loss
and mystery.

In this final example, teacher-writer Marolyn Stewart describes a night when the moon did not appear but remained hidden behind rain clouds.

February 19, 1996, a dark rainy day, ended in a chromium radiance, in a glow that might easily be mistaken for moonlight; except there will be no moonlight tonight. Rain-sodden clouds will postpone what would have been the debut of the new moon. The lunar curtains will remain drawn, at least for us watchers-of-the-moon in southern California. But as we sit in our snug houses listening to the light tapping of the evening rain, or as we step onto the patio for a heady draft of night-blooming jasmine, we know that if we could somehow transport ourselves through this drooping ceiling of clouds, as we rose higher and higher, the ceiling would become a puffy, cotton comfort, a fitting nursery for the infant moon, the tiny sliver above.

Author Byrd Baylor scorns a January celebration of the New Year, preferring a warm day in spring for her personal choice. I would choose a night such as this, a night of cleansing for the Earth, a night of rebirth for the Moon, a night of renewal for me.

In their entries, e-mailed messages, letters, and poems these teacher-writers have demonstrated another very important reason for keeping a personal Moon Journal. It is true that the process of inquiry, a classroom community, and an instructional program will all benefit greatly from the teacher's participation. But keeping a Moon Journal becomes a personal blessing as well—a journey into yourself, your past, and your dreams via the world of nature and the lunar cycle.

Author Katherine Paterson (1981) writes that "to give the children of the world the words they need is to give them life and growth and refreshment." Teachers need the same gifts. We give of ourselves daily to students, parents, and colleagues; it is a choice that brings pleasure and satisfaction. But to remain fresh we also need to create and experiment, becoming energized by personal engagement and the excitement of new learning. In his video "Eric Carle: Picture Writer," author and artist Eric Carle describes how in his studio he can "become like a child again, having fun." In your Moon Journal, you can experience that same feeling as you splash images across the white paper and paint pictures with your words. We who are so busy, who need to do so many things at one time, who make decisions every minute of our working day, can slow down our lives and give ourselves the gift of beauty and quiet, focusing our attention on the natural world.

In *The Sense of Wonder* (1984) naturalist Rachel Carson writes:

> If I had influence with the good fairy who is supposed to preside over the christening of all children I should ask that her gift to each child in the world be a sense of wonder so indestructible that it would last throughout life, as an unfailing antidote against the boredom and disenchantments of later years, the sterile preoccupation with things that are artificial, the alienation from the sources of our strength. . . . The lasting pleasures of contact with the natural world are not reserved for scientists but are available to anyone who will place himself under the influence of earth, sea and sky and their amazing life.

We need to give ourselves the same gifts we offer to children. Then, because we will have walked the land and traveled the skies, we can become their guides.

Creative Patterns

It's hard to know
where to weave the web,
The places the wind blows
are so vast,
And the first stitch
takes the most courage.

In one small spot
between the streams of moonlight,
among the multitude of passageways,
I spin strands of silk
that connect me to possibilities,
the promises I must catch.

And there I wait,
balancing in the center
of a delicate orb,
waiting in anticipation,
and often fear,
they will not find me this time.

Sometimes I cannot see
until I close my eyes,
And respond to the tiny tuggings
on spokes of heartstrings.
Creative patterns
enticing prey, again.

Gold threads
binding quickly,
Treasure bundles
I will digest another day,
When I untangle the words
that spin the tale.

   Gina Rester-Zodrow

Afterword: Beyond Moon Journals

The cycle is over, the moon has disappeared, and the journals are completed. The story of this month's moon has been told. But, as every storyteller knows, when you tell enough stories you begin to find new ones everywhere you go. And, as every writer knows, writing becomes a habit. And the artist? Once you start to see the world through art's wide lens and begin to represent your impressions visually, you are no longer satisfied with words alone. You speak a second language—one that is more precise than the first, one that communicates your personal vision of the world with all its colors, textures, fragrances, sounds, and feelings.

Conversations and correspondence await the journalist. Insects, birds, reptiles, and flowers have their own stories to share. The beach, the mountains, forests, deserts, prairies, and city streets invite journeys through lands that are filled with songs and poems waiting to be recorded. The Moon Journalist makes the creative leap to new settings without a conscious shift of gears. Knowing how to focus attention, ask questions, and discover small changes become a passport to appreciation and composition in words and pictures.

Most students who have participated in a studio workshop know where to find new topics to write about and represent. A teacher doesn't need to provide the material; as Anne Lamont writes, *life* is material. What the children need, however, are continued opportunities to create: time, choice, response, and access to tools and materials that will allow them to express their thoughts and impressions.

When our students finish their Moon Journals, many choose to continue to make nightly recordings. For example, a comet recently made an appearance in the sky and several children wrote and illustrated entries about this exciting phenomenon. But it's not just the spectacular events that trigger a response. Moon Journalists have learned to find small treasures in daily living: moonlight spilled on a bedroom floor, the glowing harvest moon, or a daytime lunar appearance. We remind the children that new entries can always be added to a Moon Journal. On the last day of the cycle, we extend this invitation by offering them a few blank pages to slip into the back of their "completed" books.

As we begin other focused-inquiry studies, the children look through their Moon Journals, reminding themselves of techniques in writing and art they could apply to projects. Pete, for example, used handpainted papers to create a collage of the Amazon rain forest. Ashley scattered salt into yellow and orange water-colors to depict the sun shining over the African savanna. Kelly wrote a "Who Am I?" poem about a polar bear for her book on the arctic.

A year-long nature study of the seasons, a travel journal, the chronicles of a garden, a tree notebook, and a personal painted diary are a few of the ideas that have resulted from our moon studies. Several books offer inspiring demonstrations in writing and art and provide literary models for focused-inquiry projects. *A Circle of Seasons* (Livingston, 1982), *Linnea's Almanac* (Bjork, 1989), *Sky Tree* (Locker, 1995), *The Road to Rome: An Artist's Year in Italy* (McLoughlin, 1995), *In and Out of the Garden* (Midda, 1981), and *Amelia's Notebook* (Moss, 1995) include unique ideas for painted improvisations, poems, letters, recipes, dialog, sketches, photographs, captions, and personal responses.

Recording reflections and impressions through words and pictures is an individual inquiry project that never ends. We both keep personal journals and Artist's Books. The personal journals are very *drafty* and messy and are not meant to be shared. Our Artist's Books contain original art and color laser copies of some of our larger pieces, collaged together with written entries. Each page is a combination of text and pictures—both make up a single art form. We routinely share these Artist's Books with our students to show them our personal process and commitment to art and writing. It is our way of reminding the children that their work as writers and artists will carry on long past the time when we are together as a classroom community. Indeed, we hope it will continue throughout their lifetimes.

Asking questions, telling stories, and drawing pictures—these are what most of us did growing up. The things we put into our own children's baby books and memory boxes are the things that tug at our hearts. Little notes written on scrap paper, drawings and paintings, "first words" and recorded conversations, letters from camp, and handmade cards are the momentos of life. They are precious and priceless.

The invitations in this book extend to other projects, studies, and investigations, both public and personal. They were written to help you and your students fill journal pages and memory boxes with questions, stories, and pictures. We hope they tug at your heart as you discover the world, the heavens, and—ultimately—yourselves.

Bibliography

BOOKS ABOUT SCIENCE AND THE MOON

Adler, D.A. 1983. *All About the Moon.* Mahwah, NJ: Troll.

Asimov, I. 1994. *The Moon.* Milwaukee, WI: Gareth Stevens.

de Paola, T. 1975. *The Cloud Book.* New York: Scholastic.

Fowler, A. 1991. *So That's How the Moon Changes Shape!* Chicago, IL: Children's Press.

Galan, M. 1992. *Understanding Science and Nature: Space and Planets.* USA: Time-Life.

Guiley, R.E. 1991. *Moonscapes: A Celebration of Lunar Astronomy, Magic, Legend, and Lore.* New York: Prentice-Hall.

Haddock, P. 1992. *Mysteries of the Moon: Opposing Viewpoints.* San Diego, CA: Greenhaven.

Hiscock, B. 1993. *The Big Storm.* New York: Atheneum.

Irwin, J., with W. Emerson. 1973. *To Rule the Night: The Discovery Voyage of Astronaut Jim Irwin.* New York: Lippincott.

Jefferies, L. 1983. *All About Stars.* Mahwah, NJ: Troll.

Jeunesse, E.G. 1993. *Exploring Space.* New York: Scholastic.

Krupp, E.C. 1989. *The Big Dipper and You.* New York: William Morrow.

———. 1993. *The Moon and You.* New York: Macmillan.

McVey, V. 1989. *The Sierra Club Wayfinding Book.* San Francisco, CA: Little, Brown.

Pearce, Q.L. 1991. *The Stargazer's Guide to the Galaxy.* New York: RGA Publishing Group.

Sagan, C. 1980. *Cosmos.* New York: Random House.

Santrey, L. 1982. *Discovering the Stars.* Mahwah, NJ: Troll.

Simon, S. 1977. *Look to the Night Sky.* New York: Penguin.

Taylor, G.J., and L. Martel, eds. 1994. *Exploring the Moon: A Teacher's Guide with Activities for Earth and Space Sciences.* Washington, D.C.: NASA Office of Human Resources and Education.

PROFESSIONAL BOOKS AND ARTICLES FOR TEACHERS

Atwell, N. 1987. *In the Middle.* Portsmouth, NH: Heinemann.

Avery, C. 1993. *. . . And with a Light Touch.* Portsmouth, NH: Heinemann.

Brown, H., and B. Cambourne. 1987. *Read and Retell.* Portsmouth, NH: Heinemann.

Calkins, L.M. 1991. *Living Between the Lines.* Portsmouth, NH: Heinemann.

Caplan, R. 1984. *Writers in Training.* Palo Alto, CA: Dale Seymour.

Ernst, K. 1994. *Picturing Learning.* Portsmouth, NH: Heinemann.

Graves, D. 1983. *Writing: Teachers and Children at Work.* Portsmouth, NH: Heinemann.

———. 1994. *A Fresh Look at Writing.* Portsmouth, NH: Heinemann.

Hansen, J. 1987. *When Writers Read.* Portsmouth, NH: Heinemann.

Hansen, J., T. Newkirk, and D. Graves. 1985. *Breaking Ground: Teachers Relate Reading and Writing in the Elementary School.* Portsmouth, NH: Heinemann.

Harwayne, S. 1992. *Lasting Impressions.* Portsmouth, NH: Heinemann.

Healy, J.M. 1990. *Endangered Minds.* New York: Simon and Schuster.

Johnson, P. 1993. *Literacy Through the Book Arts*. Portsmouth, NH: Heinemann.

Paterson, K. 1981. *Gates of Excellence: On Reading and Writing Books for Children*. New York: Elsevier/Nelson Books.

Rief, L. 1992. *Seeking Diversity*. Portsmouth, NH: Heinemann.

Short, K., J. Harste, with C. Burke. 1996. *Creating Classrooms for Authors and Inquirers*. Portsmouth, NH: Heinemann.

Smith, F. 1992. "Learning to Read: The Never-Ending Debate." *Phi Delta Kappan* February, 432–441.

Smith, M.A., and M. Ylvisaker. 1993. *Teachers' Voices: Portfolios in the Classroom*. Berkeley, CA: National Writing Project.

BOOKS, MAGAZINES, AND ARTICLES ABOUT NATURE

Barasch, L. 1993. *A Winter Walk*. New York: Ticknor and Fields.

Baylor, B. 1986. *I'm in Charge of Celebrations*. New York: Charles Scribner's Sons.

Bjork, C. 1989. *Linnea's Almanac*. New York: R&S Books.

Carson, R. 1984. *The Sense of Wonder*. Berkeley, CA: The Nature Co.

George, J.C. 1992a. *Thirteen Moon Series: Moon of the Deer*. New York: HarperCollins.

———. 1992b. *Thirteen Moon Series: The Moon of the Winter Bird*. New York: HarperCollins.

———. 1993. *Dear Rebecca, Winter Is Here*. New York: HarperCollins.

Hindley, J. 1990. *The Tree*. New York: Clarkson N. Potter.

Katz, A. 1986. *Naturewatch*. New York: Addison-Wesley.

Killion, B. 1992. *The Same Wind*. New York: HarperCollins.

Kroll, V. 1993. *Naomi Knows It's Springtime*. Honesdale, PA: Caroline House.

Locker, T. 1995. *Sky Tree.* New York: HarperCollins.

Markle, S. 1993. *A Rainy Day.* New York: Orchard.

Martin, B., and J. Archambault. 1988. *Listen to the Rain.* New York: Henry Holt.

Muir, J. 1988. *My First Summer in the Sierra.* San Francisco, CA: Sierra Club.

Orion. Great Barrington, MA: Orion Society and Myrin Institute.

Schwartz, C. 1984. "That's my sky." *Orion Nature Quarterly* Winter, 20–25.

Silver, D. 1993. *One Small Square: Backyard.* New York: W.H. Freeman.

Sobel, D., et al., 1993. "A Pocketful of Stones: Memories of Childhood." *People and Nature Orion* Spring, 28–37.

Thomas, R. 1996. *The Old Farmer's Almanac.* Dublin, NH: Yankee.

Thoreau, H.D. 1991. *Walden or, Life in the Woods.* New York: Random House.

Watson, W. 1978. *Has Winter Come?* New York: Putnam.

Winkler, F.E. 1993. "The Wisdom of Childhood." *People and Nature Orion* Spring, 8–10.

Zolotow, C. 1967. *Summer Is . . .* New York: Abelard-Schuman.

PICTURE BOOKS USED AS LITERARY MODELS FOR WRITING AND ART

Ahlberg, J., and A. Ahlberg. 1986. *The Jolly Postman.* Boston, MA: Little, Brown.

Asch, F. 1995. *Water.* New York: Harcourt Brace.

Autumn, W.D. 1992. *The Great Change.* Hillsboro, OR: Beyond Words.

Bilezikian, G., 1990. *While I Slept.* New York: Orchard.

Bragg, R.G. 1992. *Colors of the Day.* Saxonville, MA: Picture Book Studio.

Caduto, M.J., and J. Bruchac. 1988. *Keepers of the Earth.* Golden, CO: Fulcrum.

———. 1991. *Keepers of the Animals.* Golden, CO: Fulcrum.

Carle, E. 1969. *The Very Hungry Caterpillar.* New York: Scholastic.

———. 1991. *Papa, Please Get the Moon for Me.* Saxonville, MA: Picture Book Studio.

———. 1992. *Draw Me a Star.* New York: Philomel.

———. 1995. *The Very Lonely Firefly.* New York: Philomel.

Coerr, E. 1993. *Sadako.* New York: Putnam.

Collins, P. 1992. *I Am an Artist.* Ill. R. Brickman. Brookfield, CT: Millbrook.

Keats, E. 1974. *Dreams.* New York: Collier.

Langen, A., and C. Droop. 1994. *Letters from Felix.* New York: Abbeville.

Lionni, L. 1967. *Frederick.* Toronto, Ontario: Random House.

———. 1970. *Fish Is Fish.* New York: Knopf.

McGilvray, R. 1993. *Don't Climb Out of the Window Tonight.* New York: Dial.

Moss, M. 1995. *Amelia's Notebook.* Berkeley, CA: Tricycle.

Nixon, J. 1988. *If You Were a Writer.* Ill. B. Degen. New York: Four Winds.

Schuett, S. 1995. *Somewhere in the World Right Now.* New York: Knopf.

Tan, A. 1992. *The Moon Lady.* New York: Macmillan.

Ungerer, T. 1966. *Moon Man.* New York: Delacorte.

Yolen, J. 1987. *Owl Moon.* Ill. J. Schoenherr. New York: Philomel.

Zolotow, C. 1993. *The Moon Was the Best.* Photo. T. Hoban. New York: Greenwillow.

PICTURE BOOKS: LEGENDS AND MYTHS

Bruchac, J., and J. London. 1992. *Thirteen Moons on Turtle's Back: A Native American Year of Moons.* Ill. T. Locker. New York: Philomel.

Cole, J. 1991. *The Moon, the Sun, and the Coyote.* New York: Simon and Schuster.

Esbensen, B.J. 1988. *The Star Maiden.* Boston, MA: Little, Brown.

Moroney, L. 1995. *Moontellers: Myths of the Moon from Around the World.* Ill. Greg Shed. Flagstaff, AZ: Northland.

Osofsky, A. 1992. *Dreamcatcher.* New York: Orchard.

Wood, N. 1995. *Dancing Moons.* New York: Bantam.

Young, E. 1993. *Moon Mother.* New York: HarperCollins.

POETRY

Baylor, B., and P. Parnall. 1981. *Desert Voices.* New York: Charles Scribner's Sons.

Bolin, F.S. 1994. *Poetry for Young People by Emily Dickinson.* New York: Sterling.

Booth, D. 1989. *'Til All the Stars Have Fallen.* London: Viking.

Gudis, C. 1992. *Sweet and Bitter Bark: Selected Poems by Robert Frost.* Berkeley, CA: The Nature Co.

Livingston, M.C. 1982. *A Circle of Seasons.* New York: Holiday House.

———. 1986. *Earth Songs.* New York: Holiday House.

———. 1992. *Light and Shadow.* New York: Holiday House.

Moyers, B. 1995. *The Language of Life.* New York: Doubleday.

Neruda, P. 1995. *Odes to Opposites.* Boston, MA: Little, Brown.

Nye, N.S. 1994. *Red Suitcase.* Brockport, NY: BOA Editions.

———. 1992. *This Same Sky.* New York: Four Winds.

Soto, G. 1992. *Neighborhood Odes.* San Diego, CA: Harcourt Brace Jovanovich.

Spooner, M. 1993. *A Moon in Your Lunch Box.* New York: Henry Holt.

Worth, V. 1987. *All the Small Poems.* Ill. Natalie Babbitt. New York: Farrar, Straus and Giroux.

Zolotow, C. 1992. *Snippets: A Gathering of Poems, Pictures, and Possibilities.* Ill. Melissa Sweet. New York: HarperCollins.

BOOKS ABOUT WRITING (TRADE)

Cameron, J. 1992. *The Artist's Way.* New York: Putnam.

Ferra, L. 1994. *A Crow Doesn't Need a Shadow.* Layton, UT: Gibbs Smith.

Estes, C.P. 1992. *Women Who Run with the Wolves.* New York: Ballantine.

Fox, J. 1995. *Finding What You Didn't Lose.* New York: G.P. Putnam.

Goldberg, N. 1986. *Writing Down the Bones: Freeing the Writer Within.* Boston, MA: Shambhala.

———. 1990. *Wild Mind: Living the Writer's Life.* New York: Bantam.

Heard, G. 1989. *For the Good of the Earth and Sun.* Portsmouth, NH: Heinemann.

———. 1995. *Writing Toward Home: Tales and Lessons to Find Your Way.* Portsmouth, NH: Heinemann.

Janeczko, P.B. 1994. *Poetry from A to Z.* New York: Bradbury.

Lamott, A. 1994. *Bird by Bird.* New York: Pantheon.

Oliver, M. 1994. *A Poetry Handbook.* Orlando, FL: Harcourt Brace.

Tucker, S. 1992. *Writing Poetry.* Glenview, IL: Scott, Foresman.

BOOKS ABOUT ART

Appellof, M., ed. 1992. *Everything You Ever Wanted to Know About Watercolor.* New York: Watson-Guptill.

Arnosky, J. 1982. *Drawing from Nature.* New York: Lothrop, Lee and Shepard.

———. 1984. *Drawing Life in Motion.* New York: Lothrop, Lee and Shepard.

———. 1988a. *Sketching Outdoors in Autumn.* New York: Lothrop, Lee and Shepard.

———. 1988b. *Sketching Outdoors in Summer.* New York: Lothrop, Lee and Shepard.

Brommer, G. 1994. *Collage Techniques: A Guide for Artists and Illustrators.* New York: Watson-Guptill.

Brookes, M. 1986. *Drawing with Children*. Los Angeles, CA: Tarcher.

Brust, B.W. 1994. *The Amazing Paper Cuttings of Hans Christian Anderson*. New York: Ticknor and Fields.

Butterfield, M. 1993. *Fun with Paint*. New York: Random House.

Couch, T. 1987. *Watercolor: You Can Do It!* Cincinnati, OH: North Light.

Cummings, P. 1992. *Talking with Artists*. New York: Bradbury.

———. 1995. *Talking with Artists: Volume Two*. New York: Bradbury.

de Paola, T. 1989. *The Art Lesson*. New York: G.P. Putnam.

Edwards, B. 1979. *Drawing on the Right Side of the Brain*. Los Angeles, CA: Tarcher.

Franck, F. 1979. *The Awakened Eye*. New York: Random House.

———. 1993. *Zen Seeing, Zen Drawing*. New York: Bantam.

Fuentes, C. 1995. Introduction to *The Diary of Frida Kahlo: An Intimate Self-Portrait*. New York: Abrams.

Irvine, J. 1987. *How to Make Pop-Ups*. Ill. B. Reid. Toronto, Ontario: Kids Can Press.

Johnson, C. 1990. *The Sierra Club Guide to Sketching in Nature*. San Francisco, CA: Sierra Club.

———. 1992. *Creating Textures in Watercolor*. Cincinnati, OH: North Light.

———. 1995. *First Step Series: Painting Watercolors*. Cincinnati, OH: North Light.

La Plantz, S. 1995. *Cover to Cover: Creative Techniques for Making Beautiful Books, Journals, and Albums*. Asheville, NC: Lark.

London, P. 1989. *No More Secondhand Art*. Boston, MA: Shambhala.

Martin, J. 1992. *The Encyclopedia of Pastel Techniques*. Philadelphia, PA: Running Press.

McLoughlin, M. 1995. *The Road to Rome: An Artist's Year in Italy*. San Francisco, CA: Chronicle Books.

Midda, S. 1981. *In and Out of the Garden.* New York: Workman.

O'Reilly, S. 1993. *Block Printing.* New York: Thomson Learning.

Pullinger, K., and J. Rothenstein, eds. 1995. *The Writer's Drawing Book.* Boston, MA: Shambhala.

Robins, D. 1993. *Step-by-Step: Making Prints.* New York: Kingfisher.

Ryan, J. 1990. *Traveling with Your Sketchbook: A Step-by-Step Guide to Travel Sketching with Emphasis on Pen-and-Ink.* San Antonio, TX: Butterfly.

Smith, K. 1991. *Non-Adhesive Binding: Books Without Paste or Glue.* New York: keith smith.

Sohi, M.E. 1993. *Look What I Did with a Leaf.* New York: Walker.

Speckman, G. 1995. *Wet-into-Wet Watercolor: The Complete Guide to an Essential Watercolor Technique.* New York: Watson-Guptill.

Stowell, C. 1994. *Step-by-Step: Making Books.* Ill. J. Robins. New York: Kingfisher.

Szabo, Z. 1974. *Creative Watercolor Techniques.* New York: Watson-Guptill.

Thomas, J. 1990. *Masterpiece of the Month.* Ill. B. Apodaca and T. Wright. Huntington Beach, CA: Teacher Created Materials.

Tofts, H. 1989. *The Print Book: Fun Things to Make and Do with Print.* New York: Simon and Schuster.

Vaughan-Jackson, G. 1990. *Sketching and Drawing for Children.* New York: Putnam.

Wilmes, L., and D. Wilmes. 1993. *Paint Without Brushes.* Ill. T. McGinnis. Elgin, IL: Building Blocks.

VIDEOTAPE ON ART

Carle, E. 1993. "Eric Carle: Picture Writer." New York: Philomel.